Inside/Outside Nietzsche

A VOLUME IN THE SERIES

Psychoanalysis and Social Theory

edited by

C. FRED ALFORD AND JAMES M. GLASS

Inside/Outside Nietzsche

PSYCHOANALYTIC

EXPLORATIONS

Eugene Victor Wolfenstein

CORNELL UNIVERSITY PRESS

ITHACA AND LONDON

First published 2000 by Cornell University Press

Printed in the United States of America

"Redemption Song," written by Bob Marley
Copyright © 1980 Fifty-Six Hope Road Music, Ltd. and Odnil Music, Ltd.
Used by permission. All rights reserved.

Library of Congress Cataloging-in-Publication Data
Wolfenstein, E. Victor.
    Inside/outside Nietzsche : psychoanalytic explorations / Eugene Victor
Wolfenstein.
        p.   cm.—(Psychoanalysis and social theory)
    Includes bibliographical references and index.
    ISBN 0-8014-3703-2 (cloth : alk. paper)
    1. Nietzsche, Friedrich Wilhelm, 1844–1900.   2. Psychoanalysis and philosophy.
3. Critical theory.   I. Title.

B3317.W618 2000
193—dc21
                                                                99-045645

Cornell University Press strives to use environmentally responsible suppliers and materials to the fullest extent possible in the publishing of its books. Such materials include vegetable-based, low-VOC inks and acid-free papers that are recycled, totally chlorine-free, or partly composed of nonwood fibers. Books that bear the logo of the FSC (Forest Stewardship Council) use paper taken from forests that have been inspected and certified as meeting the highest standards for environmental and social responsibility. For further information, visit our website at www.cornellpress.cornell.edu.

Cloth printing   10 9 8 7 6 5 4 3 2 1

In reremembrance of Maxine,

whose mother's love has always been my best thing

Contents

Preface

Perhaps I should begin with why I became involved in a psychoanalytic exploration of Nietzsche's philosophical world and how this exploration came to be joined to the problematics of critical theory.

I studied Nietzsche briefly and superficially in the late 1960s but soon set his work aside in favor of Hegel, Marx, and Freud. By the early to mid 1970s, I had become deeply involved with Freudian-Marxism and critical theory more generally. These theoretical interests were linked to practical political ones and, beginning in 1975, to the exigencies of psychoanalytic training and clinical practice. *The Victims of Democracy: Malcolm X and the Black Revolution* (1981) and *Psychoanalytic-Marxism: Groundwork* (1993) emerged from this nexus of concerns.

Sometime in the mid-1980s, Geoffrey Howard, then a UCLA undergraduate student, asked to do an independent studies course on Nietzsche. I agreed, although this meant returning to Nietzsche's writings after a twenty-year hiatus. This time around, I found them much more interesting, no doubt as a result of the inwardizing effects of my psychoanalytic experience. I gravitated first to *On the Genealogy of Morals*, which now seemed significantly deeper than most psychoanalytic studies of morality (Freud's *Civilization and Its Discontents* included), and I slowly worked my way into the other major texts as well.

Geoff went on to do an outstanding honors thesis, and I proceeded to incorporate Nietzsche into my pedagogy. I used him first as the historical and philosophical antipode to Plato in my introductory political theory course and then began a more detailed examination of his work in my graduate courses. Over time, a very specific conceptual problem began to take shape: what was the relationship between the will to power and what I call the "determinacy of pleasure and pain" (the basic human propensity to be pleasure-seeking and pain-avoiding)? For it became increasingly evident that these Nietzschean and psychoanalytic principles were incompatible. Because, as I view it, the determinacy of pleasure and pain is foundational for psychoanalytic theory and practice, a Nietzschean perspective requires a most unwelcome transvaluation of psychoanalytic values. Moreover, I believe that these psychoanalytic principles are also basic to critical theory. So the stakes were doubled: could psychoanalysis in particular and critical theory more generally withstand the Nietzschean challenge? Could they overcome the resistance he offers to their fundamental values and interpretive principles? Thus we have the central problem and most general framing of the present inquiry, the place where it both begins and ends.

Yet I do not treat Nietzsche's philosophy simply as a middle term, a means to psychoanalytic and critical theoretical ends. Quite the opposite: Nietzsche created and lived within an extraordinary psychophilosophical world. How could I resist the temptation to enter it—despite knowing that it would also enter me? How could I refuse the dare of playing psychoanalyst to his psychologist and allowing his psychologist to play on my psychoanalytic identity? Wasn't just such deep engagement the risk that Nietzsche asks us to take, so that the risks he took would not be in vain? And the risks are, or can be, quite real. We can play at being philosophical ice dancers and skate across his surfaces, but these surfaces are the thin ice of a new day, and there are waves of passion and pain beneath them. I take Nietzsche at his word when he says "I am dynamite," and it passes through my mind that explore and explode differ by one letter only.

In any case, this inquiry focuses on and treats with due respect central Nietzschean concepts and concerns—the will to power, perspectivism, eternal return, the feminine, and the genealogy of morals. It is partially textual, partially biographically contextual. And it is, in a certain sense, pragmatic: it presupposes that concepts are to be developed and used, not merely transcribed, represented, or interpreted. Foucault once said that "it is important to have a small number of authors with whom one thinks, with whom one works, but about whom one does not write" (in Kritzman 1988, p. 250). I am temperamentally inclined to agree with him on two of the three counts. My way of thinking has been shaped by engagement with a relatively small number of thinkers—Hegel, Marx, and Freud most prominently—about whom I have also chosen to write. I have always tried to recognize their objectivity, their autonomous existence outside my engagement with them, but I have also internalized them, metabolized them, and—in the process—modified their concepts to meet my theoretical and practical needs. In previous work, I have given my own meaning to Freud's three principles of mental functioning and Melanie Klein's notion of the paranoid-schizoid position. In the present instance, I've put to pragmatic use D. W. Winnicott's conception of transitional space, Julia Kristeva's conception of abjection, and Foucault's conceptions of juridico-discursive power and biopower. And, most important, I have placed the will to power and perspectivism in the service of a psychoanalytic will to knowledge.

The way in which the will to power and perspectivism are psychoanalytically appropriated is suggested by my titular "inside / outside Nietzsche." As a matter of theory, the will to power begins outside the determinacy of pleasure and pain and ends up inside it. It is transformed in the process, but it also has, as one would expect, transformational effects. As a matter of method, the inquiry involves a kind of dance between perspectivism and dialectical reason that ends in the recognition that they are truly inside / outside each other—that they oscillate through and around a common conceptual axis.

My thanks to the many students who have shared my search for Nietzsche's peculiar truths; to Roger Haydon, Carol Betsch, and Nancy Raynor, for editorial guidance; to Larry Tipton, for the index; to Fred Alford and Jim Glass, who have been supportive of the project from first to last; to Candice Ward, who helped me turn my own Nietzschean corner; and to my wife and best friend, Judy, who read the text thoroughly and compassionately and who helped me to bear the not inconsiderable clinical travails that accompanied its birth.

Eugene Victor Wolfenstein

Beverly Hills, California

Inside/Outside Nietzsche

1

Enter Nietzsche

The stocks of dynamite used in the building of the Got-
thard Tunnel were marked by a black flag, indicating
mortal danger. Exclusively in this sense do we speak of
the new book by the philosopher Nietzsche as a dangerous book.

> —J. V. WIDMANN, review of *Beyond Good and Evil*,
> in Christopher Middleton,
> *Selected Letters of Friedrich Nietzsche*

1.

Nietzsche asked himself the question, "Under what conditions did men devise these value judgments good and evil; *and what value do they themselves possess?*" In pursuing the matter, he reports, "I discovered and ventured diverse answers; I distinguished between ages, peoples, degrees of rank among individuals; I departmentalized my problem; out of my answers there grew new questions, inquiries, conjectures, probabilities—until at length I had a country of my own, a soil of my own, an entire discrete, flourishing world, like a secret garden the existence of which no one suspected" (Nietz-sche 1887 [hereafter *GM*], p. 17). What follows is primarily a psychoanalytic exploration of the philosophical world Nietzsche created for himself. I take up in turn the will to power, perspectivism, eternal return, women and the feminine, and the genealogy of moral valuations. The inquiry also has a reflexive element: the will to power and perspectivism are brought to bear on both psychoanalysis and critical social theory.

I use the term "critical theory" to include not only the first-generation Frankfurt school philosophers with their predecessors and successors but also a variety of left Freudians, psychoanalytic-marxists, and those postmodernists who view themselves as continuing the struggle for human emancipation. Nietzsche is sometimes placed in this company, and when he is, a rather considerable difficulty is obscured. Critical theory is guided by utilitarian and hedonic values broadly defined. That is, the necessary conditions for human flourishing or well-being are presumed to include the realization of material interests and/or pleasures and the gratification of desire. Yet Nietzsche contends that all such values are metaphysical and life-denying. We are life-affirming, he claims, only when we identify ourselves with the will to power—when we take the overcoming of resistance as the goal, as the ultimate value, and not merely as a means to hedonic and utilitarian ends. Moreover, the will to power has its epistemological complement and expression in Nietzsche's radical perspectivism. A perspective might be characterized as the "whence" of the will to power and the will to power as the "whither" of a perspective. Power and knowledge are joined at the root, and objective reality slips from view. Critical theory, however, must claim knowledge of the real world it seeks to transform. Thus the question becomes, can a critical theory of human emancipation withstand the challenge of a perspectivist epistemology identified with the will to power?[1]

The will to power and perspectivism link the concerns of critical theory to the problematics of psychoanalytic theory and practice. I argue below that the first principle of psychoanalytic theory is the determinacy of pleasure and pain—not Freud's pleasure principle, but the simpler notion that human activity is rooted in the psychophysiological drive to experience pleasure and not to experience pain. I also have defended the view that psychoanalytic knowing, in practice as well as in theory, is a dialectical process. But the will to power displaces the determinacy of pleasure and pain as a first principle, and perspectivism has a dissolving effect on dialectical reason. Again a settling of accounts with Nietzsche is required.[2]

The reflexive aspects of the inquiry will tend to have a disruptive impact on all participating parties. The will to power will emerge as overcoming pain to gain pleasure, including the pleasure of overcoming pain. A clinical imperative will be derived from this redefinition of the will to power: the practice of psychoanalysis demands of the analyst the disciplined suspension or restrained employment of the will to power. And this imperative, adapted to the exigencies of political as well as clinical practice, will become the desideratum of learning to tolerate the maximum of anxiety with the minimum of defense. These formulations seem unlikely to please Nietzscheans, psychoanalysts, or critical theorists. Perhaps, therefore, I should speak of an unsettling rather than a settling of accounts.

2.

If I aimed only at the self-clarification of psychoanalysis and critical theory, there would be no need to go beyond the will to power and perspectivism. But there are good reasons for proceeding more deeply into Nietzsche's world. There is first a purely scholarly concern. Although Nietzsche has been and continues to be the object of intense interpretive scrutiny, a fairly pronounced tendency exists to divorce his philosophy from his biography.[3] This has made it difficult, I believe, to grasp the full significance of eternal return. Eternal return was the transformational event in Nietzsche's life, an experience of inspiration in which thinking and being were utterly fused— far more fused than ever they were in Hegelian dialectics. This same experience gave rise to both the will to power and the overman; these three concepts, joined together in their birth, constitute *the* Nietzschean perspective. This is not to say that Nietzsche has nothing else to teach us, but we are poor students if we fail to see his world from this angle.

A second point is closely related to the first. In describing the experience of eternal return and the subsequent genesis of *Thus Spoke Zarathustra*, Nietzsche prankishly figures himself as a female elephant. This play on gender identity is not an isolated incident. Rather, the ambiguities of gender are pervasive in his life and thinking. One does not have to "read for gender" to interpret him this way. He does it himself. But his explorations of gender bear the marks of an internalized battle of the sexes. On the one hand, his perspective is emphatically masculine. On the other, his masculinity is recurrently threatened by an enticing femininity. This opposition is not, however, quite what it appears to be. The femininity with which Nietzsche struggles is far less an attribute of women than it is a component of masculine identity and phantasy.

This leads to the third point. Although I attempt to honor Nietzsche's self-representations, I also interpret him from the perspective of a psychoanalytic theory of individuation and gender development. So doing leads to the conclusion that he philosophized from within a specific psychic location, a transitional space in which selfhood is both made and unmade, gender identity is notably unstable, and sublimity consorts with the most abject misery. This is Nietzsche's "entire discrete, flourishing world," an abysmally deep internal world with only the most fragile of links to the external one.

We might summarize these three points in the form of a biographical question: What must a philosophy be like, if it is built on a foundation of all but intolerable pain and loneliness? And—to turn the question in our direction—how far can and should we go in making this philosophy our own?

3.

Topologically, the investigation forms three concentric circles, with the concerns of critical theory on the periphery, Nietzsche at the center, and psychoanalysis in between, linking the extremes. This structure mirrors or mimics the psychoanalytic situation, in which the distinctive rules and procedures of clinical inquiry mediate the relationship between the patient's (and the analyst's) external and internal worlds.

I might extend the metaphor. Classically, one enters the psychoanalytic consulting room through one door and exits through another. Within the consulting room, the external world slips away and an interior one takes form. Patient and analyst are then in a position to explore this often dangerous and seductive interior. When the hour ends, the external world reforms as the patient reenters it. Sometimes, however, it is transformed as it reforms—that is, the patient is able to see it and live it differently. In parallel fashion the present investigation begins in our own historical situation (Chapter 1). We then enter a philosophical / psychoanalytic space, reconstituting it through engagement with the will to power and perspectivism as we go (Chapters 2 and 3). Once this work has been accomplished, we proceed to the investigation of eternal return and the feminine (Chapters 4 and 5). Finally, we come to Nietzsche's genealogy of morals and, going beyond it, return to the political starting point (Chapter 6).

Thus the inquiry is staged to resemble the outside-inside-outside rhythm of psychoanalytic practice. But the resemblance to the clinical situation is not simply a matter of staging. Whether thought of in dialectical or perspectival terms, psychoanalytic practice is unavoidably phenomenological and inductive. Patient and analyst proceed from surface to depth without knowing in advance what they will find, and such knowledge as they gain must be built up piecemeal from fragments of memory and desire. Moreover, the knowledge gained is of a peculiar sort. It is as much affective as cognitive, far more a telling of tales than a making of arguments, and less a set of interpretations about oneself than a way of thinking and being with oneself.

Although our inquiry is not literally clinical, it too proceeds phenomenologically, inductively, and as a telling of tales. And its truth, such as it might be, is in the process as well as the product. To say it once again, "the real issue is not exhausted by stating it as an aim, but in carrying it out, nor is the result the actual whole, but rather the result together with the process through which it came about" (Hegel 1977, p. 2).

4.

We begin, as indicated, in our own time, seen from the perspective of critical theory, or at least one version of critical theory. This way of looking at things is challenged by taking up Foucault's quite Nietzschean critique of the left Freudians in volume 1 of *The History of Sexuality*. I attempt to meet this challenge by bringing my own interpretive perspective to bear on the Foucauldian critique. But the encounter ends inconclusively and leads to a more thoroughgoing engagement with Nietzsche and the will to power.

I. Critical Theory in Hard Times

5.

"It is not difficult to see," Hegel wrote in 1807, "that ours is a birthtime and a period of transition to a new era" (1977, p. 6). Speculative philosophy, he believed, heralded the breaking of the dawn. By 1820 Hegel's mood, if not necessarily his philosophical perspective, had shifted: "When philosophy paints its grey in grey, then has a shape of life grown old. By philosophy's grey in grey it cannot be rejuvenated but only understood. The owl of Minerva spreads its wings only with the falling of the dusk" (1967, p. 13).

How are we to characterize our own time? There are those who, like the young Hegel, hasten to announce the dawning of a new age—in this case, the age of truly global capitalism, capitalism as *the* world system, unrivaled and unsurpassable.[4] And with the demise of the Soviet Union and the fall of the Berlin Wall, this same party (although not only this party) is celebrating a springtime of peoples and the triumph of democracy. The birth pangs associated with the globalization of capitalist democracy are acknowledged, but no serious doubts concerning its viability and desirability are entertained.

From another perspective, the view is considerably more wintry. This party looks back on the time it looked forward to a postcapitalist future. Now its projected future has become the unfulfilled dream of its past, and the social order it sought to relegate to the dustbin of history has become its future. Where once these most practical of all dreamers interpreted the world in order to change it, now they interpret it in order not to be changed by it. No longer even thinking about the criticism of arms, they nonetheless refuse to relinquish the arm of criticism. And sometimes they are chilled by the thought that they are merely painting philosophy's grey in grey, only conjuring up the shapes and shadows of life grown old.

Although the final collapse of the Left's revolutionary project is a recent event, it was not entirely unanticipated even by those who placed their hopes in it. To take only the most obvious example, in *One-Dimensional Man* Herbert Marcuse identifies critical theory with two basic valuations: "the judgment that human life is worth living, or rather can be and ought to be made worth living . . . [and] the judgment that, in a given society, specific possibilities exist for the amelioration of human life and specific ways and means of realizing these possibilities" (1991, pp. xlii–xliii). In advanced capitalist societies, however, there seems to be no way to realize these emancipatory possibilities. Bourgeoisie and proletariat continue to exist, but "capitalist development has altered the structure and function of these two classes in such a way that they no longer appear to be agents of historical transformation." And in "the absence of demonstrable agents and agencies of social change, the critique is . . . thrown back to a high level of abstraction. There is no ground on which theory and practice, thought and action meet" (p. xlv). Critical theory regresses, or at least tends to regress, from praxis to philosophy.

The revival of the Left in the late 1960s and early 1970s made Marcuse's analysis of the emancipatory project appear unduly pessimistic. Some thirty years later it seems severely realistic. We need not join him in limiting meaningful political action to the project of revolutionary transformation. There is plenty of work to be done within the constraints imposed by the capitalist mode of production. But we can no longer envision a world beyond the capitalist horizon.

6.

Whether or not critical theory is attached to a realizable project of social transformation, it is necessarily at odds with its own time. This tension between historical reality and philosophy is explicit in virtually all Nietzsche's work. In the *Untimely Meditations* of the early 1870s, for example, he places himself in opposition to existing German culture, which he characterizes as philistine, and invites his contemporaries to join him in the project of cultural renewal. The possibility of realizing this project seems rather slim, however, because Nietzsche already sees himself as condemned to isolation and misunderstanding. An especially striking fragment in his notebooks reads in part: "Do I still hear you, my voice? Are you whispering as you curse? And yet your curses should cause the bowels of the earth to burst open! But the world continues to live and only stares at me ever more glitteringly and coldly with its pitiless stars. It continues to live as dumbly and blindly as ever, and only *one thing* dies—man" (in Breazeale 1990, p. 33). Hence the appropriateness of the title given to another set of unpublished notes from this period, "Philosophy in Hard Times" (ibid., pp. 101–23).

If critical theory is identified with the leftist opposition to capitalist society, then Nietzsche cannot be placed within its ranks. If we identify it with untimeliness, however, he is necessarily included. The same ambiguity characterizes the relationship between critical theory and psychoanalysis, at least psychoanalysis in its Freudian articulation. Early and late, Freud was culturally critical without being politically radical. But in Freud's case as in Nietzsche's, it is possible to extract a theoretical kernel from the ideological shell. Such a critical appropriation would not be worth the effort if Marxism had been able to make good on its revolutionary promises. But the practical shortcomings of the left opposition in the advanced capitalist nations put this task on the political and philosophical agenda.

The rapprochement between Marxism and psychoanalysis was initiated by Wilhelm Reich in "Dialectical Materialism and Psychoanalysis" (1929), but the paradigmatic attempt to shore up critical theory with psychoanalytic concepts is Marcuse's *Eros and Civilization* (1966). Nietzsche also plays a role in this exemplary text, although not quite the one that Marcuse intended.[5]

Marcuse locates his "philosophical inquiry into Freud" beyond the pleasure principle—that is, in the territory of Freud's late drive (or instinct) theory. We will revisit this philosophical / psychological space in Chapter 2, but for the moment, the point is how Marcuse interprets it. Freud sets love and hate, sexuality and aggressivity, life-drive and death-drive in dire opposition. Marcuse redefines the death-drive as a protest against pain and a yearning for an absence of tension and "integral quiescence" (p. 29). He thereby deprives the death-drive of its Freudian sting and arrives at a unitary conception of human nature: man is the erotic animal.

From this human-ontological perspective, Marcuse evolves a dialectical conception of civilization, in which the antitheses are the pleasure principle, identified with instinctual gratification, and the reality principle, identified with instinctual restraint in the interest of survival. If we think of values as basic goods or conditions of well-being, then the opposition is between hedonic and utilitarian values. This contradiction is not antagonistic in the first instance. Civilization as such or in the abstract is a function of the basic repression of instinct. Basic repression, by giving us the "power to restrain and guide instinctual drives, to make biological necessities into individual needs and desires," increases rather than reduces gratification (p. 38). The same cannot be said for civilization in the form of domination and alienation. To take the relevant case (and to state it a bit more concretely than Marcuse himself): capitalism is a system for the production of surplus value, and surplus value is produced through the extraction of labor-power from the worker. The production of the worker, in turn, requires the repression of instinctual demand—so that libido can be transformed into labor-power—and the desexualization of the body—so that "libido becomes concentrated in one part of the body, leaving the rest free for use as the instrument of labour" (p. 48). This surplus repression—more accurately, excess repression that generates a libidinal surplus value—is enforced not by the reality principle per se but rather by the performance principle. Thus where orthodox Marxism aims at the abolition of private property, Marcuse aims additionally at the abolition of the performance principle. Human emancipation is erotic liberation.

Erotic liberation has a spatial dimension (for example, the libidinization of the body as a whole) and a temporal one. The latter includes the obvious idea of reducing the time spent in alienated labor to an absolute minimum and the less obvious idea of changing the human experience of time altogether. This is where Nietzsche enters into Marcuse's story. He is taken to be a critic, perhaps the ultimate critic, of the linear temporality of the performance principle:

> Nietzsche's critique is distinguished from all academic social psychology by the position from which it is undertaken. Nietzsche speaks in the name of a reality principle fundamentally antagonistic to that of Western civilization. The traditional form of reason is rejected on the basis of experience of being-as-end-in-itself—as joy (*Lust*) and enjoyment. The struggle against time is waged from this perspective: the tyranny of becoming over being must be broken if man is to come to himself in a world which is truly his own. (Pp. 121–22)

Here Nietzsche appears in his role as the philosopher of eternal return, which is interpreted as "the total affirmation of the life instincts, repelling all escape and negation." It is "the will and vision of an *erotic* attitude toward being for which necessity and fulfillment coincide" (ibid.). Thus eternal return is taken to be the temporal expression of the drive toward integral quiescence, and Nietzsche's untimeliness becomes the suprahistorical perspective of critical theory.

Although one can raise various questions about Marcuse's interpretation of Freud and his fusion of psychoanalysis with Hegelian-Marxism, he quite successfully attaches Freud to the emancipatory project of the left opposition. He is not nearly as successful in the case of Nietzsche. As we shall see in Chapter 4, eternal return is more nearly the conquest of being by becoming than the conquest of becoming by being. This is necessarily the case because the life that eternally returns is will to power: "And life itself confided this secret to me: 'Behold,' it said, 'I am *that which must always overcome itself*'" (Nietzsche 1883–85 [hereafter *TSZ*], p. 227). There is no escape from the infinite cycle of resistance and resistance overcome. Nietzsche aims at anything but integral quiescence. Yet Marcuse, intent on fusing eternal return with erotic liberation, insists that "the will to power is not Nietzsche's last word" (1966, p. 119). When, by contrast, we take Nietzsche at *his* word, this interpretation is ruled out. We are not free to go beyond the will to power or to identify eternal return with hedonic valuations. And because such values are foundational to critical theory, Nietzsche cannot be brought within its purview.

That Nietzsche stands outside the relatively civilized domain of critical theory does mean we need to follow him into a philosophical wilderness. Quite apart from an autonomous interest in Nietzschean territory, however, there are at least two reasons for taking this step. First, the definitional value of critical theory is thinking critically and self-critically—in Marx's words, the *"ruthless criticism of everything existing"* (in Tucker 1978, p. 13). To leave the Nietzschean challenge unanswered would be an act of intellectual bad faith. Second, in these hard times we cannot forgo the interpretive advantages that come from taking the will to power seriously.

II. Michel Foucault against Critical Theory

7.

The latent opposition between Nietzsche and critical theory in *Eros and Civilization* becomes manifest in volume 1 of Michel Foucault's *History of Sexuality* (1990). The text was originally titled *La volenté de savoir*, or "the will to know." The will to know is the scientific, philosophical, or epistemological form of the will to power. As this implies, Foucault's approach to his subject is decidedly Nietzschean.[6] Moreover, *The History of Sexuality* is framed as a critique of the Freudian Left in general and the Marcusean version of critical theory in particular; it centers on the psychoanalytic construction of sexual knowledge; and it is concerned with the practice of psychoanalysis as well as the theory. Thus engaging Foucault will take us further into both Nietzschean and psychoanalytic territory.

Foucault begins by characterizing the model of historical development he is going to contest, the core of which is the empirical claim that, beginning in the seventeenth century, sexual repression is increasingly characteristic of European society. Earlier "a certain frankness was still common. . . . It was a time of direct gestures, shameless discourse, and open transgressions." But "twilight soon fell on this bright day, followed by the monotonous nights of the Victorian bourgeoisie" (1990, p. 3). Although yet another historical grey in grey, for the left Freudians the shift is not without meaning:

> By placing the advent of the age of repression in the seventeenth century, after hundreds of years of open spaces and free expression, one adjusts it to coincide with the development of capitalism: it becomes an integral part of the bourgeois order. The minor chronicle of sex and its trials is transposed into the ceremonious history of the modes of production; its trifling aspect fades from view. A principle of explanation emerges after the fact: if sex is so rigorously repressed, this is because it is incompatible with a general and intensive work imperative. At a time when labor capacity was being systematically exploited, how could this capacity be allowed to dissipate itself in pleasurable pursuits, except in those—reduced to a minimum—that enabled it to reproduce itself? (Pp. 5–6)

But the darkest hour comes just before the dawn. Sex is a drive, an imperative force in human nature; repression eventuates in a return of the repressed. "And the sexual cause—the demand for sexual freedom, but also for the knowledge to be gained from sex and the right to speak about it—becomes legitimately associated with the honor of a political cause: sex too is placed on the agenda for the future" (p. 6).

Thus Foucault establishes the polemical framework of his investigation. He does not discuss the proponents of the repressive hypothesis in any depth, but it is clear who he has in mind. He cites Reich as an early advocate of this position; he alludes to the "great Refusal" and "hyper-repressive desublimation," hence to Marcuse's version of critical theory (pp. 96, 114); he invokes the New Left sexual rebellion of the 1960s, in which Reichian texts and Marcuse himself played a part (p. 5); and at times he engages in an imagined dialogue with an anonymous critic, who speaks from a specifically French Freudian position (pp. 36, 53, 81, 150). So, while one might complain about his scholarliness, he has taken on the versions of critical theory that had the greatest practical effect—precisely Reich's sex-pol movement in the interwar years and the Marcusean / New Left theories of sexual-cum-political revolt of the 1960s.

Foucault's relationship to this left Freudian history of sexuality is complex. On one level he does not challenge it; he too sees important changes beginning in the seventeenth century. At times he seems to grant that sexual repression is at least a significant feature of the last several centuries, if not the most basic one, and he also evinces a certain respect for the Freudian achievement. Although he raises doubts about the repressive hypothesis, he claims that the doubts are "aimed less at showing it to be mistaken than at putting it back within the general economy of discourses on sex in modern societies since the seventeenth century" (p. 11). And he holds, if weakly, to the project of going beyond the existing sexual regime.

More closely considered, however, Foucault is rather more than a doubting Thomas. He asks:

> Is sexual repression truly an historically established fact? . . . Do the workings of power, and in particular those mechanisms that are brought into play in societies such as ours, really belong primarily to the category of repression? . . . Did the critical discourse that addresses itself to repression [that of Freud and his leftist successors] come to act as a roadblock to a power mechanism that had operated unchallenged up to that point, or is it not in fact part of the same historical network as the thing it denounces (and doubtless misrepresents) by calling it "repression"? (P. 10)

In raising these questions, Foucault is executing a glissade through which he has already answered them. He intends nothing less than a radical shift in the perspective from which sex and sexuality are to be analyzed, a shift that will bring to light a very different history of modern sexuality.

Let's cut directly to the central issues. In its earliest and simplest version, psychoanalysis characterizes sex as a drive with highly determining effects on apparently nonsexual mental processes and modes of social interaction, as well as on sexual behavior itself. Repression is an intrapsychic technique for managing this disruptive force. It prevents the sexual wishes of, especially, infancy and early childhood from emerging into consciousness. It is reinforced by repression in the more general social sense (for example, religious prohibitions). In combination, the two forms of repression mobilize social pressure against the force of the sexual drive through the institution of internalized moral authorities. The kingdom of the mind becomes hierarchically ordered, in a veritable image of the political kingdom. Morality is enthroned, while the sexual drives are either domesticated or outlawed.

Thus the classical psychoanalytic model combines the notion of sex as a drive with a conception of power relations as hierarchical and restrictive. In the left Freudian and Marcusean instance, capitalism is introduced as the power behind the throne—that is, as the situational explanation for sexual repression. Power mediates the relationship between capitalism as a mode of production and the sexual drives of individuals in such a way as to turn sexual energy, libido, into labor-power: labor is alienated libido.

Foucault sets out to challenge the foundations of this argument. Instead of taking sex as a drive, a biological given, he asks the historical question, how does sex come to be seen as a drive? Sex may be the god in the machine, but who built the machine, under what circumstances, and with what consequences? Instead of begging the question of how sexuality evolves historically by positing sex as an a priori principle, Foucault wants to call the sex drive itself to historical account.

The Foucauldian critique includes not only the idea of repressed sexuality but also the concept of repression itself. In sexual repression one party (social or psychological, as the case may be) is exerting power over another. Power is prohibitive, on the one side, and rebellious, on the other. Foucault does not deny that such relationships exist. He contends, however, that power in general more nearly resembles a contingently interwoven network of strategic interactions that only occasionally takes on the form of stabilized and repressive hierarchies. When, consequently, prohibition is put forward as the paradigmatic form of power, a part has been allowed to (mis)represent, indeed to disguise and occlude, the whole. Foucault aims to elucidate this larger domain of power relationships.

Foucault not only broadens the definition of power, he also relocates it. Although both psychoanalysis and critical theory include the analysis of power, in each instance power plays its familiar role as mediator, as a means to an end external to it. But for Foucault, power itself is the interpretive perspective. He does not follow Nietzsche in interpreting power ontologically. Rather, he intends to keep ontological claims to an absolute minimum. As "Maurice Florence" puts it, Foucault's "first methodological rule" is "to circumvent anthropological universals to the greatest possible extent, so as to interrogate them in their historical constitution" (in Gutting 1994, p. 317).[7] This is the skeptical approach he takes to the claim that the sexual drive is constitutive of human nature. It is also the approach he would have to take to the anthropological universalization of a will to power. But short of this perhaps metaphysical extreme, power is his privileged interpretive perspective.

8.

We may think of *The History of Sexuality* as consisting of three dimensions: a challenge to the empirical-conceptual claims of the "repressive hypothesis," along with an initial reconstruction of the discursive history of sexuality; an articulation of the perspective of power, especially in the form of the will to knowledge; and the development of a more general historical narrative within which to place power, knowledge, and sexuality. In short, we have a critique, an alternative perspective, and an alternative historical interpretation.

First the critique. Empirically, Foucault does not deny that "new rules of propriety" and "a policing of statements" developed during the modern period. But the appearance of censorship and silencing is misleading: "around and apropos of sex, one sees a veritable discursive explosion" (1990, pp. 17–18). The Catholic confessional of the premodern period, in which sex was both directly named and to be spoken about in detail, changes in one respect but not in the other. Sex is not spoken of so directly, but the confessional mode is maintained and enlarged. The essential point is this "incitement to discourse": "What is peculiar to modern societies, in fact, is not that they consigned sex to a shadow existence, but that they dedicated themselves to speaking of it *ad infinitum*, while exploiting it as *the* secret" (p. 35).

This emergent sexual discourse takes shape as a science with characteristic means of gaining knowledge and characteristic objects of knowledge created by these very means. In the former regard, we have a confessional science, of which psychoanalysis is clearly the most elaborated form. Its attributes include a clinical codification of the inducement to speak; the postulate of a general and diffuse causality, with sex as the cause of even manifestly nonsexual phenomena; therefore a latency of sexuality, an unconscious sexuality that can be forced to speak; a method of interpretation that brings forth this truth about sexuality; and the medicalization of the process, the inscription of sexuality within the domain of medical therapy (pp. 65–67). In the latter regard, this process of interrogation generates four principal objects of knowledge: "the hysterical woman, the masturbating child, the Malthusian couple, and the perverse adult" (p. 105). Thus the analytic question becomes not only how and why a sexual science emerged but also why it constructed precisely these objects of knowledge.

9.

Like the critical theorists, Foucault ties his investigation of sexuality to the evolution of the capitalist system; unlike them, he does not anchor the analysis in the problematics of labor and libido. As indicated above, he operates from the perspective of power and with a distinctive conception of power itself.

Foucault begins his discussion of power by imagining a French psychoanalytic (Lacanian) critic of his critique of the repressive hypothesis. The critic accuses him of conflating the early Freudian or Reichian / Marcusean model of sexual drive and moral prohibition with the sophisticated psychoanalytic view of the constitutive role of the law (that is, the Law of the Father) with respect to desire. The latter, in which desire is never outside of the power of the law, is itself a refutation of the former. This conflation, the critic claims, permits Foucault to play a double game:

> You confuse your adversaries by appearing to take the weaker position, and, discussing repression alone, you would have us believe, wrongly, that you have rid yourself of the power of the law; and yet you keep the essential practical consequence of the principle of power-as-law, namely, the fact that there is no escaping from power, that it is always-already present, constituting the very thing which one attempts to counter it with. (P. 82)

Not so, Foucault responds. He is perfectly willing to acknowledge the variations in psychoanalytic theory. But whatever the differences between the two versions of the theory, in both cases the exercise of power is identified with prohibition:

> Underlying both the general theme that power represses sex and the idea that the law constitutes desire, one encounters the same putative mechanics of power. It is defined in a strangely restrictive way, in that, to begin with, this power is poor in resources, sparing of its methods, monotonous in the tactics it utilizes, incapable of invention, and seemingly doomed always to repeat itself. Further, it is a power that only has the force of the negative on its side, a power to say no; in no condition to produce, capable only of posting limits, it is basically anti-energy. (P. 85)

This conception of power has a historical foundation. It grew up alongside European monarchies and the legal systems associated with them (even if the association sometimes took on the form of opposition). But such a "juridico-discursive" conception of power, of "power that has its central point in the enunciation of the law" (p. 90), is only part of the story. One must expand the conception to grasp the manifold ways in which power interacts with sexuality.

Just here we come to the neo-Nietzschean heart of Foucault's analysis. I say "neo-Nietzschean" because Foucault does not fully embrace a will to power. Rather, his expanded conception of power appears to be more descriptive than explanatory, more a way of mapping interactive processes than a way of theoretically explaining them. Of course, this appearance might be deceptive. A power-drive may be implicit in or even required for his conception of power relations. Alternatively, it may be that he has rid Nietzsche's philosophy of a residual homunculus of subjective causality. Either way, his conception of power bears an unmistakable Nietzschean stamp:

> Power must be understood in the first instance as the multiplicity of force relations immanent in the sphere in which they operate and which consti- tute their own organization; as the process through which, through cease- less struggle and confrontations, transforms, strengthens, or reverses them; as the support which these force relations find in one another, thus form- ing a chain or a system, or on the contrary, the disjunctions and contradic- tions which isolate them from one another; and, lastly, as the strategies in which they take effect, whose general design or institutional crystallization is embodied in the state apparatus, in the formulation of the law, in the var- ious social hegemonies. (Pp. 92–93)

When Foucault adds that "where there is power, there is resistance" and that "resistance is never in a position of exteriority in relation to power" (p. 95), we come very close to a pervasive will to power which "can manifest itself only against resistances" and which therefore "seeks that which resists it" (Nietzsche 1901 [hereafter *WP*], p. 346).

When sexuality is viewed from this broadly Nietzschean perspective, its Freudian features fade away. Sex is no longer seen as "a stubborn drive, by nature alien and of necessity disobedient to a power which exhausts itself trying to subdue it and often fails to control it entirely." It appears

> rather as an especially dense transfer point for relations of power: between men and women, young people and old people, parents and offspring, teachers and students, priests and laity, an administration and a population. Sexuality is not the most intractable element in power relations, but rather one of those endowed with the greatest instrumentality: useful for a num- ber of maneuvers and capable of serving as a point of support, as a linchpin, for the most varied strategies. (Foucault 1990, p. 103)

The task is then to see how power relations immanently constitute the field of sexual knowledge as well as to explain the historical evolution of this power / knowledge relationship.

10.

Foucault approaches this task from two, mutually reinforcing directions. First, he contends that within the ruling classes the system of kinship alliances tended to be replaced by the surveillance of sexuality. Second, and more broadly, he depicts a shift from juridico-discursive power to biopower. Both transitions find expression in and are mediated through the creation of the sexual sciences.

The first point might be approached negatively. The Reichian / Marcusean version of critical theory also depicts a two-stage modern history:

> The first phase corresponded to the need to form a "labor force" (hence to avoid any useless "expenditure," any wasted energy, so that all forces were reduced to labor capacity alone) and to insure its reproduction (conjugality, the regulated fabrication of children). The second phase corresponded to that epoch of *Spätkapitalismus* in which the exploitation of wage labor does not demand the same violent and physical constraints as in the nineteenth century, and where the politics of the body does not require the elision of sex or its restrictions solely to the reproductive function; it relies instead on a multiple channeling into the controlled circuits of the economy—on what has been called a hyper-repressive desublimation. (P. 114)

Foucault responds that this depiction of sexual history is backward and upside down. Sexual discipline and surveillance began with members of the bourgeoisie, who imposed it on themselves, and spread only belatedly and incompletely to the lower classes (pp. 119–22). Hence the historical question becomes, what functions did the sexual sciences perform for the bourgeoisie?

To put the answer in Nietzschean terms, the deployment of the sex / power / knowledge relationship was the vehicle for the bourgeoisie's self-overcoming, the discipline through which it created itself as a class. The effect of this new regime on the lower classes was a secondary matter:

> The primary concern was not the repression of the sex of the classes to be exploited, but rather the body, vigor, longevity, primogeniture, and descent

of the classes that "ruled." This was the purpose for which the deployment of sexuality was first established, as a new distribution of pleasures, discourses, truths, and powers; it has to be seen as the self-affirmation of one class rather than the enslavement of another: a defense, a protection, a strengthening, and an exaltation that were eventually extended to others— at the cost of different transformations—as a means of social control and political subjugation. (P. 123)

Or, to extend the Nietzschean interpretation of this passage, the deployment of sexuality derives from the will to power of the bourgeois classes, just as the deployment of alliances derived from the will to power of feudal and early modern aristocracies.[8]

The history of the deployment of sexuality, Foucault now claims, "can serve as an archaeology of psychoanalysis" (p. 130). On the one hand, psychoanalysis is the archetypal confessional science for the bourgeoisie, the characteristic vehicle for its sexual self-formation. On the other, it helps effect the transition from the system of alliance to that of sexuality by symbolically preserving the former in the latter:

> But despite everything, psychoanalysis, whose technical procedure seemed to place the confession of sexuality outside family jurisdiction, rediscovered the law of alliance, the involved workings of marriage and kinship, and incest at the heart of this sexuality, as the principle of its formation and the key to its intelligibility. The guarantee that one would find the parents-children relationship at the root of everyone's sexuality made it possible— even when everything seemed to point to the reverse process—to keep the deployment of sexuality coupled to the system of alliance. (P. 113)

Hence the logic and limits of the Reichian intervention. Reich waged war against the system of alliance as it presented itself within the deployment of sexuality. He did not, however, call into question the deployment of sexuality itself. It therefore is "apparent why one could not expect this critique to be the grid for a history of this very deployment. Nor the basis for a movement to dismantle it" (p. 131).

11.

If the Reichian/Marcusean version of critical theory cannot provide a "grid" for the history of the deployment of sexuality, what can? Or, to vary the question, what is the relationship between the deployment of sexuality and the evolution of capitalism?

Again, there is first a negative answer: The deployment of sexuality is not a function of the purely economic requirements of the capitalist mode of production. This point is made explicit in Foucault's lecture of January 7, 1976, at the Collège de France, in which he takes up the question of how to analyze power. He asks, "Is the analysis of power or of powers to be deduced in one way or another from the economy?" (Gordon 1980, p. 88). Is it that "the constitution of political power obeys the model of a legal transaction involving a contractual type of exchange," as we find in liberal versions of economism? Or is it that "power is conceived primarily in terms of the role it plays in the maintenance simultaneously of the relations of production and of a class domination which the development and specific forms of the forces of production have rendered possible," as we find in the instance of Marxist economism? Or must one drop the assumption of a primary economic causality to make possible a "non-economic analysis of power," even if "it effectively remains the case that the relations of power do indeed remain profoundly enmeshed in and with economic relations and participate with them in a common circuit?" (pp. 88–89).

Put too simply perhaps, Foucault is arguing for viewing capitalism as a system of power relations. If adequately conceptualized, this view would constitute the grid for the history of the deployment of sexuality.

Here we return, at an historically more concrete level, to the misleading tendency to subsume all power relations under the juridico-discursive model. Juridico-discursive power, Foucault contends, developed around early modern monarchical claims of sovereignty. The monarch's sovereignty was materialized in practices of "deduction" (*prélèvement*). The populace lived as it would live, outside the monarch's control. He imposed himself only at its boundaries—through processes of economic extraction and the right to kill offenders (those who threatened his power) (1990, pp. 135–36). Power in this sense was associated with the system of ruling–class alliances. And this conjuncture was both symbolized and mediated by blood. Blood was "*a reality with a symbolic function*" (p. 147). Bloodlines were to be maintained in their purity, blood was to be appropriately shed, and so on.

These practices and their symbolization have not disappeared. Nonetheless, since "the classical age the West has undergone a very profound transformation of these mechanisms of power" (p. 136). Power now flows through the (individual and social) life process itself. This is "biopower," and it operates through two principal modalities: the disciplines of the body and the regulation of populations. And in these we have the historical explanation for the emergence of the sexual sciences; sex was the "pivot" linking the two modalities of biopower: "On the one hand, it was tied to the disciplines of the body: the harnessing, intensification, and distribution of forces, the adjustment and economy of energies. On the other hand, it was applied to the regulation of populations, through all the far-reaching effects of its activities. It fitted in both categories at once" (p. 145). Both modalities converged in constituting the objects of sexual knowledge. The sexualization of children, hysterization of women, reproductive narrowing of marital sexuality, and the psychiatrization of the perversions functioned to bring life processes into the domain of biopower.

It might be protested—indeed, Foucault himself enters the protest (p. 151)—that the analysis of biopower presupposes precisely sex. How else could sex function as the constitutive medium of biopolitical relationships? Foucault's response is to distinguish between embodied sexualities and "sex *in itself*" (p. 152). He does not intend the exclusion of biology and the physiological realities of sexuality from history. Quite the contrary: biopower is a conceptualization of a specific mode of their historicization. But he insists on a distinction between these multiform sexualities and an a priori sexual principle, a sexual essence with a variety of existential manifestations. The latter is constituted through and is the symbolic center of the former. Just as commodities and money function as fetishes in political economy, so sex functions as the fetish in the sexual economy. In short, "sex is the most speculative, most ideal, and most internal element in a deployment of sexuality organized by power in its grip on bodies and their materiality, their forces, energies, sensations, and pleasures" (p. 155).

From this perspective, the left Freudian project of human emancipation is doubly misguided. It is anchored in an economistic conception of power, on the one side, and it fetishizes sexuality, on the other. What, then? Rather than liberating sexuality, we need to liberate ourselves from sexuality:

> We must not think that by saying yes to sex, one says no to power; on the contrary, one tracks along the course laid out by the general deployment of sexuality. It is the agency of sex that we must break away from, if we aim— through a tactical reversal of the various mechanisms of sexuality—to counter the grips of power with the claims of bodies, pleasures, and knowledges, in their multiplicity and their possibilities of resistance. The rallying point for the counterattack against the deployment of sexuality ought not to be sex-desire, but bodies and pleasures. (P. 157)

Breaking away from the idealism of sex does not carry with it the promise of human emancipation, but it might permit us to enjoy ourselves as embodied beings.

III. Critical Theory against Michel Foucault

12.

Foucault provides us with a virtual mirror image of the Marcusean version of critical theory. Instead of seeing the sexual drive as a determinant of social interaction, he sees historically variable patterns of social interaction determining the conceptualization of sex. Instead of seeing sexual liberation as a vital aspect of human liberation, he argues that it is vital to free ourselves from the project of sexual liberation. This inversion is accomplished by using an approximation to the will to power rather than biological imperatives as the theoretical optic.

How are we to respond to the Foucauldian critique? The prudent course would be to follow Plato's advice in the *Phaedo*. If someone were to challenge a "supposition" in your argument, Socrates says to his friends, "you would let him be and would not answer, until you examined the consequences to see if they were in agreement or discord together." Only if the challenge could not be met by attacking the attacker would one turn from offense to defense: "and when you must give account of that supposition itself, you would do it . . . by supposing another supposition, whichever seemed best of the higher suppositions, until you came to something satisfactory" (in Rouse 1956, p. 505).

If we were to play this dialectical game, we first would attempt to defend critical theory by defeating Foucault. We would seek out the inadequacies in his critique of the left Freudians and in his own history of sexuality. If these were of a sufficient magnitude, we could rightly claim that the criticism did not touch us. Only if Foucault survived the assault would we be forced to clarify further or reform our own positions. But the problem with proceeding in this fashion is that the desire to win can usurp the desire to know, in such a way as to preclude additional theoretical development. Everything turns into battles along the perimeter, and the central issues are never truly engaged. So we will invert the discursive rule and adopt a less defensive strategy.

We put ourselves in the position of Foucault's interlocutor: "If Marxism is identified with economic determinism, psychoanalysis with sexual reductionism and critical theory with the project of sexual liberation, then one might well kick over the theoretical traces. But we have available to us 'suppositions' or premises that are quite different from those of Reich, Marcuse, and the left Freudians. These premises must be specified, if the debate between us is to be meaningful."[9]

13.

Let's begin with the classic anthropological question: What do all human individuals have in common, by virtue of which we characterize them as human and distinguish them from that which is not human? We must not ask this question naïvely. Recall Foucault's desire "to circumvent anthropological universals to the greatest possible extent, so as to interrogate them in their historical constitution." But granting that we wish to interrogate such universals, is it necessary to circumvent them? And in any case, aren't some anthropological assumptions always embedded in social theory? Might it not be better to explicate these assumptions, if for no reason other than to make them available for interrogation?

To put it another way, we are not so naïve as to attempt to conceptualize "human nature as such." Rather, we aim at specifying those minimal features of human beings that help us to understand the variable forms of human interaction with which we happen to be concerned. When it is appropriate, we can also investigate the "historical constitution" of these concerns and the ways in which they shape our "anthropological universals."

Four anthropological "suppositions," then: human individuals are inherently interactive; human interaction is structured by the interpenetrating modalities of sensuousness, work, desire, and consciousness; the gateway between sensuousness and properly mental functioning—that is, the first stage of self-formation—is the oscillation between the paranoid-schizoid and depressive positions; and normatively, girls and boys pass through this gateway—which is also the passageway to individuality—in different fashions.

14.

Human Interaction. In the inner world as in the outer one, we always find more than one of us. The monad, the solitary individual, is a result of psychosocial processes, not their premise. The "individual as such," like "sex as such," is a fetish. We therefore begin with the interaction of two or more human individuals.

With Foucault in mind, these interactions can be arranged along a continuum. At one extreme, one individual or group of individuals has absolute control over another. At the other extreme, power is absolutely equalized, with the consequence that it has no determining effect on the interaction. We will suppose that in the latter situation mutual recognition is possible, whereas in the former one it is not. Or, to vary the normative framework, in the one case we have the possibility of freedom, in the other the possibility of domination. Between these extremes, there are different kinds of interaction—varyingly cooperative, competitive, mutualizing, mutually resistant, and antagonistic. Nothing in "human nature" can be assumed to determine a priori which types or patterns of interaction are going to predominate—except that, for better or for worse, children in their immaturity are going to be subjected to the power of adults.

15.

Sensuousness, Work / Desire, Consciousness. All human individuals, whatever the differences between them, are creatures of sensuousness, work, desire, and consciousness. Likewise, all interactions can be characterized in terms of these interpenetrative modalities.

- Sensuousness: Human individuals are psychophysiological organisms. As such, they are oriented toward pleasure and away from pain. Let us call this the "determinacy of pleasure and pain." Because at this elementary level pleasurable experiences tend to be life-sustaining and painful ones (if sufficiently intense) life-threatening, the determinacy of pleasure and pain does not contradict the imperative of self-preservation.

  From the ontogenetic beginning, actual experience tends to mix pleasure and pain. Aggression may be understood as the force mobilized in human individuals, when pain must be overcome to secure pleasure.

- Consciousness: The psychophysiological determinacy of pleasure and pain links us to other animate species. Our capacity for conscious mentation through the mediation of language differentiates us from them. Especially with respect to those species nearest to us, the difference is not absolute, but it does meet the old dialectical criterion of a transformation of quantity into quality.

- Work / desire: Between sensuousness and consciousness we may specify two humanizing modalities of interaction. On the one hand, and as Marx emphasized, human beings learn to work in ways that distinguish us from other species. On the other, and as psychoanalysts emphasize, human desires (not just sexual desire) are distinctively polymorphous and displaceable. They lack the automatic fixity of purely animal instinct. Thus in both regards we are creatures of imagination. Human beings are, one might say, the nonliteral animals or, more precisely, the least literal animals.

Next we picture these aspects of human individuality interactively. The interaction can be represented as "I—I," so long as the first-person singular is not essentialized—that is, it is not taken to mean something more than or different from the potentially self-unifying manifold of sensuous activity, work / desire, and consciousness. Moreover, the "I" can signify a collectivity as well as an individual. This does not mean that collectivities should be thought of as selves but rather that, at the present level of abstraction, the distinction between individual and collective function is barely emergent.

Using this representation, we can specify various relationships:

"I—I": The relationship is indeterminate.

"I = I": The relationship is one of equality. If power is involved, it has been equalized or is equally shared. The two individuals are the same as each other, in one or more respects.

"I ≠ I": The relationship is one of inequality, although not necessarily inequalities of power. Minimally, the two individuals are different from each other, in one or more respects.

"I > I": This is a relationship of inequality, in which one individual has more power than the other. The magnitude of the power differential and its field of operation are unspecified. In the model used here, the limiting case is when the power of the first party is absolute and operative in all spheres (consciousness, work / desire, and sensuousness).

No positive normative claims are built into this model. We could posit a value for human life itself, but this position turns in the well-known logical circle that the value of human life must be presupposed if human life is to be valued. We can, however, put forward a restricted negative claim: our anthropology provides no a priori basis for valuing one individual or collectivity of individuals over another. And if we arbitrarily take the additional step of affirming human life, then the substantive dimensions of the model do suggest four positive values: reduction of unnecessary pain; satisfaction of needs and creative work; gratification of desire and fulfilling relationships; and some version of mutual recognition. Yet what counts as unnecessary pain and so on is notoriously variable. Hence these values are thin, not thick, as well as existentially indeterminate.

16.

Self-Formation: Paranoid-Schizoid Position and Depressive Position. The paranoid-schizoid and depressive positions are among the fundamental building blocks of Melanie Klein's version of psychoanalytic theory (see, for example, Klein 1952). Because my general conception of psychoanalytic theory and perforce of these concepts as well departs quite considerably from hers, it seems prudent to retell the developmental tale.

Picture an infant, female or male, in the early months of postnatal life. We'll assume its psychophysiological needs are to be satisfied through interaction with its mother. She (the mother) has needs, desires, and a mind of her own. We know that she is not reducible to the performance of maternal functions, but this knowledge is not shared by her baby.

The baby's life moves in a rhythmic, metabolic circle. At one extreme there is interaction with the mother, organized around alimentation. At the other extreme there is sleep. The rhythm of life is the movement from alimentation into sleep and from sleep into alimentation. The emergent meaning of this experience is subject to the determinacy of pleasure and pain.

This depiction is not particularly psychological and certainly not psychoanalytic. The baby and its mother could figure in a variety of narratives, even Marxist or Foucauldian ones. But when we speculate on the ways in which the infant's external world shapes the formation of its internal world, we move into properly psychoanalytic territory.

To begin with, the infant's inner world is not, strictly speaking, mental. It is not differentiated from the body but rather permeated by sensations. These sensations are organized around the polarities of alimentation and somnolence. As they are mentalized, the inner world becomes structured by images of interaction, on the one side, and aloneness, on the other. Each side is also affectively colored, as are the processes that link and disjoin them.

The habitability of the emergent inner world depends on the degree of pleasure to be found in the actual metabolic process. Pleasure is a function of the adequacy of care, and adequacy of care is a function of both the mother's capacity for caregiving and the infant's capacity to make use of caregiving. In optimal situations, mother and infant find ways of cooperating in this momentous endeavor. The infant's experience is then relatively pleasurable, and the inner world is relatively easy to inhabit. But the more the actual process of mother-child interaction is experienced as painful and the more, therefore, aggressivity is mobilized, the more the inner-world polarity of interaction becomes paranoid and persecutory and the more the inner-world polarity of aloneness becomes schizoid and withdrawn.

Additionally, pain and the expectation of pain are accompanied by both anger and anxiety. These affective states can interact in such a way as to be mutually amplifying. This adds to the need for paranoid-schizoid defenses, which may or may not be adequate to contain potentially explosive affective intensities. The greater the intensity, the more rigid the defenses, until the point is reached at which the paranoid-schizoid position breaks down and psychic chaos ensues.

The paranoid-schizoid position, characterized here in its emergence, is a variable attribute of human psychological experience, but also a highly ubiquitous one. Note that it lacks the primary moral criterion of concern for the well-being of others. It is not in this regard immoral but rather premoral. According to Klein, a moral orientation begins to be formed during the first year of life, in the emotional attitude she characterizes as the depressive position. The baby begins to experience the (m)other as a separate person and as someone who can be damaged by its hostile impulses. Complex patterns of guilt and reparation come into being, along with the experience of gratitude to the (m)other for maintaining her loving and nurturing despite the emotional storminess of the situation. When all goes well, the infant emerges with precisely a "capacity for concern" (Winnicott 1963). Subsequently, the infant who becomes a child and the child who becomes an adult will oscillate between the ruthlessness of the paranoid-schizoid position and the concern for others of the depressive position, depending on how well established the depressive position is in the first instance and on the level of uncertainty, stress, anxiety, and deprivation to which the person is subjected, in the second.

17.

Individuation and Gender Differentiation. As noted above, the oscillating field established by the paranoid-schizoid and depressive positions is the gateway between sensuous and properly emotional experience. It is also the space in which individuality is constituted and in which the formation of gender begins. This is not to deny that the gendering of children by their parents can begin even before they are born, or that the process of gender formation is prolonged, complex, and often unstable. Nor is it to claim that individual identity is constituted once and for all. It is to put forward the claim that the emergence from sensuousness, individuation, and gender formation are interdependent and equally foundational processes.

In *Group Psychology and the Analysis of the Ego* Freud distinguished between relationships of identification, in which one would like to "be" the other, and relationships of object-choice, in which one would like to "have" the other (1921, p. 106). Both terms are problematic, in themselves and in any possible empirical application. But they will do to distinguish between a primary relationship, in which the infant does not clearly distinguish itself from its mother, and a secondary relationship, in which the infant is capable of making and (to a greater or lesser extent) maintaining the distinction. At its simplest, the movement from one situation to the other is all that is meant by "individuation."

Individuation does not mean becoming an individual in either a monadic or a mutualizing sense. Either outcome is possible—or both outcomes at different times. Which form of individuality emerges depends in part on the psychic position the person comes to occupy: insofar as individuality is a function of the paranoid-schizoid position, it is monadic (as well as predatory); insofar as it is a function of the depressive position, it tends to be empathic and mutualizing.

Although psychoanalysts have long maintained that girls and boys negotiate the passage to individuality in different ways, the predominant models of this developmental process have been rife with patriarchal and phallocentric assumptions. The critique of these models and their reconstruction has been the work of feminist psychoanalysts, some of whom base themselves on the work of Klein and "middle school" psychoanalysts such as D. W. Winnicott.[10] This, very briefly, is the story that they tell.

For girls, the primary feminine / maternal identification is maintained. Individuation has to occur despite this gendered entanglement. A third party or position is required to permit individuation within continued same-sex gender identification. Archetypally, this party or position is masculine, in a twofold respect. On the one hand, the little girl accepts her father (who is normatively the bearer of masculinity) as the object of erotic desire. On the other, she partially identifies with him, both to differentiate herself from her mother and to maintain her mother as an object of erotic desire. It is this latter component of feminine gender identity that is so often repressed in patriarchal cultures. When repression is successful, the girl who becomes a woman takes her assigned position within a perfectly binary (either / or) sexual order, in which assertiveness, initiative, and desire for union with a woman are gendered masculine.

For boys, the primary maternal identification is simultaneously rejected and devalued in the process of individuation. To be male is to be not-female, to be a boy is to be not-a-girl. The boy must not only repress but also split off—rigorously separate himself from—the part of himself that is identified with his mother and her desire. He must identify instead with his father and with the father's desire. The signifier of this twofold identification is the phallus (the magical, phantasied, or imaginary version of the penis).

We see, then, that (normatively) masculine and feminine identity are alienated, mirror images of each other. They are not, however, equivalents. The phallus signifies not only selfhood and desire but also power and its legitimated derivatives—the authority of the Law, the right of public speech, and so forth. In this latter regard, and not only in this latter regard, the girls who become women are the have-nots in the relationship between the sexes.

At this juncture, a not unkindly critic might object that such a depiction of self-formation, individuation, and gender differentiation goes well beyond the boundary of the anthropological. Especially when one introduces normative conceptions of gender formation, one is unquestionably in the realm of historical variation. I quite agree. Indeed, I would add that we have also begun to encounter the repressive mechanisms and familial drama of which Foucault is so skeptical. This proves, if proof were needed, that anthropological suppositions quickly slip back into the historical manifold from which they have been abstracted, revealing in the process the interests, desires, or will to power of their originator. So I will break off our anthropological construction at this point. Note, however, that the present model does not include the fetishistic "sex as such" that is the object of Foucault's analysis and criticism. On the contrary, insofar as Foucault is a critic of psychoanalytic metaphysics—of psychic energy, disposable libido, and the like—we are his allies and not his opponents.

18.

Even at the discursive level of anthropology, the identity of human individuals soon gives way to the differences between them—differences between one generation and another, one gender and another, one sexual orientation and another, and one individual and another. And when inevitably the distinction between individual and collectivity or between one collectivity and another emerges, we think of differences between races, ethnicities, and nationalities—also social classes, patterns of belief, and so on.

At this point the most unproductive of debates can occur, with one side insisting on what human beings have in common and the other on the ways in which we differ from each other. But just as in formal (or dialectical) logic we cannot think difference without identity or identity without difference, so empirically human interactions involve fluctuating patterns of identity and difference. The more productive questions are not, therefore, essentialist (Is x essentially the same as or different from y?) but situational and relational: when do differences make a difference? Is the difference or identity a good thing or a bad thing, judged by what standard, and with respect to which party? When do identities mask differences, and when do differences mask identities? In other words, if we put to one side the essentialism of *either* identity *or* difference, we ask, more concretely, when is the relationship of identity and difference problematic?

There are various ways of answering this question. Referring back to our anthropological categories, I would say the relationship between two parties becomes problematic when there are metabolic incompatibilities, oppositions of interest, disjunctive affects and opposed desires, and impediments to mutual understanding. These points of tension constitute the field of contestation between individuals and collectivities of individuals (or between collectivities and individuals). How the contest plays out depends, perhaps most importantly, on the degree and extent of antagonism structuring the field and on the power differentials active (or activated) within it. In fields of interaction with low levels of antagonism and relative equalization of power differentials, relationships of identity and difference are not especially problematic. Identity tends to be mutualizing; difference tends to be individuating. Differences, to put it another way, tend to be mutually enriching. But the greater the antagonism structuring the field, the more identity functions as constraint and difference as a basis of opposition. And the greater the power differential in such circumstances, the more one approaches the situation in which both identities and differences become the instrumentalities of domination.

19.

Where do we now stand with respect to critical theory, psychoanalysis, and Michel Foucault?

We have, first, an anthropological groundwork or perhaps only a scaffolding for the analysis of the capitalist mode of production—one in which new problems (for example, gender relations) present themselves for solution. Second, we have joined Foucault in his critique of the sexual fetishism of the left Freudians and have, to that extent, immunized psychoanalysis and critical theory from his critique. To be sure, once gender differentiation is introduced, the interpretive nexus of the family and juridico-discursive power reemerges. But because our analysis of gender is more historical than anthropological, we can follow Foucault in studying gender relationships in their situational specificity.

Third, the reformulated version of critical theory permits the subsumption of the better part of Foucault's history of sexuality. Let's consider only his major thesis, namely, that the sexual sciences are instrumentalities of emergent biopolitical relationships, replacing the system of blood and alliance that constituted the field of operation for juridico-discursive power. I'll leave to one side the possible objection that juridico-discursive power is not tied so tightly to the early modern system of alliance as Foucault seems to maintain—that its mechanisms continue to operate within the field of biopower relations, perhaps with greater subtlety but with no loss of efficacy.[11] The present point is rather that both forms of power can be analyzed from our own perspective. For example, using the anthropological notions outlined above, one can conceptualize the way in which the capitalist mode of production permeates and disrupts even the sensuous or metabolic level of social interaction while operating through structures of economic, sexual, and racial domination that resemble the Hegelian configuration of lordship and bondage (Wolfenstein 1993, chap. 8). Focusing on the sexual sciences as disciplinary and regulative forms of power linking the capitalist disruption of life processes to the more obtrusive macro-formations of domination would enrich this interpretation, but it would not overthrow its premises.

Let these three points and the preceding arguments stand as a defense of critical theory. We now may ask, what, if any, critical or interpretive leverage do our anthropological suppositions provide with respect to Foucault's work?

This question could initiate an internal critique of Foucault's position. We could ask whether Foucault's data are adequate to his interpretations or whether, for example, he must implicitly rely on Marxist or psychoanalytic categories whose use he explicitly excludes. Or we could attempt a critique through comparison, as might be done by analyzing specific empirical and pragmatic issues from Foucauldian and critical theoretical perspectives. But we again will depart from Plato's recommended strategy and offer only an interpretation of Foucault's analytic orientation, one that might or might not be viewed as a criticism.

Simply put, Foucault conceptualizes power and knowledge from the perspective of the paranoid-schizoid position. A recurring theme in *The History of Sexuality* is the productivity of power, the objects of knowledge it creates rather than the ignorance that it generates. At a minimum, power brings things into view—forces them to speak—hence the link between the psychoanalytic consulting room and the church confessional. In each instance sexuality must be brought to the surface and subjected to the gaze of the inquisitor. The power that brings things to light is persecutory. Enlightenment is a stripping away of defenses, an overcoming of resistances, the establishment of universalizing patterns of surveillance, regulation, and discipline. Yet these patterns are formed quite dispassionately and coldly. They do not proceed from the monarch's desire, they are not assertions of sovereignty and acts of revenge, nor are they even adequately configured in the image of Bentham's panopticon, which has, after all, a central point from which all the prisoners' actions and words can be monitored. Instead one needs to think in terms of a decentered panopticism: "There is no need for arms, physical violence, material constraints. Just a gaze. An inspecting gaze, a gaze which each individual under its weight will end by interiorising to the point that he is his own overseer, each individual thus exercising this surveillance over, and against, himself" (in Gordon 1980, p. 155).[12] No wonder, then, that Foucault is discontent with the repressive hypothesis. Power in the paranoid-schizoid position shines its light ever more brightly. The impression of repression is only the resistance to enlightenment, an artifact of the productivity of power.

In the interview just cited, Foucault claims he is not reducing power to this malign version (or vision) of enlightenment. Insuring visibility is only one of the strategies operative in modern society. Yet it seems fair to take knowledge-as-surveillance as paradigmatic or exemplary for Foucault. And, I suggest, the psychological basis for such a conception is the paranoid-schizoid position, in which the possibility of persecution is combined with impersonal coldness.

This interpretation helps us to understand both Foucault's appeal to those who are interested in emancipatory struggles and the difficulties involved in using his ideas to justify such efforts. On the one hand, his perspective insinuates that Big Brother (or a host of little brothers) is watching you—indeed, that being watched does not even require someone to do the watching. On the other, empathy and mutual recognition, guilt and reparation, are features of the depressive position. These values, vital for the moral or ethical grounding of political action, are simply absent in a paranoid-schizoid world. And if this world is the only world, then emancipatory efforts lack a justificatory basis.

One can, to be sure, beg the question of justification. Society is a biopolitical state of war in which overcoming the resistance of the other is always fair game. Especially because Foucault encourages us to see the operations of power at the microlevel, there is no difficulty in conceptualizing actions opposing the extension of disciplinary power. But at best—that is, if successful—any such action can only reconfigure the distribution of forces.

It cannot alter the nature of the game. This is strikingly clear in Foucault's own attempt to articulate an emancipatory project. "The rallying point for the counterattack against the deployment of sexuality ought not to be sex-desire," he proclaims, "but bodies and pleasures." Granting that sexual liberation is not the goal, rallying around the body and pleasures is not liberating. Splitting apart body and mind in this fashion, placing "the body" at the center of the struggle, is itself fetishistic, a thingification of the self and the reduction of a whole (no matter how complex and multicentered) to a part. "The body," like "sex as such," is the product of affective distancing and dissociation, an artifact of paranoid-schizoid mentation. Panopticism creates the body as its object; it cannot be resisted on that basis.

Finally, when viewed from this angle, we can also see why Foucault would minimize the emancipatory claims of clinical psychoanalysis. The paranoid-schizoid position rules out mutual recognition. One does not share feelings with another or see things from the other's point of view. Instead clinical interaction necessarily appears as a power struggle, one that the patient cannot win. Certainly, she or he can evade or thwart the analyst's will to know and thereby defeat the analysis, but these are schizoid and paranoid maneuvers, which leave the psychic situation unchanged. Surveillance has not been extended, because no analysis has taken place. The patient must be brought into the purview of the analyst's will to know, the disciplinary gaze must not be averted or subverted, and the analyst must be internalized if the analysis is to be successful. And in this instance yet another piece of psychic territory has been assimilated into the power domain of enlightenment.

20.

Various objections can be raised to this interpretation of Foucault. One might follow Plato's advice and seek out the possible internal contradictions in the argument, with the hope of being able to dismiss it. Alternatively, one could lessen the critical force of the interpretation by narrowing the distance between critical theory and Foucauldian power/knowledge. It might be granted that Foucault's world has a paranoid-schizoid structure—not, however, because his perspective is paranoid-schizoid but because the modern social world is structured in this fashion. Or one could argue that in his last years Foucault was venturing beyond the power principle and, in the process, opening up the possibility of grounding an ethics of resistance. But these strategies, although legitimate enough in their own right, evade the real nexus of contestation. The more powerful objection is that our interpretation of Foucault is an imposition of meaning on him—yet another instance of the object of knowledge being swallowed up by the knowing subject. The paranoid-schizoid position is in the eye of the beholder, and interpreting *The History of Sexuality* in these terms is precisely an example of a power/knowledge relationship. Transparently, a psychoanalytic will to know aims at overcoming the resistance of Foucauldian social theory. Or, to put it another way, the problem with my interpretation of Foucault is that it presupposes the validity of anthropological principles that he is entitled to call into question. He may not be positing an ontological will to power, but he is using the principle of overcoming resistance as his interpretive perspective. He is free to examine our premises, no less than those of Marcuse and the left Freudians, in this light. And he might well see them as normalizing and regulative, as part and parcel of the regime of biopower, even if they do not center on the fetish of "sex as such."

Because Foucault raises questions concerning the nature of clinical interaction and the play of social power in our own historical situation, we will resume the conversation with him at the inquiry's end. But at this juncture, he must be replaced by Nietzsche. Foucault does not really push his arguments to their limits. Although there is a quite genuine modesty in this deference, there is also evasiveness, an unwillingness to take responsibility for the implications of a given line of reasoning. This permits him to back away from his most extreme and provocative positions. And because he avoids ontological or foundational questions, he can always retreat to the position that power is just one perspective among many, not to be privileged over interests and desires. This is a more reasonable (commonsensical) position, of course, but it does not constitute a fundamental challenge to either psychoanalysis or critical theory. Nietzsche, by contrast, takes his arguments as far as they will go and, in so doing, challenges the hedonic and utilitarian presuppositions of more conventional forms of social theorizing. We cannot rest content with either our own anthropological conceptions or our interpretation of Foucault until we have settled our accounts with him and with the will to power.

2

Overcoming Resistance

The will to power can manifest itself only against resistances; therefore it seeks that which resists it.

—Nietzsche, *The Will to Power*

I. Prelude: The Magic Mountain

1.

The focus now narrows. The will to power confronts the determinacy of
pleasure and pain in this chapter; perspectivism is deployed as an epistemology of psychoanalytic practice in the next. In both instances we advance
phenomenologically from surface to depth, while questions concerning the
status of dialectical reason hover in the background.

Because Nietzsche joins the will to power to perspectivism, I'll recount an
incident in which this conjunction is evident. It took place at an interdisciplinary psychoanalytic meeting. The participants were academics who use
psychoanalytic theory in their work, some clinically trained, some not, as
well as psychoanalytic psychiatrists affiliated with university training hospi-
tals. The meeting was held at a mountain retreat, which at times created a
somewhat magical mood—not quite the "6000 feet beyond man and time"
where the idea of eternal recurrence came to Nietzsche (Nietzsche 1888b
[hereafter *EH*], p. 295) but sufficiently removed from the everyday world so
that the boundaries between inner and outer reality could blur somewhat. It
resembled, therefore, the transitional space first conceptualized by D. W.
Winnicott—that is, a space in which playing is possible just because it is not
necessary to settle the question of what is real and what is not (1971).

We had just viewed Joan Campion's film *Sweetie* and were preparing to discuss it. Three women, none of whom was a clinician and all of whom were involved in literary studies, led the discussion. They began by ruling out "clinical"—that is, diagnostic—interpretations. The group accepted this limitation and proceeded to work on the meanings of the film. We managed to stay close to the narrative and, importantly, adopted alternately the perspectives of the film's main characters—especially of the two sisters who embody painfully twisted forms of feminine identity. For some of us, the experience was both pleasurable and creative, but in time one of the psychiatrists mildly protested that the initial interdiction prevented him from "demonstrating his power." His request for inclusion was accepted, and the discussion took a more diagnostic turn.

I cannot unpack all the meanings of this complex interaction, but I would like to focus on four points. First, the group leaders were aware that the film lent itself to psychiatric as well as psychoanalytic reduction. They foresaw the possibility that the language of the film would be transformed into diagnostic categories and that the protagonists would be reduced to clinical types. They were attempting to avoid this eventuality and were successful. Second, the means the leaders used to accomplish their end did involve a prohibition, thus the psychiatrist could quite legitimately appeal to the rules of discursive fair play in protesting his exclusion. It was striking to me, however, that he did not appeal to these rules directly but rather chose to protest the limitation of his power. One could take this simply as his way of saying he was not being given the opportunity to express what he really thought. But I had the impression that he was protesting, if politely, a narcissistic injury—that is, he felt resentful because he was not permitted to use all his thinking apparatus. In any case, and with whatever affective valence, he was reacting to a real feature of the situation: the leaders had exercised power to limit power.

Third, the leaders were epistemologically sophisticated. They recognized that psychological interpretation involves and reflects various kinds of power relationships. They not only were self-aware in their exercise of power; they also were demonstrating how power constitutes knowledge by providing the group with an explicit experience of prohibitive processes (juridico-discursive power, Foucault would say) that usually operate implicitly.

Fourth, it was an unmistakable feature of this incident that interpretive categories and the power / knowledge experience were gendered. Women were running the group, and only (some of the) men protested the group process. The psychiatric categories once deployed moved away from a cinematic domain richly evocative of women's emotional lives and into an apparently gender-neutral realm of concepts and categories—precisely the apparent neutrality that so often masks masculinist thinking.

I should also mention what I later learned about the origins of the leaders' discursive strategy. The previous evening one of the three women had been talking with a group of people, including a couple of the psychiatrists. She had casually mentioned that she identified with Sweetie in the film. Sweetie is a sexually unrepressed and emotionally uncontrolled woman who is set off against her sexually repressed and emotionally inhibited sister. She is very much daddy's little girl, trapped in eternal childhood out of the need to please and perform for him. And she is the family "bad object," the container of all its unwanted impulses and desires. In expressing her identification with Sweetie (not in all particulars, it should be noted), the woman at the conference was simultaneously acknowledging painful features of her own childhood and affirming her own identity: she did not need to disavow or split off the Sweetie part of herself.

The psychiatrists in the group interpreted this communication in their own terms, with the consequence that the narrator felt that she had been reduced to a diagnostic category. If, therefore, the discussion leaders erected defenses against reductive interpretation, it was to prevent a recurrence of this experience, this time with respect to the women in the film. To put it a bit differently, to open up a space where the film could be empathically experienced, a species of unempathic reductionism had to be ruled out in advance.

Thus we seemingly have a straightforward tale of power and knowledge, but it is possible to have second thoughts. What about the protesting psychiatrist? I don't really know what motivated his intervention. Perhaps my experience of it as the expression of resentment was simply its meaning in group context—for us and not for him, as the Hegelians would say. Perhaps, indeed, my perception of resentment was the result of projection: maybe I was unconsciously angry at him for disrupting the aesthetic space we had been occupying and attributed my anger to him. Moreover, it might seem that I am of two or even three minds about the incident. From one angle, the incident turns on pain—vulnerability, injury, emotional response to injury. From another, the issue is power—who gets to do what to whom. From yet a third, the core issue is gender, not merely as a matter of who/whom but also as an ontological question: what "really" happened, is there indeed something that really happened, or are there only feminine and masculine realizations occurring in an otherwise unfilled time/space? Thus we have contending psychoanalytic, Nietzschean, and feminist interpretations, not reducible, the one to the other, without a standard that legitimates the reduction, and with each position claiming to be the standard-bearer.

Additional doubts arise. What is the meaning of this multiplication of perspectives? It might seem to be a failure of nerve, an anxiety-driven retreat from the preceding critique of psychiatric power/knowledge, another failed oedipal rebellion, resulting in intellectual self-fragmentation. Conversely, multiplying perspectives is a characteristically Nietzschean exercise of interpretive power in which there is no need to settle the matter but rather the strength to interpret without a central point of reference. On this reading, it is anxiety that results in clinging to one perspective, overcoming anxiety that allows the interpretive process to float without an anchor. And then what? Are we speaking in body language? Is assertion and sticking to the point phallic? Is a web of interpretations, deep but without a defined bottom, vaginal or uterine?

Lest it seem that I am becoming lost in obsessional rumination, think of the ordinary clinical situation. An interpretation is offered, sometimes with an inner sense of conviction leading the analyst to view the patient's anger and objections as resistance. At other times this sense of conviction is a countertransference—for example, the analyst's resistance to the emergence of something anxiety-producing that she or he does not understand. Sticking to the interpretation then might be seen as a defensive deployment of the will to power. At yet other times an interpretation seems doubtful from the beginning but must nonetheless be put forward. And so very often the analyst is confused and/or anxious and must try to interpret her or his own dysphoric experience.

In sum, both our interdisciplinary vignette and clinical psychoanalysis raise questions of perspective as well as power. For just this reason they lend weight to Foucault's idea of power/knowledge relationships. They also suggest a question concerning perspectivism itself: when is perspectivism a defense against a painful or difficult truth, and when is the assertion of a truth a defense against painful and difficult perspectival ambiguities?

2.

We might use the *Sweetie* incident to raise an additional question of method. The power/knowledge strategy of the group leaders was designed to prevent reductionist interpretations of the film. Analytic reduction was viewed as an instrument of discursive warfare. It had to be ruled out to secure a feminine and aesthetic territory from masculine and psychiatric invasion. Reduction is also the primary method of phenomenological advance, the way in which secondary meanings are stripped away so that the simplest, perhaps even essential, meanings of an object are brought to light. We must employ it if we wish clearly to represent the will to power. But isn't the one use of reduction at odds with the other? Doesn't the will to power *in* analytic reduction undermine any attempt to investigate the will to power *through* analytic reduction?

Maybe so. Although the question can be questioned, I would not deny that a psychoanalytic will to power plays a significant role in the investigation. Yet the aim is to make psychoanalytic use of the will to power and not just to overcome a Nietzschean resistance to psychoanalytic knowing. This requires the exercise of a measure of epistemic restraint: we must grant the autonomous or objective existence of Nietzsche's thinking and strive to represent it accurately.

In the next chapter it will emerge that at times Nietzsche himself seems to accept just such epistemic restraints. He also—often and ultimately— throws them off. Let's stick to the present issue. I suggested at the outset and will argue in what follows that Nietzsche treats a perspective as the "whence" of the will to power and the will to power as the "whither" of a perspective. A "perspective" is a position from which meaning is imposed, and the imposition of meaning is a function of the will to power. Here we have the ultimate analytic reduction, an ontological / epistemological monism.

If Nietzsche's philosophy did not include this important monistic aspect, there would be no reason to consider monisms further. As it is, we might specify one of the epistemological problems they involve. The sociologist Marion Levy, from whom I took a course many years ago, liked to say that monisms were either meaningless but true or meaningful but false. Take, for example, Hegel's rejection of abstract idealism. The ontological assertion that subject equals object ($A = A$) is true, he claims, but trivial—a "night in which . . . all cows are black" (Hegel 1977, p. 9). This meaninglessness is overcome if the subject-object relationship is conceptualized dialectically. Then it can be seen that "wherever there is movement, wherever there is life, wherever anything is carried into effect in the actual world, there Dialectic is at work" (Hegel 1892, p. 148). This monistic interpretation of life is determinate; it has a specific content and is not meaningless. But it is not true. One can easily point to nondialectical movements and life processes or to equally plausible interpretations of life processes. For example, what can be interpreted as dialectical process from one perspective might be interpreted as will to power from another. Hence the universalized version of dialectics is false as well as meaningful.

Levy, I would emphasize, was not claiming that all monisms are epistemologically useless. Monisms of the second type, no doubt paradoxically, teach us something about reality by falsifying it. This paradox is not limited to monisms. By leaving something out of a manifold of phenomena, analytic reduction necessarily falsifies it. The truth adduced in this fashion is one-sided relative to the many-sidedness of the manifold itself. Thus monisms are simply the paradox of analytic reduction laid bare, the point at which establishing the truth about things becomes hard to distinguish from falsifying them.

Levy does not push the analysis of analytic reduction this far, but I might take it a Nietzschean step further: if analytic reduction is an expression of the will to power and monistic interpretations are the ultimate analytic reductions, then monistic interpretations are the ultimate expression of will to power. Put more concisely—that is, with the middle term dropped out—the monistic interpretation of things *as* will to power is the ultimate expression *of* will to power.

With this statement, the initial stage of our descent is complete and we have entered Nietzsche's world. I turn first to the explication of the will to power and then to a series of thought experiments in which, ultimately, the will to power finds its place within the determinacy of pleasure and pain.

II. "This world is the will to power— and nothing besides!"

3.

The title of this section is taken from *The Will to Power*, the collection of Nietzsche's notes published by Nietzsche's sister after his death. The thought continues and the book concludes with, "And you yourself are will to power—and nothing besides!" (*WP*, p. 550).

It is appropriate to begin the explication of the will to power at this end point because one of the issues that arises in interpreting Nietzsche is how to use the material in his notebooks. Bernd Magnus differentiates between "lumpers," who feel free to use these notebooks, and "splitters," who view them as suspect: "In particular lumpers and splitters often divide over the importance of the concept of the will to power (which is mentioned rarely in the published work) and the cosmological version of the doctrine of eternal recurrence (which appears only in the unpublished work)" (Magnus and Higgins 1996, p. 58).[1]

Meaningful differences exist between the works Nietzsche himself published and those he did not, but I do not think they divide in the way specified by Magnus. The will to power is first named in *Thus Spoke Zarathustra*. It is the guiding principle or presiding force of part 2 of that work; it provides the content to the form of the overman, who is the dominant figure in part 1; and it is the force that permits the affirmation of eternal return in part 3. Thereafter it occupies a strategic position in the first part of *Beyond Good and Evil* and is the basic interpretive principle in *On the Genealogy of Morals* and *The Antichrist*. Moreover, the will to power is a way of thinking about things as well as the most general proposition from which Nietzsche's more specific arguments can be derived. It is there in the published works if one has eyes to see it.

As to eternal return, Nietzsche introduces it in *The Gay Science* as an ontological hypothesis (What if things recur eternally?) and treats it ontologically in *Thus Spoke Zarathustra*. It is also the implied standard of postmoral judgment in his later work. He does not, it is true, put forward arguments in support of its cosmological status in his published works, while by contrast he does attempt such arguments in *The Will To Power*. This disjunction can be interpreted in various ways, including the possibility that Nietzsche was trying to work out a satisfactory defense of the idea but was not yet satisfied with his results. Be that as it may, the difference between the published and unpublished works is not in the concept of eternal return itself but in the presence or absence of argument in its support.

At least with respect to will to power and eternal return, therefore, I fail to see any *contradiction* between what Nietzsche published and what he did not. Moreover, we cannot take the work he published as his final say, especially when he himself believed that he had more to say. *The Antichrist* was one of Nietzsche's last completed works. Yet he intended it to be the first of four parts of a revaluation of all values. Viewed this way—prospectively and open-endedly rather than as the detritus of a totalized body of work—the notebooks would be interpreted as work in progress.

How, then, does one distinguish between work that Nietzsche viewed as finished—that is, as fit for publication—and work that is by definition unfinished? In two ways, I would say. First, the expectations and standards of judgment differ in the two cases. The very act of publication creates the position of the author who puts before the public what he intends to say and who expects to be judged for what has been said. In reading unpublished work, we invade the author's privacy. We cannot, by rights, hold him accountable the same way. We also should be expecting to find incomplete lines of argument, unsuccessful as well as successful thought-experiments, and so forth. These are, however, the author's thoughts, and—to return to Nietzsche and the will to power—just these lines of argument and thought-experiments help us to understand what the concept meant to him.

Second, in the published works Nietzsche mainly *employs* the concept of a will to power, while in the unpublished ones he also attempts to *explicate* it.

The same holds true for perspectivism and at least the background thoughts that crystallize in eternal return. Taken together, these thoughts constitute a way of thinking. In the published works we primarily see the results of Nietzsche's thinking through them; in the notebooks we also see him thinking them through.

Because we are interested in the possible psychoanalytic employment of the will to power and perspectivism, Nietzsche's thought-experiments cannot fail to be of interest to us. This would not be the case if we were primarily concerned with the persona of the author or the artistry of his creations. Thus, while I would not deny Magnus's claim that "the position that scholars take on the status of the unpublished material often has repercussions for how significant they consider certain themes in Nietzsche's work as a whole" (Magnus and Higgins 1996, p. 58), I also would argue that one's judgment of the significance of certain themes in Nietzsche's work has repercussions for the choices one makes concerning the use of the unpublished manuscripts.

That said, I will trace the genesis and presence of the will to power in Nietzsche's published work before representing his experiments with it in the manuscripts.

4.

Nietzsche published his first book, *The Birth of Tragedy out of the Spirit of Music*, in 1872, when he was twenty-eight years old.[2] His argument turned on two animating principles of Greek culture, which he termed the "Dionysian" and the "Apollonian." The works he published over the next ten years, although certainly not devoid of sustained argument, point of view, distinctive sensibility, and the like, lacked explicit interpretive principles of this kind. But toward the end of this period, he began to experience occasional euphoric states, out of which the will to power, eternal return, and the other characteristic principles of his later philosophy emerged.

The will to power is initially announced in the first part of *Thus Spoke Zarathustra*, but the elements from which it is formed are clearly visible in *The Gay Science*. Kaufmann draws our attention to section 13 of book 1, in which Nietzsche expands on the notion that "benefiting and hurting others are ways of exercising one's power upon others; this is all one desires in such cases" (Nietzsche 1882 [hereafter *GS*], p. 86). This anticipates a psychological application of the will to power. But two other sections come closer to the concept itself and not just to its application.

Section 118 is on benevolence. Where benefiting and hurting others were derived in section 13 from the desire to experience power, here the virtue of benevolence is derived from the impulse to assimilate or be assimilated:

> *Benevolence.*—Is it virtuous when a cell transforms itself into a function of a stronger cell? It has no alternative. And is it evil when the stronger cell assimilates the weaker? It also has no alternative; it follows necessity, for it strives for superabundant substitutes and wants to regenerate itself. Hence we should make a distinction in benevolence between the impulse to appropriate and the impulse to submit, and ask whether it is the stronger or weaker that feels benevolent. Joy and desire appear together in the stronger that wants to transform something into a function; joy and the wish to be desired appear together in the weaker that wants to become a function. (Pp. 175–76)

Thus Nietzsche explains the two forms of benevolence from the perspective of assimilative and appropriative relationships between stronger and weaker parties. These processes will later constitute the mode of operation of the will to power. Moreover, these psychological relationships are analogized to intercellular processes. This is not to say that the explanation of values in terms of assimilation and appropriation is biologically or bio-ontologically grounded. But Nietzsche could not analogize society and biology if he did not see them as having something in common. To this extent, the boundary between the natural and the human is breached, although it is a moot point as to which one is the stronger party.

In the next passage (section 119), Nietzsche challenges the notion that self-sacrifice (allowing oneself to be assimilated) is altruistic:

> *No altruism!*—In many people I find an overwhelmingly forceful and plea-surable desire to be a function: they have a very refined sense of all those places where precisely they could "function" and push in those directions. Examples include those women who transform themselves into some func-tion of a man that happens to be underdeveloped in him, and thus become his purse or his politics or his sociability. Such beings preserve themselves best when they find a fitting place in another organism. If they fail to do this, they become grumpy, irritated, and devour themselves. (P. 176)

Some organisms are fulfilled when they are appropriated by and function within another. This is not altruism but rather self-realization. The example chosen to make this point are women who perform a function that completes a man. This aligns such women with the weaker and submissive beings of the preceding passage.

In this example, Nietzsche is not putting forward a claim about all women and all men, nor is he deriving his analysis of assimilative relationships from sexual ones. Assimilative processes are the generality, and gender complementarity the particularity, and only particular men and women are being depicted. If, however, we have license to interpret these sections as anticipations of the will to power and if we generalize from some cases to all cases, then the implication would be that the male will to power is oriented toward assimilation and mastery, whereas the female will to power is oriented toward being assimilated and being mastered. This is not so much the human, all-too-human as it is the familiar, all-too-familiar. The polarities of the emergent will to power are isomorphic with sexual relationships of male dominance.

In book 4, section 310, we go beyond the determinate relationships specified above:

> *Will and Wave.*—How greedily this wave approaches, as if it were after something! How it crawls with terrifying haste into the inmost nooks of this labyrinthine cliff! It seems that it is trying to anticipate someone; it seems that something of value, high value, must be hidden there.—And now it comes back, a little more slowly but still quite white with excitement; is it disappointed?—But already another wave is approaching, still more greedily and savagely than the first, and its soul, too, seems to be full of secrets and the lust to dig up treasures. Thus live waves—thus live we who will—more I will not say. (P. 247)

This apostrophe to ocean reflects the inspired states of mind that Nietzsche was beginning to experience. From his elevated perspective, he sees wave upon wave, the soul of each seeming to lust after treasure. The simile is anthropomorphizing, the human is projected into the natural. But the recoil ("thus live waves, thus live we who will") brings the power of the waves into the domain of the human will. This could be read as simply a restatement of the Dionysian principle in *The Birth of Tragedy*, with its resonances of Schopenhauer's world as will. In this instance, however, the world is not identified with suffering and privation, as it is by Schopenhauer, nor is there an Apollonian idea or representation to oppose it. Rather, as the waves rise above him, Nietzsche asks them, "Are you angry with me? . . . Are you afraid I might give away your whole secret?" If so, they need not fear: "Everything suits me, for everything suits you so well, and I am so well-disposed toward you for everything: how could I think of betraying you?

For—mark my word!—I know you and your secret, I know your kind! You and I—are we not of one kind?—You and I—do we not have *one secret?*" (p. 248). The movement from the human into the natural and the reflux of the natural into the human culminate in the identification of the one with the other. There is one secret in both will and wave, and—although it is not named, perhaps because Nietzsche did not yet have a name for it—we do have another aspect of the will to power, to wit, the restless, acquisitive mobility of wave upon wave.

5.

As noted, the initial published articulation of will to power is in the first part of *Thus Spoke Zarathustra:* "A table of the good hangs over every people. Behold, it is the tablet of their overcomings; behold, it is the voice of their will to power" (*TSZ*, p. 170). The will to power underlies and animates historically variable moral valuations. In each instance values specify the aim of a people, hence also that which they must overcome and master. Good and evil are valuations of this kind, and especially powerful ones. The overman's task is to overcome them and to create values beyond good and evil.

The idea of overcoming and being overcome unifies the various experiences and phenomena we saw in *The Gay Science*, and the will to power provides them with a name. Overcoming is also the unifying motif in *Thus Spoke Zarathustra*. At the outset the overman is announced as the one who overcomes conventional morality, and in the end Zarathustra must overcome his dread of eternal return. In between, he must overcome those of his own experiences that seem most likely to overcome him—the ones that threaten to preclude his affirmation of eternal return. He must, in short, overcome himself.

The relationship between Zarathustra's self-overcoming and the will to power is evident in the placement of two sections in the second part of the text. In "The Tomb Song" Zarathustra evokes the experiences that threatened to overwhelm or undermine him and then calls forth his will as "the shatterer of all tombs" (p. 225). In the next section, "On Self-Overcoming," he articulates the concept itself.

Zarathustra addresses himself to thinkers and truth-seekers, those who are animated by a "will to truth." Their will to truth, he claims, is a will to "*make* all being thinkable," to make it "yield and bend" so it can serve as their "mirror and reflection": "That is your whole will, you who are wisest: a will to power—when you speak of good and evil too, and valuations" (ibid.). The will to truth—Foucault's will to know—is the epistemic version of the will to power. This is not its only form. "Where I found the living," says Zarathustra, "there I found will to power" (p. 226). Although the term "the living" is socially inflected and Zarathustra is primarily interested in human relationships of obedience and command, social processes are treated as instances of life processes more generally: "And life itself confided this secret to me: 'Behold,' it said, 'I am *that which must always overcome itself.* Indeed, you call it a will to procreate or a drive to an end, to something higher, farther, more manifold; but all this is one, and one secret'" (p. 227). We are reminded of the waves, whose secret Nietzsche promised not to betray. But rhetorically, it is neither Nietzsche nor Zarathustra who breaks the silence. Life is given a voice that the waves did not possess. It can and does speak for itself. It reveals its secrets, so to speak, willingly.

6.

The monistic ontology of *Thus Spoke Zarathustra* is maintained in *Beyond Good and Evil.* Here, however, analytic reduction replaces ecstatic pronouncement.

Nietzsche's use of analytic reduction follows from what he terms, in section 13, a methodological "economy of principles" (1886 [hereafter *BGE*], p. 21). This methodological orientation requires the elimination of "*superfluous* teleological principles." Hence, he argues: "Physiologists should think before putting down the instinct of self-preservation as the cardinal instinct of an organic being. A living thing seeks above all to *discharge* its strength— life itself is *will to power;* self-preservation is only one of the indirect and most frequent results" (p. 21). There is no need to multiply ontological principles by positing self-preservation as a primary drive of living organisms, so long as self-preserving activities (such as nutrition and procreation) can be economically explained or described from the perspective of will to power. To be sure, we could reverse the position of the terms and still apply Occam's razor. Then we might claim that so long as the will to power can be described from the perspective of self-preservation, no need exists to posit it as a primary drive of living organisms. But our current task is to represent Nietzsche's position, not to contest it.

The actual reduction of the manifold of phenomena to the will to power proceeds as follows. In section 36, Nietzsche asks:

> Supposing nothing else were "given" as real except our world of desires and
> passions, and we could not get down, or up, to any other "reality" besides
> the reality of our drives—for thinking is merely a relation of these drives

to each other: is it not permitted to make the experiment and ask the question whether this "given" would not be *sufficient* for also understanding on the basis of this kind of thing the so-called mechanistic (or "material") world? (P. 47)

Might it not be the case, he continues, that material reality is "a more primitive form of the world of affects in which everything still lies in a powerful unity before it undergoes ramifications and developments in the organic process . . . as a *pre-form* of life?" Further, assuming we believe in causality of any kind and in the will as an efficient cause, then mustn't we push explanation to "its utmost limit" ("to the point of nonsense," he adds parenthetically) and "risk the hypothesis whether will does not affect will wherever 'effects' are recognized"? And wouldn't the last step of the reduction be to explain "our entire instinctive life as the development and ramification of *one* basic form of the will—namely, of the will to power":

> Suppose all organic functions could be traced back to this will to power and one could also find in it the solution to the problem of procreation and nourishment—it is one problem—then one would have gained the right to determine *all* efficient force univocally as—*will to power*. The world viewed from the inside, the world defined and determined according to its "intelligible character"—it would be "will to power" and nothing else. (P. 48)

The reductive process, at once epistemological and ontological, results in the will to power as the perspective from which all other perspectives are to be both interpreted and evaluated. Thus when we identify ourselves with the will to power, we are able to view the world from the inside and from the inside out.

Defining the world as will to power does not define will to power itself. We know from *Thus Spoke Zarathustra* that it is overcoming and self-overcoming, hence also being overcome. Section 13 of *Beyond Good and Evil* (cited above) specifies as an additional feature of the concept that a living thing seeks to "discharge its strength." This was an implied attribute of will to power in the earlier text as well. For example, at the beginning of the second part, Zarathustra is filled with the wisdom of the will to power. He is impatient to release it: "The tension of my cloud was too great: between the laughter of lightening bolts I want to throw showers of hail into the depths. Violently my chest will expand, violently will it blow its storm over mountains and thus find relief" (*TSZ*, p. 197). Here Nietzsche evokes the will to power in Zarathustra's overpowering need to articulate it. But the discharge of strength is not explicated as an attribute of the concept. In *Beyond Good and Evil*, by contrast, there is a hint of conceptual analysis.

There are other hints of this kind in the later text. Of these the broadest is in section 259, where Nietzsche argues that exercising restraint, refraining from violence, and so forth can in exceptional circumstances be simply a mark of good manners. But when taken as a "fundamental principle of society" it represents "a will to the *denial* of life, a principle of disintegration and decay" (*BGE*, p. 203). This is because

> life itself is *essentially* appropriation, injury, overpowering what is alien and weaker; suppression, hardness, imposition of one's own forms, incorporation and at least, at its mildest, exploitation. . . .
>
> Even the [social] body within which individuals treat each other as equals, as suggested before—and this happens in every healthy aristocracy—if it is a living and not a dying body, has to do to other [social] bodies what the individuals within it refrain from doing to each other: it will have to be an incarnate will to power, it will strive to grow, spread, seize, become predominant—not from any morality or immorality but because it is *living* and because life simply *is* will to power. (Ibid.)

The terms used in this social depiction of will to power give additional content to the idea of overcoming. They make manifest its latent martial meaning. Moreover, Nietzsche uses the martial articulation of the concept to distinguish healthy social bodies from disintegrating, decaying, and dying ones. The former directly incarnate the will to power, the latter turn against and deny it.

For clarity's sake, let's pull together the various anticipations and articulations of the will to power thus far considered. The will to power is life, life is will to power. The identification of the one with the other is secured through the concept of overcoming. This is the secret of the restless, acquisitive mobility of will and wave. Stated in biological terms, it is the tendency of cells to assimilate other cells—mirrored in a certain sense by organisms that realize their own purposes through being assimilated by and functioning within another. Assimilation has a link, not clearly specified, to discharge of strength. Neither assimilation nor the discharge of strength are means to the end of self-preservation; rather, self-preservation is merely a by-product of these more fundamental forces. Moreover, at the social or cultural level, the will to power is expressed in all forms of benevolence, while social valuations and moral codes articulate the will to power of a people. In the instance of healthy societies, these valuations are martial; in the instance of diseased societies, the will to power is inhibited and turned against itself—life denying life.

7.

The reduction of all drives to will to power in section 39 of *Beyond Good and Evil* is, Nietzsche states, an "experiment." How are we to interpret this epistemological modesty? On the one hand, experimentalism can be interpreted as perspectivism in a methodological mode. This fits with Nietzsche's announced orientation toward philosophizing, as when he names the philosophers of the future "attempters" (p. 52). On the other hand, and more speculatively, I am inclined to believe that he had not worked out all the problems associated with the will to power. Either way, he is to be interpreted as an experimenter. His published works present the (never final) results of his experiments; the unpublished works are a record of the experimental process.[3]

That being said, Nietzsche assigns quite definite meanings to the concept of a will to power in the notes published as *The Will to Power*. Hence I will temporarily bracket the problems that arise when perspectivism is applied to the will to power, in order to deepen understanding of the concept itself.

The "will" in the will to power is not the will of popular psychology, the moral will of Kant, or the free will of Hegel. It is closer to the cosmological will of Schopenhauer's *The World as Will and Representation* (1969), in the sense that this conception presents the problem the will to power was intended to solve. Schopenhauer identifies the will with privation, deficiency, or lack. It aims at overcoming this deficiency, hence at overcoming itself, by achieving a state of purposeless rest or repose. As Stambaugh puts it: "Underlying the purpose of the will of coming to a purposeless rest is its essential determination of being a lack, and the suffering resulting from that lack. The will suffers because it is insufficient for itself, and strives for redemption" (1987, p. 25).[4] But if the will *is* privation and suffering, to will a condition of repose is to will will-lessness. The will therefore aims at its own annihilation, which, because the will is the world, is a contradiction in terms.

In *The Birth of Tragedy*, Nietzsche identified the Dionysian with the will in the Schopenhauerian sense and the Apollonian with the aim of redemptive repose. He left unsolved the problem of willing will-lessness—that is, of nihilism. The will to power does solve it. Willing will-lessness is retained as one expression of the will to power: nihilism in its many forms proceeds from the will to power of the weak and decadent. The will to power of the strong and healthy, however, overcomes any such nihilistic tendencies. Superabundant, it takes even nihilism as a stimulus and an incitement. When the Dionysian reemerges in Nietzsche's later work, it is identified with the superabundance of the will to power and not the primal lack of the Schopenhauerian will.

What do the nihilistic and Dionysian forms of the will to power have in common? Stated most generally—that is, in the sphere of the inorganic—the will to power is a relationship among centers of force. There are no "things" at this level, "only dynamic quanta, in a relationship of tension to all other dynamic quanta" (WP, p. 339). Each of these quanta—each "quantum of power"—is "designated by the effect it produces and that which it resists. . . . It is essentially a will to violate and to defend oneself against violation" (p. 338). Hence the "degree of resistance and the degree of superior power—this is the question in every event" (p. 337).

Despite the impression left by the arrangement of sections in *The Will to Power*, Nietzsche does not proceed linearly from the inorganic to the organic. He does relate the one to the other:

> The connection between the inorganic and the organic must lie in the repelling force exercised by every atom of force. "Life" would be defined as an enduring form of processes of the establishment of force, in which the different contenders grow unequally. To what extent resistance is present even in obedience; individual power is by no means surrendered. In the same way, there is in commanding an admission that the absolute power of the opponent has not been vanquished, incorporated, disintegrated. "Obedience" and "commanding" are forms of struggle. (P. 342)

This formulation adds considerable specificity to the idea that life itself is will to power. Will to power is an ongoing struggle between unequal centers of force, a relationship of resistance that does not end even in stabilized conjunctures of command and obedience.

We see, then, that "will" cannot be divorced from "power." The former does not precede the latter, either logically or ontologically. "There is no such thing as 'willing,' but only a willing *something*" (p. 353). Hence what Schopenhauer called the "will" is "a mere empty word" (p. 369). Starting with nothing, he ends with nothing; nihilism is inevitable.

The "will" in will to power is something like directedness, the "whither" of a process (see Stambaugh 1987, p. 99 ff). Power is the activity itself, the accumulating and discharging of force. And because the will is *to* power, will to power is not teleological. It does not aim beyond itself but only at the experience of itself. The ends of action are collapsed into the means—into overcoming resistance. In overcoming resistance, the accumulation and expenditure of force are conjoined: "Not merely conservation of energy, but maximal economy in use, so the only reality is the will to grow stronger [characteristic] of every center of force—not self-preservation, but the will to appropriate, dominate, increase, grow stronger" (*WP*, p. 367). Once again:

> The will to power can manifest itself only against resistances; therefore it seeks that which resists it—this is the primeval tendency of the protoplasm when it extends its pseudopodia and feels about. Appropriation and assimilation are above all a desire to overwhelm, a forming, shaping and reshaping, until at length that which has been overwhelmed has entirely gone over into the power domain of the aggressor and increased the same. (P. 346)

The will to power is neither teleological nor nihilistic. It is essentially active—a "reaching out for power" (p. 347). Passivity is only inverse activity: "To be hindered from moving forward: thus an act of resistance and reaction" (p. 346). Passive resistance (as it were) can be overcome, but overcoming resistance cannot be surpassed.

We already know that Nietzsche views self-preservation as an unintended and problematic consequence of the will to power. We can now say that the will to power in living organisms aims at the experience of overcoming resistance, even at the expense of the life of the organism. The will to power does not calculate utilities. Nor does it balance pleasures and pains. To the contrary, Nietzsche contends that pleasure "is only a symptom of a feeling of power attained, a consciousness of a difference" (p. 366). It is not the aim of action. Indeed, insofar as we wish to view pleasure and pain as motive forces, it would be more accurate to say that we are displeasure-seeking: "As a force can expend itself only on what resists it, there is necessarily an *ingredient of displeasure* in every action. But this displeasure acts as a lure of life and strengthens the will to power!" (p. 369). Moreover, pain and pleasure are not opposites:

> There are even cases in which a kind of pleasure is conditioned by a certain *rhythmic sequence* of little unpleasurable stimuli: in this way a very rapid increase of the feeling of power, the feeling of pleasure, is achieved. This is the case, e.g., in tickling, also the sexual tickling in the act of coitus: here we see displeasure at work as an ingredient of pleasure. It seems, a little hindrance that is again overcome—this game of resistance and victory

arouses most strongly that general feeling of superabundant, excessive power that constitutes the essence of pleasure. (P. 371)

Pleasure accompanies the accumulation of force, the accumulation of force comes from overcoming resistance, overcoming resistance is accompanied by displeasure. Sexual pleasure involves accumulation of power through rhythmic overcoming of successive displeasures; it is the experience of victory over resistance. Thus, if we are to have recourse to the language of cause and effect, we would say that Nietzsche has effected a reversal. Pleasure and pain are consequences, not causes. Theories in which they are viewed as causally efficacious have it backward.

A striking feature of the example of sexuality in Nietzsche's analysis is that there seems to be no room for postcoital experience. Perhaps orgasm is implied, as the final overcoming of resistance and the fullest feeling of power. But what about the quiet pleasure that follows satisfying sexual interaction—"integral quiescence," to reintroduce a Marcusean notion?

We already know the answer to this question. Nietzsche does not ignore quiescence, but he hardly views it as integral. Quiescence is a retreat from life and a sign of decadence (of a weakening of the will to power). In contrast to the displeasure that is necessary to and stimulates the feeling of power is "displeasure following an overexpenditure of power." Then there is exhaustion and an "inability to resist." The only pleasure still felt in this state is "falling asleep": "The exhausted want rest, relaxation, peace, calm—the happiness of the nihilist religions and philosophies" (p. 374). Brought back to the sphere of sexuality, we have detumescence as depression and decadence.

Thus we return from the conceptual generality of the will to power to its particularization in the distinction between healthy/active/life-affirming and decadent/reactive/life-denying tendencies. But doesn't this tidy duality leave us with the inverse of the problem Nietzsche inherited from Schopenhauer? Schopenhauer identifies the will with privation and therefore can conceive of plenitude only as quiescence. Nietzsche identifies the will with plenitude and therefore can conceive of quiescence only as privation.

Let me put the matter another way. I am not, for the moment, objecting to the characterization of life as will to power but rather to the characterization of the will to power itself. On the one hand, Nietzsche—employing the weapon of analytic reduction and guided by the rule of parsimony—cuts his way down to the generality of the concept. On the other, he articulates its opposing affirmative and nihilistic expressions. In the nature of the case, the particular forms must be derivable from the generality. But Nietzsche's most general formulation of the will to power *is* the affirmative version. He performs a kind of glissade or sleight of hand in which the will to power as affirmation is slipped in behind the will to power as such. The generality is reduced to a particularity. This maneuver permits him to identify passivity, inactivity, or quiescence with decadence or weakness—to view them as pathological forms of the will to power or as the will to power of the weak. But more closely considered, it leaves him without a sufficiently general premise from which to derive these phenomena.

There is a psychological problem contained within the logical or ontological one. Stated as a question: are we really content to equate not-resisting, or the absence of resistance, with life-denial?

III. Thought-Experiments

8.

In *Beyond the Pleasure Principle* (1920), Freud describes a small boy (his grandson Ernst) struggling with the experience of being left by his beloved mother. The boy created a game—the *fort! da!* game—in which he would make a reel attached to a string first disappear and then reappear.[5] Why would he thus re-create a painful experience? Because, Freud answers, "at the outset he was in a *passive* situation—he was overpowered by the experience; but, by repeating it, unpleasurable though it was, as a game, he took an *active* part" (p. 16). "These efforts," he continues, "might be put down to an instinct for mastery that was acting independently of whether the memory was in itself pleasurable or not." Nietzsche might be willing to equate this instinct for mastery with the reactive form of the will to power and, on this basis, accept the interpretation of the incident. But Freud is not satisfied with this view of the matter. He offers another interpretation that restores the theoretical position of the pleasure principle. The compulsion to repeat the painful experience, he hypothesizes, was motivated by an impulse toward revenge: the little boy gained the compensatory pleasure of throwing away his mother as he himself had been thrown away (ibid.).[6] Nietzsche would probably just shake his head: "Isn't it obvious," we can hear him saying, "that no recourse to the pleasure principle is warranted? The two interpretations are one and the same. The transformation of passivity into activity motivated by the desire for vengeance is precisely an expression of the will to power of the weak." And he might commend to Freud's attention the discussion of the slave revolt in morals in *On the Genealogy of Morals*.

The *fort! da!* game is an example of an empirical phenomenon that can be plausibly interpreted from the standpoint of either the pleasure principle or the will to power. And that is not all. In *Beyond the Pleasure Principle*, Freud identifies stimulation with pain and therefore life with privation, and he postulates a fundamental, nirvanic aim of escaping from life's suffering into the quiescence of inorganicity. Hence, from Nietzsche's perspective, he is a nihilist, virtually a reincarnation of Schopenhauer. Conversely, from Freud's perspective, Nietzsche's philosophy looks like a version of the *fort! da!* game—that is, an attempt to turn the tables on the goddess of necessity. Thus the relationship between the two theorists is strikingly dialectical. Their positions are bound together by mutual antipathy.

This way of characterizing the relationship between Nietzsche and Freud suggests the possibility of the dialectical sublation of the antagonism. Such a Hegelian aim is, however, rather too ambitious or perhaps even wrong-headed. More modestly, the goal is to bring the will to power into a working relationship with the determinacy of pleasure and pain. Yet a kind of dialectical thought-experiment will be of some use in this regard.

Here is what I have in mind: Section 39 of *Beyond Good and Evil* and the speculations in *The Will to Power* are Nietzsche's thought-experiments with the will to power. Freud states that the central line of argument in *Beyond the Pleasure Principle* is "speculation, often far-fetched speculation, which the reader will consider or dismiss according to his individual predilection." He adds that the argument is "an attempt to follow out an idea consistently, out of curiosity to see where it will lead" (p. 24). In short, he offers us a thought-experiment with the pleasure principle. Moreover, the experimental setting is the same in both instances—that is, the time or space separating and joining the inorganic and the organic—the origins of life. This ontological space, an abstraction from a manifold of phenomena, is reached by explicit or implicit analytic reduction. It parallels in this regard the state of nature in classical liberal political theory or the setting Hegel creates for the battle of recognition in chapter 4 of *The Phenomenology of Spirit*.

Our thought-experiment joins these two settings and will take place in three stages. I will, first, set up a contest of interpretations concerning the origins of life. The battle will end in a stalemate. Second, in an attempt to get beyond this impasse, I will reconceptualize the will to power and the determinacy of pleasure and pain, so as to narrow the gap between them. Third, I will restage the confrontation between them in a psychological rather than ontological space, namely, the space of neonatal experience. This thought-experiment will, finally, permit us to say something about the role of the will to power in psychoanalytic practice.

9.

We have already considered Nietzsche's creation myth, so we turn to Freud's. In the beginning, the "attributes of life were . . . evoked in inanimate matter by the action of a force of whose nature we can form no conception" (Freud 1920, p. 38). Because there is a tendency (presumably in all nature) to restore earlier states of being and reduce and, if possible, eliminate tension or stimulation, life at first eliminated itself. The "tension which then arose in what had hitherto been an inanimate substance endeavored to cancel itself out." Easy come, easy go. But in these fleeting moments of life "the first instinct came into being: the instinct to return to the inanimate state" (ibid.), in other words, the death-drive. External exigencies somehow rendered the work of the death-drive more difficult with the passage of time. Organisms began to live longer, and so the return trip to inorganicity took longer. Nonetheless, the drive toward inorganicity—toward a stable, unstimulated condition—remained not only operative but ultimately determinative as well.

We now picture a "little fragment of living substance . . . suspended in the middle of an external world charged with the most powerful energies." It protects itself by the development of a "special envelope or membrane resistant to stimuli," consisting of bound or quiescent investments of energy. This membrane is semipermeable. It permits the organism to sample its environment and to resist intrusion by excessive amounts of force. Any significant breaching of this shield, however, "is bound to provoke a disturbance on a large scale in the functioning of the organism's energy and to set in motion every possible defensive measure" (p. 27). Energies are mobilized to bind and render quiescent the stimuli impinging from outside, and in this situation, self-defense takes priority over all other functions.

Given the basic viability and defensive capabilities of the organism, a second drive comes into play—a drive toward the prolongation of life. This drive operates through the joining of one organism to another and, to a certain extent, resembles the will to power: "The germ-cells themselves . . . behave in a completely 'narcissistic' fashion. . . . [They] require their libido, the activity of their life instincts, for themselves" (p. 50). Unlike the will to power, however, these organisms seem to be regulated by the invisible hand of an intercellular market: "the life instincts or sexual instincts which are active in each cell . . . partly neutralize the death instincts (that is, the processes set up by them) in . . . [other] cells and thus preserve their life; while the other cells do the same for *them*, and still others sacrifice themselves in the performance of this libidinal function" (ibid.). Here we have exchange for mutual benefit. This does not mean that Freud denies conflict and destructiveness in the natural order. Destructive tendencies are conceptualized as derivatives of the death-drive, so that organicity can be understood as the struggle of life against death.

Thus far we (apparently) have learned nothing about pleasure and pain, and for good reason. Freud was led back to inorganicity and the primordial chaos of life by the need to explain the compulsion to repeat even painful experiences. The compulsion to repeat seemed both to disregard the pleasure principle and to have a drivelike quality. The death-drive, conceived as a universal tendency to restore a prior state of being, covered the phenomenon. It did not preclude the possibility of pleasure in repetition, as in the *fort! da!* game, but it established a set of prior conditions for the operation of the pleasure principle. Once these conditions have been met—narrowly, the death-drive operating according to the Nirvana principle (stimulus elimination); more broadly, the binding of the death-drive by the life-drive—activity is guided by the pleasure principle and its modification, the reality principle.

I have contended elsewhere that Freud's argument is not only speculative but also incoherent (Wolfenstein 1985, 1993). Yet I would not deny that it has a certain appeal and elegance, perhaps even that it appears to permit Freud to have it both ways. On the one hand, he explains the compulsion to repeat without having to grant an independent drive toward mastery (which would have brought him perilously close to Nietzsche's will to power and a genuine overturning of the pleasure principle). On the other hand, he only seemingly goes beyond his version of the pleasure principle. From the beginning—for example, in that other grand piece of speculation, the "Project for a Scientific Psychology" (1895)—he had grounded his thinking in the principle of constancy ("neuronal inertia" in the "Project"), of which the pleasure principle is a subsidiary form. The Nirvana principle is simply another name for the principle of constancy. By ontologizing the Nirvana/constancy principle and differentiating it from the pleasure principle, he has in essence split the pleasure principle into two parts: an absolute part that retains the aim—unrealizable by living organisms—of total stimulus elimination and stability, and a relative part that aims at the degree of stimulus reduction and stability appropriate to living organisms.

To put it differently, splitting the pleasure principle provides a defense against the criticism that, because without stimulation there is no life, pleasure defined as the absence of stimulation cannot be experienced by living organisms. Quite right, Freud can now respond. We are unable to realize the aim of the pleasure principle in a double sense. First, when measured by the standard of the Nirvana principle and the demand for stimulus elimination, living organisms always fall short. To be alive is to be in pain. Second, each organism has developed its own proper balance between the death-drive, which is stimulus-reducing, and the life-drive, which is stimulus-seeking. But reality does not permit the consistent maintenance of this balance. It routinely bombards the organism with excessive stimuli and hence with added increments of pain. Some of this pain can be reduced, however, through changed behavior—that is, adaptation in accordance with the reality principle. In this derivative sense there is a principle of mastery—not for its own sake, however, but in the interest of maintaining the integrity of the organism and reducing pain.

Thus we find ourselves back where our discussion of Freud began. Freud did not write *Beyond the Pleasure Principle* to provide a non-Nietzschean explanation for the drive toward mastery, but that is the result. It is as if he had heeded Socrates' advice in the *Phaedo* and jumped the level of argument. Confronted by the stubborn resistance of the will to power to psychoanalytic reduction, Freud retreated to the principle of constancy, stripped of its organic derivatives, and then came down to a conclusion that subsumed Nietzsche's position.

Nietzsche would not be impressed. He would point out that *absence* of stimulation is an empty notion, yet another metaphysical night in which all cosmic cows are black. The aim of stimulus elimination—the principle of constancy—is nihilistic and, as such, explicable in terms of the will to power. Moreover, the constancy principle is an ontological nonstarter. It is nothing in itself, and nothing can be derived from it. And so far as life processes are concerned, it is counterfactual. Freud himself must confess that it is not descriptive of any actual living organism. Consequently, it is not compelling either as an explanation of phenomena or as a critique of the will to power. By contrast, the will to power is a principle of activity. It is generative and creative. Life extends rather than contradicts its preorganic meaning.

I do not believe that Freud has an adequate defense against this line of attack. His vulnerability does not result from his adherence to the pleasure principle, however, but from his nihilistic conflation of stimulation and pain. Hence he could retreat to a this-worldly version of the pleasure principle and again put forward the position that the will to power is a philosophical version of the *fort! da!* game. But Nietzsche could claim that Freud is just begging the question. "Your argument presupposes what it ought to prove," he might say, "namely, the determinacy of pleasure and pain. And just because you presuppose this banal hedonic position, you persistently reduce the will to power to its reactive form. By contrast, the will to power in a healthy state is like the tension of a bow and the release of the arrow. The greater the tension, the more powerful the release, the longer the flight. Those who cannot bend the bow, the weak and the diseased, are destructively envious of those who can. Their will to power has the form of *ressentiment* and the craving for revenge. You, however, fail to recognize this distinction. Perhaps as a result of your own decadence, you persist in reducing the will to power to a child's game."

Freud would not be silenced. Following the argument in Section 7 above, he would point out that Nietzsche is not entitled to his particularization of the will to power. Hence he might decline to proceed any further until the meaning of the concept had been clarified. Correspondingly, Nietzsche might claim that the determinacy of pleasure and pain is largely undetermined—that this concept, too, is lacking in definition.

At this juncture we must leave Nietzsche and Freud to their own devices. In truth we have already abandoned or compromised the position that each of them is forced to maintain. They are locked into a battle for recognition. If, by contrast, we wish to establish a modus vivendi between the will to power and the determinacy of pleasure and pain, we must take the work of conceptual clarification into our own hands.

10.

First, the will to power, which according to Nietzsche is the overcoming of resistance. Resistance, we may suppose, is a quantum of force, energy, or power (whether bound/quiescent or unbound/mobile, to use Freud's terms).[7] When a resistance is overcome, there is a release of energy, either the energy of the resistance itself or the energy that the resistance held in check. But in the Nietzschean example of the tensed bow, the release of energy results more from a relaxation or facilitation than an overcoming. Similarly, *Thus Spoke Zarathustra* begins on a note of overflowing, not overcoming. In the prologue Zarathustra asks the sun's benediction: "Bless the cup that wants to overflow, that the water may flow from it golden and carry everywhere the reflection of your delight" (*TSZ*, p. 22). And it was in precisely this mood of overflow that Nietzsche wrote, with great rapidity, the first three parts of *Thus Spoke Zarathustra*. This implies that there is an experience of power that comes from not resisting or ceasing to resist.

Thus even Nietzsche's affirmative conceptualization of will to power as overcoming resistance is one-sided. If, for example, Sisyphus were to succeed in pushing his boulder over the top of the mountain, the release of energy would indeed be an overcoming. But Zarathustra in the prologue is not Sisyphus. Hence the will to power cannot be defined simply as overcoming resistance.

Perhaps we can cover both types of experience if we interpret the will to power as a dialectical manifold. Picture, first, an indifferent or immediate relationship (whether internal or external) between two centers of force.[8] Each center of force has an active and a passive pole. Second, the relationship between the two centers of force is mediated. They come up against each other, in one of several ways: each center of force is passive and no development occurs; one force is active and one is passive, so that the active force advances without resistance; both forces are active and one overcomes the other. The last form of engagement, and only the last form, leads on to an approximately dialectical resolution of an antagonism, in which a new constellation of forces or a determinate relationship of forces is possible. But this outcome can be achieved in two different ways. Force encounters force, and one party simply overpowers the other, absorbing it into itself. This is the martial conception of the will to power that Nietzsche explicitly conceptualizes. Alternatively, as the pressure of the encounter intensifies, one force may shift its posture from active to passive (or from resistance to facilitation, to use a classically psychoanalytic vocabulary). There is then the release of energy which Nietzsche depicts but which his more formalized presentation of the will to power does not include.

Given this more inclusive conceptualization of the will to power, we might imagine a continuum of experiences falling within its purview. The most intense experience of power would involve a high level of tension or resistance, brought to a sudden end in such a way that the distinction between overcoming resistance and resistance overcome would dissolve (such as orgasm). The least intense experience of power would involve a release or relaxation when there is little initial tension (such as normal breathing). In between these extremes would be varying intensities and constellations of forces and resistances.

This reconceptualization of the will to power alters quite radically the meaning of health and decadence. "Health" would be defined as a kind of rhythm of overcoming, resisting, and not resisting. Which modality predominates would be situationally variable. "Illness," "weakness," or "decadence" would be a deviation from this rhythm. It could be either too active or too passive, too fast or too slow. Thus both Nietzsche's hyperactivism and Freud's hypoactivism (his aim of stimulus elimination) would be interpreted as symptoms of decadence.

As a psychological principle, the will to power is a prime example of a monism that is meaningful but false. Although the dialectical manifold of overcoming resistance is an element in an extremely wide range of human interactions, it cannot be maintained that it is the determining principle in all of them. Likewise—to recur to the Freudian instance—the elimination of stimulation cannot be adduced as the determining principle of any and all human activity. It is sometimes the case, however, that overcoming resistance or stimulus elimination is the consciously or unconsciously intended aim of an action. For just this reason the question arises, when do the will to power and the Nirvana principle determine the aims of human activity, and when do they function as means to other ends?

I think we can answer this question from the perspective of the determinacy of pleasure and pain.[9] Pleasure, we will assume, is an organism-specific rhythm or set of rhythms of stimulation; pain is a break in or disruption of such rhythms. Pain is not, as with Freud, identified with stimulation. Rather, pain can involve excessive or insufficient stimulation, as well as patterns of stimulation that are inappropriate for a given organism.

Stimulation can be interpreted from the perspective of power, and all stimulation involves some process of resistance and facilitation. It is therefore fair to say of the will to power what Hegel said of the dialectic: where there is life, there is will to power. But one could equally say, where there is life, there is pleasurable and painful stimulation. These two claims are not contradictory. A resistance consists of stimuli in a "bound" although not quiescent form; stimuli are constellations of resistance. Or, to put the point in terms both psychoanalytic and Nietzschean, resistances and stimuli are quanta of force or energy. When we attempt to determine the direction of organic activity, however, sensations of pleasure and pain are the initial differentiating factors: we are oriented toward pleasure and away from pain. In the first instance, therefore, the will to power functions as a means to these ends.

We may borrow the idea of a life-drive (cell-to-cell attraction in *Beyond the Pleasure Principle*) to describe the potential for and orientation toward pleasurable experience. It warrants this name because certain pleasurable experiences (alimentary ones most obviously) are simultaneously life-preserving. Thus we come into this world as little hedonists and utilitarians— not as a matter of moral choice but as a matter of psychophysiological predisposition.

Just as we are driven toward pleasurable stimuli, we are driven away from painful ones. The aim of stimulus reduction is specific to experiences of pain. In the limiting instance, however, when life has become nothing but pain, the drive is to bring life to an end—to eliminate stimulation altogether. In this sense, the drive to reduce painful stimulation is a death-drive, and we may so name it. But we must remember that the death-drive is simply the dialectical opposite of the life-drive, the life-drive in negative form.

If we take the step of formulating regulative principles, we would say that the two drives are guided by organism-specific tendencies to maintain appropriate rhythms and levels of stimulation. The pleasure principle states this tendency in the positive form, the Nirvana principle in the negative form.

It will be observed that these two drives and their associated principles rarely operate in anything approaching pure form, most importantly because pleasures so often come tangled up with pains. This is especially the situation with respect to the vital needs. The task then becomes to disentangle pleasure from pain or, put more concretely, to overcome pain to gain pleasure. Stated differently, it becomes necessary to overcome a level or form of stimulation experienced as a resistance. Moreover, this process of overcoming resistance may in time come to be experienced as pleasurable in itself, although in the first instance it is merely a painful means to a pleasurable end. Thus we have, psychoanalytically reformulated, the will to power: *overcoming pain to gain pleasure, including the pleasure of overcoming pain.*

12.

Although we cannot work out all the implications of this reconceptualization of the will to power, several points do need to be made if we are to bend the concept to our own interpretive purposes.

Drives and emotions. The life-drive, death-drive, and will to power are more basic features of human experience than either affects or ideas, but affects and ideas grow out of and accompany drive activity. Loving feelings tend to accompany the life-drive; fear or even dread tend to accompany the death-drive. The affective valence of the will to power is not so simply fixed but depends on whether a situation is predominantly pleasurable or painful. In the former case, the will to power gravitates toward lust, excitement, and erotic desire; in the latter, it is pushed toward rage, depression, and hatred.[10] Aggression, destructiveness, and hatred are functions of the will to power and not, as Freud would have it, derivatives of the death-drive. But because the death-drive is set in motion by pain, there is a tendency for its operations to be characterized by hostility and for the breaking off of contact to be used destructively.

Creativity and destructiveness. The preceding analysis helps us to distinguish between healthy / active and decadent / reactive forms of the will to power. The drive to overcome pain in order to experience pleasure, as well as to experience the pleasure of overcoming pain, is a primary feature of healthy human functioning, as is seeking out situations that provide the opportunity for such experiences. In these instances, the will to power is aligned with the life-drive and is fundamentally creative. It may also give rise to the feeling of overflow and the desire to give gifts that characterize Zarathustra at the beginning of each of the first two parts of *Thus Spoke Zarathustra*. When, however, the level of pain begins to exceed one's capacity for taking pleasure in overcoming it, the death-drive comes forcefully into play. The will to power then serves the Nirvana principle. It becomes destructive and nihilistic, and it can give rise to envy and *ressentiment*. If the tormented individual struggles against fate and if she or he is confronted by someone who is alive and creative, the vision of health and well-being may add to the torment. Then she or he will be driven to devalue or destroy that which she or he cannot be.

At this juncture it might seem that we have simply recast Nietzsche's genealogy of noble and base valuations in psychogenetic terms. But Nietzsche, I would argue, conflates two distinguishable phenomena: the healthy or creative version of the will to power and the will to dominate. The former is assertive and aggressive without being cruel and sadistic. Cruelty and sadism are rather nihilism in active form. Moreover, "active" does not necessarily mean "outward." Cruelty may be turned inward and may even be used to master feelings of envy and *ressentiment*.

Intimations of eternal return. In the face of extreme pain in living, the will to power can become an end in itself, but again in opposed forms. In both instances it functions as a drive to master the pain of traumatic events. But in the one case, it takes the form of repetitive efforts to repair the damage caused by traumatic levels of stimulation. Here we have the compulsion to repeat explained by the will to power rather than the principle of constancy. In the other case and very uncommonly, the self becomes so deeply identified with the will to power that even traumatic experiences can be affirmed.

In sum: when the will to power is conceptualized as overcoming pain to gain pleasure, including the pleasure in overcoming pain, the phenomena of greatest concern to Nietzsche are brought into the purview of the determinacy of pleasure and pain. I would not deny that there is a psychoanalytic will to power operative in this redefinition and that other perspectives are possible—including, of course, Nietzsche's. But in my view, some such conceptualization of the will to power provides the most useful interpretive guidance for psychoanalytic theory and practice.

<h2 style="text-align:center">13.</h2>

In their ontological speculations, Nietzsche and Freud placed us at the birth of the world. Having sufficiently worked through their basic assumptions both ontologically and psychologically, let's shift the scene to the postbirth world of human infants. And with their arguments in mind, we find ourselves in a situation resembling the paranoid-schizoid position.

The paranoid-schizoid position is a bipolar psychic or even psychophysiological structure replicating and reifying the simplest rhythm of neonatal life: from sleeping to feeding to sleeping, from feeding to sleeping to feeding. In optimal circumstances, the rhythm is predominantly pleasurable. It is then characterized by considerable fluidity, and the will to power functions creatively—as a kind of mutual gift giving and empowerment of infant and caregiver. When, by contrast, frustrations in the feeding situation produce so much rage that feeding becomes, in phantasy, a matter of eat or be eaten—attack and counterattack, assault and persecutory response—the nurturing interaction becomes paranoid. Breaking off from the now paranoid feeding situation becomes a defensive maneuver, and relapse into somnolence becomes the prototype of schizoid withdrawal.

Whatever its limitations, the paranoid-schizoid position has several virtues, including its imposition of structure on a potentially chaotic situation. Hence it can be interpreted as a defense against forces that threaten to overwhelm the neonatal self, or as a kind of mastery, the monistic imposition of form *and meaning* on the neonatal world. Here is perhaps the primal instance of a monism that is meaningful but false—meaningful because it is falsifying. Here also is the creation of meaning on the edge of meaninglessness, as well as a psychic situation in which any attempt to re-create meaning (for example, in the course of psychoanalytic treatment) risks the loss of meaning altogether.[11]

Probably the fit between the paranoid-schizoid position and the pathological extremes of the will to power is evident. The paranoid extreme of the structure is determined by the will to power in its most aggressive, assimilative form. The schizoid extreme is embodied nihilism, a retreat to an apparently lifeless and desireless condition. The resulting appearance of inorganicity then functions as a resistance to hostile forces. Thus we have schizoid resistance to persecutory attack or, conversely, ruthless attack on schizoid defenses. And these are the positions occupied by Freud and Nietzsche, respectively, in their ontological confrontation.

The paranoid-schizoid position is a very primitive version of selfhood, and a quite narcissistic one. It leaves no place for the subjectivity of the nurturer. She—for typically, archetypally, and stereotypically the mother is the one who plays this role—is simply the primordial matrix of life. This is true for both her sons and her daughters. But as discussed in Chapter 1, in the course of development the male maintains the position of subject in relation to maternal object, while the female is "destined" to play the role of object. She will mother him, even when mothering takes the form of gratifying his sexual desires. He will assert his selfhood against and over her. Thus both roles in the drama of gender and sexuality express his drive to mastery. But this drive derives from impotence and not a superabundance of power, from the need to overpower and punish the apparently omnipotent mother of neonatal life—thus (to use Nietzsche's terms) from *ressentiment* and a craving for revenge.

Viewed this way, little Ernst's creation of the *fort! da!* game, with its drive to mastery and turning of the tables, is a paradigmatic instance of masculine gender formation. This does not mean that only boys exert their will to power in this fashion or that the will to power is necessarily gendered masculine. Indeed, Nietzsche's account, as well as the one here, rules out that possibility. But it might be fair to say that Nietzsche is prone to position men and women on opposing sides of the barrier of resistance. We recall from *The Gay Science* the case of "those women who transform themselves into some function of a man"—who are, so to speak, assimilated into another organism. We might also bring to mind his recurrent gendering of truth or wisdom as women to be seduced or conquered. For example, in *Thus Spoke Zarathustra* we find the aphorism, "Brave, unconcerned, mocking, violent—thus wisdom wants us: she is a woman and always loves only a warrior" (*TSZ*, p. 153). Taken as a paradigm of gender relations, this is sexual interaction in the paranoid-schizoid position. Men violently and ruthlessly overwhelm the defenses of women, and women desire nothing more than to be mockingly violated.

Again, the intent in these comments is not to define the will to power as either paranoid-schizoid or masculinist. But Nietzsche's own usage of the concept is, I would argue, strongly inflected with these meanings. And for just this reason, it focuses our attention on important clinical problems.

14.

Psychoanalysts who have been following the preceding lines of argument would be prepared to interpret the role played by the patient's will to power, especially when the patient is a man and the transference is characterized by paranoid-schizoid dynamics. Unless they are readers of Foucault or writers in the antipsychiatry tradition, however, they might be less prepared to interpret the role played by the will to power of the analyst. Yet almost nothing is more destructive to the analytic process than a lack of restraint in the analytic use of the will to power.

Think first of Freud. Psychoanalysis is made possible by two processes: the free associations of the patient in accordance with the "fundamental technical rule of analysis" (Freud 1917, p. 287), and the "evenly suspended attention" of the analyst (Freud 1912, p. 111). These processes involve a stance of not resisting the thoughts and feelings that are emerging from the unconscious. They contrast with critical thinking and the exercise of judgment that, in the clinical context, are forms of resistance. An experience of power results, although ambiguously. The patient or analyst, identified with the ego, may feel overpowered or overcome, as if a dam had burst and emotional forces are out of control. One might say, where there was ego, now there is id. Alternatively or eventually, patient or analyst may feel that the ego has been empowered, that it has been strengthened by the experience of not needing to resist the unconscious, and that new emotional energies have become available to it. Where there was id, now ego is becoming.

Not resisting is built into our expanded definition of the will to power. But with reference to its core psychoanalytic meaning (overcoming pain to gain pleasure, including the pleasure of overcoming pain), an attitude of nonresistance can be viewed as the suspension of the will to power—not suspension in the dialectical sense of supersession or sublation but simply a not-resisting where resistance comes naturally. Then we can say that we inherit from Freud the discipline of suspending the will to power.

This is no small gift. Unfortunately, the Freudian heritage also includes the idea of overcoming the patient's resistance. This arises innocently enough, as when Freud notes how difficult it is for many patients to tolerate the analytic process. The doctor tries to "compel" the patient to fit his "emotional impulses into the nexus of the treatment"; the patient resists: "This struggle between the doctor and the patient, between intellect and instinctual life, between understanding and seeking to act, is played out almost exclusively in the phenomena of the transference" (1912, p. 108). Viewed charitably, the analyst is here playing ego to the patient's id, with the aim of encouraging emotional development. It is patent, however, that Freud is describing will to power exerted against will to power—a contest in which, as Foucault points out, the analyst is heir to the moral authority of the priest, even if there has been a change in doctrinal substance. And in reading Freud's own clinical reports, one finds that this enactment of a power differential is especially notable in his relationships with women patients. He never really overcomes the attitude we find in the "specimen dream" with which the psychoanalytic enterprise is officially launched: "*I at once took . . . [Irma] on one side, as though to answer her letter and to reproach her for not having accepted my 'solution' yet. I said to her: 'If you still get pains, it's really your own fault'* " (Freud 1900, p. 107). Here we have a characteristic expression of masculine will to power, including the moment of blaming the woman for her resistance. We are reminded of the *Sweetie* incident and the ways in which women's experience can be reduced to diagnostic categories.[12]

Yet the analyst cannot utterly suspend the operation of the will to power. The basic rules of the analytic process and the very act of interpretation function in part as resistances to the will to power of the patient. But resistance in this minimal sense—the analyst's restrained employment of the will to power—must not be confused with exerting power over the patient— that is, with overcoming the patient's resistance. Moreover, the analytic frame ought to constitute a resistance to the analyst's will to power. It should create a space from which the analyst's will to power is withdrawn and within which the play of the patient's will to power becomes visible and palpable.

W. R. Bion, who was notable for his ability to tolerate the most primitive emotional experiences, was especially sensitive to the difficulty involved in maintaining the analytic space. Because the emptiness of this space evokes anxiety or even panic, analyst no less than patient is tempted to fill it. Even the exercise of such ordinary mental functions as memory, desire, understanding, and the reception of sense impressions can serve this defensive purpose. And so Bion posited that the practice of analysis requires the disciplined denial or suppression of memory, desire, understanding, and sense impressions (Bion 1970, p. 43).

Bion's formulation bears the mark of clinical truth, but it also raises a question: how is the analyst ever to offer an interpretation if these mental functions are utterly excluded? Clearly some kind of thinking must take place or no analysis is possible. Yet, Bion seems to be saying, the analyst's thinking is just what makes analysis impossible.

This contradiction can be resolved if we differentiate between thinking driven by the analyst's will to power and thinking that occurs when the analyst is able to suspend its operations. In the former instance, ordinary mental processes are activated. They impose themselves on the analytic situation, and the patient's pain is treated as a resistance to be overcome. Conversely, when the analyst is able to resist the temptation of overcoming resistance, these same processes function receptively. They create space rather than filling it. Hence we may complement Bion's clinical dictum with one of our own: *The practice of psychoanalysis requires the disciplined suspension or restrained employment of the will to power.* If this aim is realized, then the analyst achieves something approximating to the state of mind Buddhists designate as *sunyata,* or "emptiness." According to Mark Epstein, sunyata "has as its original, etymological meaning 'a pregnant void, the hollow of a pregnant womb.'" He continues: "When a therapist is able to create such a fertile condition, through the use of her own silence, the patient cannot help but come in contact with that which is still unfinished and with which he is still identified, albeit unawares" (Epstein 1995, p. 190). It should be added that this state of mind is never perfectly maintained, with the consequence that the analyst also recurrently comes into contact with that which is still unfinished in himself or herself.

3

Very Few Rules to Guide

Restraint!
What possible restraint?
— CONRAD, *Heart of Darkness*

1.

We turn now from the will to power to perspectivism. Our interest is in epistemology both pure and applied. In the former regard, the aim is to explore the limits of Nietzsche's perspectivism, both for its own sake and so that, at a later stage of the inquiry, we can work through its relationship to dialectical reason. In the latter regard, the aim is pragmatic. Perspectivism is brought forward as an epistemological precondition for learning from psychoanalytic experience.

The first part of the chapter is largely expository. In it I depict Nietzsche's perspectivism as a critique of dogmatic philosophizing, a methodological orientation constrained by a residual realism, and an antimetaphysical worldview.

The second part is both an attempt to articulate a perspectivist conception of psychoanalytic practice, based on my own psychoanalytic training and clinical experience, and a report of actual psychoanalytic experience, interpreted perspectivally.

2.

I have already introduced two applied epistemic rules or imperatives of psychoanalytic practice: Bion's dictum that the practice of analysis requires the disciplined denial or suppression of memory, desire, understanding, and sense impressions, and the related notion that psychoanalytic practice demands of the analyst the disciplined suspension or the restrained employment of the will to power. Both these notions will be further investigated in what follows, while a third imperative will be added to them: *The practice of psychoanalysis requires tolerating the maximum of anxiety with the minimum of defense.* All three dicta, I will argue, are perspectival in nature.

Very few rules to guide, therefore, and quite peculiar ones at that. Yet these alone constitute the analyst's restraint, without which it is not possible to explore—as one sometimes must—"the heart of an immense darkness" (Zabel 1976, p. 603).

I. Truth, Interpretation, and the Will to Power

3.

What we conventionally designate as Nietzsche's perspectivism consists of a cluster of elements with somewhat indefinite borders. The central epistemological or methodological idea is clear enough. As Arthur Danto puts it, "we speak of seeing the same thing from different perspectives, and we might allow that there is no way to see the thing *save* through a perspective" (1965, p. 77). The second element in this formulation does not necessarily follow from the first, but Nietzsche is certainly a perspectivist in this double sense.

Danto adds, as a third definitional element of a consistent perspectivism, that "there is no perspective which is privileged over any other" (ibid.). This claim is at the very least problematic. First, a consistent perspectivism would seem to necessitate a privileging of perspectivism itself. If there is no way of seeing a thing except through a perspective, this means that knowing in general is perspectival and that particular forms of knowing must be interpreted perspectivally. One might argue that perspectivism cannot be universalized in this fashion—that it is self-contradictory to assert that all knowing is perspectival.[1] But this is quite different from the claim that all perspectives (in this case epistemological perspectives) are equal. Second, adherence to perspectivism in general does not preclude quite definite assessments of value within or between particular epistemic domains. And, third, whatever might be our view of the matter, Nietzsche is not an epistemological egalitarian.

If a generalized perspectivism is to be maintained, the possibility of a nonperspectival truth must be ruled out. Otherwise perspectivism reduces to the banal claim that things often can be seen from more than one point of view. Thus perspectivism demands a critique of extraperspectival truth-claims.[2]

A critique of nonperspectival thinking, then, as a preface to perspectivism as method or epistemology. There is also, in Nietzsche's case, a third element, although not the one suggested by Danto—to wit, an attempt to articulate an antimetaphysical worldview. This involves two elements. First, perspectives are positions from which meaning is imposed, and the imposition of meaning is a function of the will to power. To interpret is to overcome the resistance of the interpreted object; to overcome resistance is to interpret. Thus perspectivism as epistemology virtually coincides with the will to power as ontology. Everything is seen from the perspective of restless movement, the ceaseless breaking of wave on wave. Second, Nietzsche exercises a kind of perspectival restraint. He denies the possibility of gaining true knowledge of reality itself.

These two components of Nietzsche's worldview are reconcilable so long as the will to power is treated as nothing more than an ontological hypothesis. I will argue, however, that a philosophy grounded in the will to power can offer no resistance to the overstepping of epistemic limitations—and that when these limitations are transgressed, we come perilously close to philosophical madness. Thus in the end, Nietzsche walks the line between keeping everything in perspective and losing perspective on everything.

The order of the discussion follows what will prove to be a descending line: the perspectivist critique of metaphysics; constrained perspectivism; perspectivism as an antimetaphysical worldview and as the thinnest of horizons between knowledge and an infinite darkness.[3]

4.

Nietzsche begins *Beyond Good and Evil* with the famous characterization of truth as a woman (*BGE*, p. 2): "Supposing truth is a woman—what then? Are there not grounds for the suspicion that all philosophers, insofar as they were dogmatists, have been very inexpert about women?" In the Western tradition, Nietzsche identifies Platonism with dogmatism, and he treats Christianity as Platonism for the people (p. 3). By contrast, he is presumably not a clumsy dogmatist but rather a skilled lover of the truth.

Nietzsche's gendering of philosophical issues is already familiar to us, but it is not our current concern. The present point is that Nietzsche identifies dogmatism with Platonism; the critique of the one is a critique of the other.

The object of Nietzsche's criticism appears plainly in *The Republic*. Here Plato attempts to solve the problem of being and becoming that he inherited from the pre-Socratics—that is, to reconcile the unchangeable being of Parmenides with the ceaseless becoming of Heracleitus, and likewise the logic of either / or with the logic of interpenetration. His solution is to place each in its proper location. Figuratively (in the image of the divided line), the world is separated into upper and lower regions. In the lower region we experience the changeableness of things and their apparent interpenetration. Because they are unstable, we cannot know them but can only form (better or worse) opinions about them. We interpret them, in other words, but we cannot put forward truth-claims concerning them. The upper region, by contrast, consists of stable, unchangeable elements. This is the real world, of which the lower one is a mere appearance. Here, and here alone, true knowledge is possible. True knowledge descends from the Good, ultimate Being, and conversely, one ascends to the Good through the employment of the highest form of knowledge: dialectical reason.

In Nietzsche's view, Plato's higher reality is no reality at all. The lower world is the only world, and this being the case, truths in the Platonic (that is, in any dogmatic, metaphysical, or theological) sense are falsehoods. The dialectical ladder linking the lower and higher realms must be taken apart, rung by rung. Thus we have the following propositions concerning the true and apparent worlds:

First proposition. The reasons for which "this" world has been characterized as "apparent" are the very reasons which indicate its reality; any other kind of reality is absolutely indemonstrable.

Second proposition. The criteria which have been bestowed on the "true being" of things are the criteria of not-being, of *naught*; the "true world" has been constructed out of contradiction to the actual world: indeed an apparent world, insofar as it is merely a moral-optical illusion. (Nietzsche 1888c [hereafter *TI*], p. 484)

Two more propositions follow, which we will come to in a moment. For now, the point is that the world of becoming—of "life," as Nietzsche goes on to say—is the only world. Hence, in Plato's terms, there can be only opinions, not truths.

Nietzsche does not content himself with the reduction of the supersensible to the sensible world. He also seeks to demolish our faith in the soul (the Platonic mediator between the upper and the lower ontological regions) or, in more modern terms, the Cartesian (hence also the Kantian) ego:

When I analyze the process that is expressed in the sentence, "I think," I find a whole series of daring assertions that would be difficult, perhaps impossible, to prove; for example, that it is *I* who think, that there must necessarily be something that thinks, that thinking is an activity and operation on the part of a being who is thought of as a cause, that there is an "ego," and, finally, that it is already determined what is to be designated by thinking—that I *know* what thinking is. (*BGE*, p. 23)

The *cogito* cannot be taken as an "immediate certainty" or as an unconditioned presupposition of our knowing. To the contrary, it presupposes itself, recursively: I can only know that it is I who does the thinking if I already know what thinking is and that there is an I that is capable of thought. And when I reflect on this prior I and prior thinking, I find myself in an indeterminate regressive series.

The object of Nietzsche's criticism, it should be added, is not only self-certainty but also any conception of agency or substance whatsoever. Even to say that a thought comes when it wishes—that it, the thought, thinks—is for Nietzsche an "interpretation" of a process conditioned by our inability to free ourselves from the grammatical conventions of agency and action (p. 24).

So far we have taken two steps down Plato's ontological ladder: the ultimate object of knowledge (true being) is a superstition, and the subject who knows this object is a supposition. As a third step, Nietzsche contends that the concept of causality through which the subject makes sense of the object is a logically unwarranted projection from the one to the other: "People have believed at all times that they knew what a cause is; but whence did we take our knowledge—or more precisely, our faith that we had such knowledge? From the realm of the famous 'inner facts,' of which not a single one has so far proved to be factual" (*TI*, p. 495). Like Hume, Nietzsche is here denying the objectivity of causality. But as we have already seen, he goes further. One cannot say that causality is projected subjectivity, because the subject itself is supposititious. It, along with causality, may be of practical value, may even be necessary for creatures such as ourselves. But this does not confer on these concepts the truth-value claimed for them in traditional or even Kantian metaphysics.

There is also a corollary to Nietzsche's critical interpretation of causality. While granting that we must necessarily employ the relationship of cause and effect to make sense of the world and bring it under our control, he argues that we often misapply it, in one of two ways. First, we may treat an event as an effect and impute a cause to it, as when one interprets a lightning flash, a single event, as the flash (effect) of lightning (cause). This doubling of the deed is logically supernumerary, but it may be psychologically important, as when it is used to impute an agent capable of choice to an action performed in the absence of any such capacity for agency (*GM*, p. 45). Second, the position of cause and effect may be inverted, as when one mistakes a slender diet as cause of a long life, when it is the slow metabolism of someone who is long-lived that accounts for the slender diet (*TI*, p. 492).[4]

Three of the concepts that make possible extraperspectival knowing (true object, certain subject, and the law of cause and effect) have now been removed from the philosophical field. There remains the formal concept of true reality—of the thing-in-itself. This need not be a higher reality, in the Platonic sense, but merely a reality beyond the appearance of things. In Nietzsche's view, however, any such Kantian position is simply a variation on an ontological theme. In *Twilight of the Idols* we find this series:

1. The true world—attainable for the sage, the pious, the virtuous man; he lives in it, *he is it*.

    (The oldest form of the idea, relatively sensible, simple, and persuasive. A circumlocution for the sentence, "I, Plato, am the truth.")

2. The true world—unattainable for now, but promised for the sage, the pious, the virtuous man ("for the sinner who repents").

    (Progress of the idea: it becomes more subtle, insidious, incomprehensible—*it becomes female*, it becomes Christian.)

3. The true world—unattainable, indemonstrable, unpromisable; but the very thought of it—a consolation, an obligation, an imperative.

    (At bottom, the old sun, but seen through mist and skepticism. The idea has become pale, Nordic, Königsbergian.) (P. 485)

Platonism degenerates into Christianity, which Nietzsche denigrates by gendering it feminine; Christianity degenerates into Kantianism. Degeneration is also regeneration, however. The series continues through positivism and the stance of "free spirits," ending in the Zarathustrian noon when the dogmatist's true and apparent worlds are simultaneously abolished.[5] We then find ourselves in the realm of becoming, with no place else to go. And given the path we have taken to reach it, we also find ourselves deprived of our habitual defenses against its uncertainty and impermanence.

The last point—about metaphysical and other defenses—requires clarification. Nietzsche's critique of metaphysics is at once epistemological and psychological. In the former regard he purports to have undermined the truth-claims that can be attached to a series of metaphysical notions (being, soul, cause and effect, and essences in general and things-in-themselves in particular). In the latter regard he offers an explanation, or several related explanations, of the origin and functions of metaphysical principles. Reduced to a formula: metaphysics expresses the will to power of those who are too weak to affirm life in its fullness. Thus the third and fourth theses on the true and apparent worlds from *Twilight of the Idols:*

> *Third proposition.* To invent fables about a world "other" than this one has no meaning at all, unless an instinct of slander, detraction, and suspicion against life has gained an upper hand in us: in that case, we avenge ourselves against life with a phantasmagoria of "another," a "better" life.
>
> *Fourth proposition.* Any distinction between a "true" and an "apparent" world . . . is only a suggestion of decadence, a symptom of the *decline of life.* (P. 484)

For the weak and decadent, the pain of living (whatever the nature of the pain) is experienced as inadequacy, deficiency, or lack—as in the philosophy of Schopenhauer and, so Nietzsche would have argued, of Freud. The "true world" provides consolation for this suffering and contains the promise of passing beyond it. It also bespeaks the will to power in its reactive, nihilistic form. The true, higher, or next world is an attempt to negate the value of this one. In *The Gay Science*, Nietzsche quotes Socrates' dying words, "O Crito, I owe Asclepius a rooster" (*GS*, p. 272). Because Asclepius is the god of healing, Socrates' words mean, "O Crito, *life is a disease.*" Even the Greeks could not affirm the fullness of life, even they viewed it as a disease. And so "we must overcome even the Greeks!" (ibid.).

We have here the cutting edge of Nietzsche's transvaluation of all values. For Plato and his successors, the Good, the Beautiful, and the True rise above the world of becoming and confer value on it. Deprived of these redemptive valuations, humankind is in danger of sinking into a nihilistic void. But from Nietzsche's perspective, metaphysical values are themselves nihilistic—that is, denials of the value of life. This does not mean that life has value a priori or as such. To affirm "life itself" is just as metaphysical as positing a true world in contradistinction to the apparent one. The point is rather to affirm or place value on life as it is actually lived—to will life as it is. And this provides a standard of value: the strongest valuations are those which deny life least. Thus postmetaphysical nihilism, the dread-filled confrontation with the inherent meaninglessness of things in general and suffering in particular, is not for Nietzsche a fall from grace. It is rather "a pathological transitional stage" (*WP*, p. 14), an illness, but one that may portend a greater health—a step in the direction of being able to affirm life in its own terms, that is, as will to power.

We will return to question of nihilism in Section 8, but we may already anticipate its psychoanalytic implications: metaphysical beliefs perform a variety of defensive functions. When they are analyzed and their "falsity" is revealed, we are exposed to psychic realities we previously have been able to repress or deny. The consequence may be intense anxiety and nihilistic rage. But this descent into nihilism may be a necessary condition for emotional development.

5.

In the untimely meditation "On the Uses and Disadvantages of History for Life," Nietzsche claims, as a "universal law," that "a living thing can be healthy, strong and fruitful only when bounded by a horizon" (Nietzsche 1873–76 [hereafter *UM*], p. 63). The healthier the organism, the greater the expanse of life that can be brought within its field of vision. Dogmatism and metaphysics narrow our horizons, perspectivism broadens them. It commits us to eliminating as little as possible from our viewing of the world.

Thus we come to perspectivism itself, first as method of inquiry and then as worldview. I will attend, when appropriate, to some of the epistemological and logical problems that are attached to the notion. But it seems useful to dispatch three of them at the outset.

There is, first, the question of self-reference mentioned earlier. It would seem that a statement such as, "All truth is perspectival" is self-refuting: if the statement is true and there are only perspectival truths, then—because it is stated as a universal—it is also false. The paradox arises, however, not from the truth-claim but from its implicit derivation. That is, the claim is assumed to be deductive-nomological. On this assumption, the form of the statement is at odds with its content. But for Nietzsche, any such assumption is precisely metaphysical or dogmatic—the way of thinking he is arguing against. By contrast, if we construe the statement as an inductive generalization, hence as true only so long as a counterinstance cannot be adduced, then it is self-reinforcing rather than self-refuting. This becomes explicit if we say, "All truths are perspectival, including this one." The reflexive claim might appear to make the circle of self-reference more vicious but only, I would argue, from the perspective of someone who is attempting to escape from it.

Second, a problem results from the equation of perspective and particularity. One takes the possibility or even probability that there are several valid or plausible interpretations of things and converts it into a general rule. Yet perspectivism as a generalization from experience does not rule out the possibility that, in a given instance, there may be one, and only one, valid or plausible way of looking at something.

A third difficulty arises from the assumption of perspectival incommensurability—that there can be no common measure for the assessment of perspectival claims. But again, perspectivism does not commit one to the idea that there are no perspectives which cut across perspectives—unifying them and/or permitting evaluation between them. Or, to combine the elements of this discussion, it might be that the broadest perspectival horizon would come close to being a nearly universal (although not final or absolute) standard of judgment. It might even be the case that it would serve the interests or will to power of the species as a whole.

I recognize that these positions can be contested. I would maintain, however, that they come closer to Nietzsche's position than do the alternatives. No doubt, his distinctive procedure was to multiply perspectives and to set them up against each other. He broadened horizons precisely through accentuating differences and engaging in perspectival reversals. Yet this did not prevent him from thinking across perspectival boundaries or attempting to answer extremely general epistemological and ontological questions.

So much for what perspectivism is not; now for what it is. Perspectivism, first of all, is an experimental method. It rests on the presupposition that final, uncontestable, and universal truths are unobtainable. Even if, for example, one could come up with a theory that would resolve all existing cosmological problems, one could not eliminate the possibility of new problems or new cosmological perspectives arising. Or—to take this line of argument to its limit—even if we could adequately articulate a universal human perspective, we can still know only what human beings are capable of knowing. We cannot know how reality would appear from an extrahuman position. In a section of *The Gay Science* entitled *"Our new 'infinite'"* Nietzsche contends that "we cannot look around our own corner: it is hopeless curiosity that wants to know what other kinds of intellects and perspectives there *might* be; for example, whether some beings might be able to experience time backward, or alternatively forward and backward (which would involve another direction of life and another concept of cause and effect)" (*GS*, p. 336).[6] We cannot rule out, to vary the content, the possibility of a perspective beyond human perspectivism—I would add, even the possibility of a unique perspective from which all other perspectives derive. But equally, "we cannot reject the possibility that . . . [the beyond] *may include infinite interpretations*" (ibid.). One can never know, therefore, that one has come to the end of the ontological line, and this being the case, all attempts at knowing are experiments with the truth.

It follows that, even when putting forward the boldest interpretations, a certain epistemological modesty is in order. Thus as we saw in the last chapter, Nietzsche characterizes his analytic reduction of organic life to will to power as *"my* proposition" (*BGE*, p. 48). In another instance, he asks the reader to remember that his "few truths about 'woman as such'" are "after all only—*my* truths" (p. 162). The irony and provocation in these statements is evident. They can even be read with the opposite valence: are you, the reader, worthy of *this* truth? Either way, Nietzsche took seriously the idea that the possibility of alternative interpretations always exists.

Locutions such as "my truths" have an additional implication. Perspectives are constituted through experience, both individual and collective. When Nietzsche personalizes truth-claims, he is acknowledging that they are the products of *his* experimentation and self-experimentation. Thus when he says that "every great philosophy" is "the personal confession of its author and a kind of involuntary and unconscious memoir" (p. 13), he is in part describing himself. "My philosophy," he is saying, "is unmistakably about me; but in comparison to so many others, my confession is voluntary and conscious."

Nietzsche's clearest published statements about himself as a perspectivist are in *Ecce Homo*, which begins with the riddle, "I am . . . already dead as my father, while as my mother I am still living and becoming old" (*EH*, p. 223). Two identities, two ways of living—one male, one female. Given Nietzsche's valuations of masculinity and femininity, his father should have been strong and his mother weak. But his father was "delicate" and "morbid," and Nietzsche identifies his own illnesses or decadence as a paternal legacy ("in the same year in which his life went downward, mine, too, went downward" [ibid.]). He does not, however, identify his health with a maternal inheritance, although this would seem to be the implication of "while as my mother I am still living and becoming old."

We will return to the matter of Nietzsche's parental identifications in Chapters 4 and 5. The present point is that these identifications signify his experience of both profound illness and profound health, which he takes to be basic interpretive perspectives:

> Looking from the perspective of the sick toward healthier concepts and values and, conversely, looking again from the fullness and self-assurance of a rich life down into the secret work of decadence—in this I have had the longest training, my truest experience; if in anything, I became master in this. Now I know how, have the know-how, to reverse perspectives: the first reason why a "revaluation of values" is perhaps possible for me alone. (P. 223)

The manifest claim in this statement is that Nietzsche learned to think perspectivally from his experience of health and decadence and that this experience of reversing perspectives enabled him to see the more general problem of valuation from a new angle. It also, he goes on to say, enabled him to see beyond unitary conceptions of the self: "This *dual* series of experiences, this access to apparently separate worlds, is repeated in my nature in every respect: I am a *Doppelgänger*, I have a 'second' face in addition to the first. *And* perhaps also a third" (p. 225). Thus the self who sees perspectivally is also a self perspectivally seen.

Nietzsche was not much interested in the more technical methodological questions of empirical validation, but he did have criteria by which he evaluated propositions. He valued interpretations that change our angle of vision, allowing us to see things that were hitherto not visible, as well as those which combine and / or alter perspectives, allowing us to see things from more than one angle. Both criteria are explicitly stated in the often quoted rejection of disinterested objectivity in *On the Genealogy of Morals:*

> But precisely because we seek knowledge, let us not be ungrateful to such resolute reversals of accustomed perspectives and valuations with which the spirit has, with apparent mischievousness and futility, raged against itself for so long: to see differently in this way for once, to want to see differently, is no small discipline and preparation of the intellect for its future "objectivity"—the latter understood not as "contemplation without interest" (which is a nonsensical absurdity), but as the ability to control one's Pro and Con and to dispose of them, so that one knows how to employ a variety of perspectives and affective interpretations in the service of knowledge. (P. 119)

On the one hand, Nietzsche is here commending the perspectival pluralism for which he is so well known. On the other, he puts forward the desideratum of bringing these viewpoints under one's own control, in the service of epistemic aims. The more powerful the will to knowledge, in other words, the greater the number of perspectives that can be mobilized.

In sum, Nietzsche's perspectivism includes an experimental attitude, an acknowledgment of the personal element in all knowing, the valuing of multiple perspectives and perspectival reversals, and the valorization of a philosophical will to power that can command a legion of contrasting and contending interpretations. And as we have seen, this epistemological orientation is set against the background of the rejection of metaphysical, transcendental, and all other "disinterested" conceptions of knowledge. As in the old song about class warfare in the Harlan County coalfields, in the epistemological field too, "there are no neutrals there."

6.

Perspectivism in the preceding sense is compatible with at least a residual realism. Indeed, it seems to depend on there being a real knower and a real object to be known: a real Nietzsche, who had real experiences, that enabled him to see reality from more than one angle and therefore more clearly. In *The Antichrist*, for example, Nietzsche takes Buddhism, Judaism, and Christianity as historical givens and uses the duality of ascending and descending life as his interpretive grid. The text presupposes that there is a history to be interpreted. And this is his usual stance toward the things of this world. He accepts the reality of objects existing (at a minimum) outside of *his own* interpretation of them and assumes that his interpretations must take account of and, in some sense, fit with this preinterpreted object. Hence in his actual philosophical practice, he proceeds as a constrained perspectivist—a perspectivist who accepts some version of empirical reality as an epistemic constraint—or as a perspectivally constrained realist.

So long as Nietzsche stays within the specified limits, he can use knowledge of this-worldly reality as a standard for judging otherworldly truth-claims, he can offer multiperspectival interpretations of empirical matters, and he can rely on relatively conventional definitions of truth and falsehood when investigating the value of knowledge for life. Thus, in the latter regard, he can argue that the "falseness of a judgment is . . . not necessarily an objection to a judgment" (*BGE*, p. 11). Metaphysical "truths," for example, are horizons and—at least for some people—invaluable falsifications of the actual terms of existence. More generally, it might be that "untruth" is a "condition of life" (p. 12). Or, to restate the point in psychoanalytic terms, mental health might require some defensive distortion of reality, so that "renouncing false judgments would mean renouncing life and a denial of life" (ibid.). But none of this is to deny our usual, even commonsensical, ideas about reality and about true or false knowledge.

Nietzsche is not content with this position, which, in any case, *we* have extracted from the matrix of his thinking. When we expand our interpretive horizon, we find him raising questions about both reality and knowledge that go beyond the constraints we have attributed to or perhaps imposed on him.

For example:

It is no more than a moral prejudice that truth is worth more than mere appearance; it is even the worst proved assumption in the world. Let this much be admitted: there would be no life at all if not on the basis of perspective estimates and appearances; and if, with the virtuous enthusiasm and clumsiness of some philosophers, one wanted to abolish the "apparent world" altogether—well, supposing *you* could do that, at least nothing would be left of your "truth" either. Indeed, what forces us at all to suppose that there is an essential opposition of "true" and "false"? Is it not sufficient to assume degrees of apparentness and, as it were, lighter and darker shadows and shades of appearance—different "values," to use the language of painters? Why couldn't the world that concerns us—be a fiction? (Pp. 46–47)

The first part of this passage can be interpreted in the spirit of Nietzsche's "realist" critique of metaphysics. The "apparent" world is the *actual* real world, that is, the world of becoming. True knowledge is not metaphysical "truth" but such understanding as we are able to gain of our life circumstances. This understanding is necessarily provisional, perspectival, and incomplete. One might protest that this stance does violence to the idea of the truth—that it elides the distinction between knowledge and opinion. Nietzsche is free to respond that there are only *truths* and never the "truth." Absolute truth vanishes along with the metaphysical true world; perspectival truths are all that we can know. In any case, truth thus far retains its core meaning of some kind of fit between reason and reality, such that we can continue to distinguish between true and false interpretations of the things of this world.

Nietzsche, however, takes a step beyond *this* reality principle. He plays with the idea that truth and falsity are variations on a theme, different "values" rather than opposites. Taken together, these values allow us to paint a picture of the world or tell a story about it. But pictures and stories are fabrications or fictions. Reality, knowledge of which would be the truth, lies beyond our horizon.

Two things now happen simultaneously. First, interpretation of the things of this world becomes scarcely distinguishable from telling stories about them. An empirical world is still there, but the criteria by which we judge the validity of interpretations have become ambiguous. In a word, epistemic and cognitive values have become interpenetrated with aesthetic ones. Second, the "reality" that was to ground the critique of metaphysics and function as the common object of perspectival interpretations has become little more than a thing-in-itself. Nietzsche does not merely grant that things exist independently of any particular interpretation of them; he also presupposes a reality beyond any *possible* human perspective. The experimentalist limit of his perspectivism—that "we cannot look around our own corner"—requires the belief that there is something around the corner which we cannot know. Metaphysics covers over this epistemic abyss with "truths" that the perspectival critique of metaphysics demonstrates to be falsehoods (albeit, sometimes useful or even vital ones). In the passage just cited, however, Nietzsche takes the argument one step further. To say that the world that concerns us, the world we live within, is a "fiction" implies something nonfictional with which it can be compared. And precisely this nonfictional world is inaccessible, around our own corner. Hence Nietzsche cannot escape the Kantian, or perhaps Socratic, dilemma: he knows just enough to posit the existence of a reality that he cannot know.

7.

One of the opening images of *Thus Spoke Zarathustra* is a tightrope walker who attempts to maintain his balance as he walks a rope between two towers. Overtaken by a jester on the same rope, he loses his head and plunges to his death. Nietzsche the perspectivist comes close to taking a similar plunge into an ontological abyss. But he manages to keep his head and balance rather delicately on the dividing line between the things of this world and things-in-themselves. Exercising more than a modicum of epistemic restraint, he constructs a perspectival worldview by (a) joining perspectivism to the ontological hypothesis of the will to power and (b) limiting all truth-claims through a critical analysis of the falsifying functions of both logic and language.

As to (a): We remember that, in his analytic reduction of instinctive life to will to power, Nietzsche treated the latter simply as a "proposition" (*BGE*, p. 48). Ample evidence in both the published texts and the notebooks indicates that he believed in the validity of this proposition, and he assuredly uses it to interpret historical phenomena and philosophical positions. But he does not place it outside his own experimentalist boundaries.

Hypothetically, then, the world consists of quanta of force, centers of will to power, each of which constitutes a perspective. This is the "necessary perspectivism" in all things, because "every center of force—and not only man—construes all the rest of the world from its own viewpoint, i.e., measures, feels, forms, according to its own force" (*WP*, p. 339). There is a localist tendency built into ontological perspectivism: "Even in the domain of the inorganic an atom of force is concerned only with its neighborhood." If there is a semblance of order on a large scale, it is only because "distant forces balance one another" (p. 340). Yet we are not reduced to perspectival atomism: "Every specific body strives to become master over all space and to extend its force (—its will to power:) and to thrust back all that resists its extension. But it continually encounters similar efforts on the part of other bodies and ends by coming to an arrangement ("union") with those of them that are sufficiently related to it; thus they then conspire together for power. And the process goes on" (ibid.). The overcoming of resistance proceeds from various centers. These centers can combine, resulting in a "complex form of specificity," but, as noted, the only approximation to stability in these relationships is the result of distant forces balancing one another.

At this imagined physical level, interpretation is an action, and all action is interpretive. Accordingly, Nietzsche claims that the "will to power *interprets*. . . : it defines limits, determines degrees, variations of power" (p. 342). This can be taken to soften the meaning of will to power, as if Nietzsche were saying the will to power *only* interprets—as if the meaning of interpretation had been restricted to the imparting of meaning. But the text itself does not seem to support this limitation.

The situation is not fundamentally changed when we advance from the inorganic to the organic, or even human, spheres: "It is our needs that interpret the world; our drives and their For and Against. Every drive is a kind of lust to rule; each one has its perspective that it would like to compel all the other drives to accept as a norm" (p. 267). Every drive—let's say every drive of a human individual—is an instance or specification of the will to power. Each strives for mastery. But as in the case of inorganic forces, alliances are possible, and a chain of command can be established that yields "the ability *to control* one's Pro and Con and to dispose of them, so that one knows how to employ a *variety* of perspectives and affective interpretations in the service of knowledge"—or in the service of life.

Thus to say that there is "*only* perspective 'knowing'" is to say that there are only epistemic placements of the will to power. Although these centers of force may engage in a philosophical war of all against all, they can also form not only alliances but even a grand alliance. What they cannot do is resolve disputes by appeal to principles of pure reason or impartial epistemic magistrates. Or perhaps we should say that they absolve us from needing such appellate procedures. In yet another of Nietzsche's comments on the true and apparent worlds, he notes: "The perspective therefore decides the character of the 'appearance'! As if a world would still remain over after one deducted the perspective! By doing that one would deduct relativity!" (p. 305). Our knowledge consists of perspectival relationships. Subtract the relationships and knowledge disappears at the same time. To be sure, from a metaphysical perspective this leaves us floating in an ontological void. There are no ultimate truths to serve as anchors for our thinking. But Nietzsche's intent all along has been to unanchor us from metaphysical truths.

This intention is further realized in (b), Nietzsche's analysis of the epistemic limits of logic and language. We have already seen that he treats a wide range of categories (for example, true object, certain subject, and the law of cause and effect) as metaphysical. When this line of criticism is followed to the end, however, it turns back on itself: logic and language themselves, hence also the logic and language of critique, are metaphysical. Thus he claims:

> Logic is bound to the condition: assume there are identical cases. In fact, to make possible logical thinking and inferences, this condition must first be treated fictitiously as fulfilled. That is: the will to logical truth can be carried through only after a fundamental *falsification* of all events is assumed. From which it follows that a drive rules here that is capable of employing both means, firstly falsification, then the implementation of its own point of view: logic does not spring from will to truth. (*WP*, p. 277)

Note that Nietzsche here uses "truth" in two senses. There is "logical truth" and "truth"—that is, knowledge of reality. The former, we might infer, consists of a whole network of conceptual relations within which judgments of truth and falsity are possible. But the rules of logic demand of things an equality they do not possess. This demand for equality is not inexplicable: "*the will to equality is the will to power*—the belief that something is thus and thus (the essence of *judgment*) is the consequence of a will that as much as possible *shall be* equal" (ibid.). Nonetheless, the result is that logical thinking depends on a prior falsification of the truth (in the second, presumably empirical, sense).

One might evade this epistemic aporia by splitting off logic from language—by imagining a language that is not structured by the logic of identity and difference. But Nietzsche does not hold out the possibility of such a postmetaphysical language. Rather, he treats language as a very primitive acquisition of the species, one that is intrinsically metaphysical: "In its origin language belongs in the age of the most rudimentary form of psychology. We enter a realm of crude fetishism when we summon before consciousness the basic presuppositions of the metaphysics of language, in plain talk, the presuppositions of reason" (*TI*, p. 483). Yet we cannot think otherwise: "*We cease to think when we refuse to do so under the constraint of language; we barely reach the doubt that sees this limitation as a limitation. Rational thought is interpretation according to a scheme that we cannot throw off*" (*WP*, p. 283). If we take metaphysics to mean the falsification of reality, then all thinking, because it is limited by the language of logic or the logic of language, is metaphysical.

This conclusion does not, in my opinion, undercut the validity of Nietzsche's constrained perspectivist critique of metaphysics. Within the limits of language and logic, particular metaphysical concepts can be analyzed and rejected—or, at a minimum, used with caution and self-awareness. Moreover, because the analysis points to the entrapment of perspectivism within the metaphysics of language, it functions as a self-critical as well as an antimetaphysical limit.

The elements of Nietzsche's perspectival worldview have now been sufficiently articulated. In his own words:

> That the value of the world lies in our interpretation (—that other interpretations than merely human ones are perhaps somewhere possible—); that previous interpretations have been perspective valuations by virtue of which we can survive in life, i.e., in the will to power, for the growth of power; that every elevation of man brings with it the overcoming of narrower interpretations; that every strengthening and increase of power opens up new perspectives and means believing in new horizons—this idea permeates my writings. The world with which we are concerned is false, i.e., is not a fact but a fable and approximation on the basis of a meager sum of observations; it is "in flux," as something in a state of becoming, as a falsehood always changing but never getting near the truth: for—there is no "truth." (P. 330)

Perspectivism is the epistemological technique through which narrower interpretations are overcome. Conversely, the ascendant will to power "opens up new perspectives and means believing in new horizons." This broadening of horizons is not a means to an end; it does not aim at the "truth." It is rather its own end, the expansive refalsification of the world.

Although our aim to this point has been largely expository, we might raise a question or two concerning the falsification thesis. How can we know that language and logic falsify reality if—as Nietzsche maintains—we have no true knowledge of reality on which to base this judgment? Conversely, if we have a sufficient knowledge of reality so that we can judge logic and language to be falsifying, then it can no longer be claimed, as a general rule, that logic and language are falsifying. Thus Nietzsche's equation of knowledge and falsification saddles him with yet another version of the old Kantian contradiction of knowing that the thing-in-itself is unknowable—of knowing something about which no knowledge is possible. Moreover, what Nietzsche terms the falsification of reality could with equal justice be termed its "truthification." That is, the judgments of truth and falsity are both, as he would have to grant, artifacts of logic and language. They can be meaningfully applied, in a constrained perspectivist fashion, to the things of this (our human) world, but they cannot be meaningfully applied to whatever might be around our own corner. In both regards, therefore, Nietz-sche's own position would be better secured by simply acknowledging language and logic as limits of thought.

There are alternative approaches to this issue. We might interpret "falsification" to mean simply "selection" or "simplification." Then falsification is roughly synonymous with perspective valuation and analytic reduction. I do not think Nietzsche really licenses this view, but it is another way of avoiding the Kantian impasse. Or we could interpret Nietzsche's epistemology in aesthetic terms. We might, with some justification, equate the falsification of reality with Apollonian illusion and reality itself with the Dionysian will. We could remind ourselves, in other words, that Nietzsche never quite managed to shake himself free from Schopenhauer or—to put it more affirmatively—that he continued to build on the foundation of *The Birth of Tragedy*. But this explanatory approach to his epistemological stance does not resolve the problems that are native to it.

8.

We are going to take a Nietzschean step beyond Nietzsche's perspectival limits. Before we do, let's reorient ourselves by reference to Plato's divided line. In this hierarchical arrangement of things ontological and epistemological, the upper region of reason and being is the metaphysical "true world," the lower region of opinion and becoming is mere appearance. The perspectival critique of metaphysics reveals the "true world" to be a nihilistic attack on the so-called apparent one. When it disappears, the judgment of appearance disappears along with it. The lower region of becoming is all that remains. In this world one may have opinions but not knowledge, perspectival truths but not the absolute truth. Truth-claims may be assessed and adjudicated but only by reference to one or another of the available this-worldly standards.

One major trend in Nietzsche's philosophy is to be content with experience and knowledge at this level. "Today we consider it a matter of decency not to wish to see everything naked," he says in the 1886 preface to *The Gay Science:* "'Is it true that God is present everywhere?' a little girl asked her mother; 'I think that's indecent'—a hint for philosophers! One should have more respect for the bashfulness with which nature has hidden behind riddles and iridescent uncertainties. Perhaps truth is a woman who has reasons for not letting us see her reasons. Perhaps her name is—to speak Greek—*Baubô?*" (*GS*, p. 38). In myth and in the Eleusinian mysteries, Baubô makes the mourning Demeter laugh by lifting her skirts and exposing her belly and genitals. The sexual implications of this figuration of the truth therefore are clear enough: we (men) should not look under nature's skirts; her genitals should be kept under cover. But leaving the sexual theme to the side just for the moment, Nietzsche's point is that there are reasons to leave well enough alone. The Greeks, he concludes, "were superficial—*out of profundity*" (ibid.).

The other major trend in Nietzsche's thinking is to lift nature's skirts. In this regard he is a kind of inverse Socrates. Socratic *élenchos* (questioning or interrogation) aimed to strip away error. When taken to its Platonic extreme, error includes most human beliefs. As these beliefs fall away, they are replaced by ever closer approximations to the truth, until at last the soul is fully illuminated by the light of the Good. By contrast, Nietzsche's per-spectivist questioning of all metaphysical notions takes him ever further from the Good and ever more deeply into a world where truth is scarcely distinguishable from falsity. Still, empirically constrained perspectivism can be defended in recognizably philosophical terms so long as, first, ontologi-cal propositions are treated as hypotheses, to be tested by their interpretive consequences, and, second, perspectivist thinking is accepted as self-limiting. We then live in a world of thought-experiments and pragmatic adjustments. This is a disquieting world, rife with uncertainty and therefore anxiety. It is human, all-too-human and, for just this reason, profoundly sane.

We could stop at this point and, in fairness to Nietzsche, perhaps we should. But how is one to resist the two temptations that are built into his worldview? Aren't we driven, on the one hand, to know what really is there? Doesn't our will to power demand that we overcome the resistance with which reality opposes our epistemic efforts? And aren't we forced, on the other, to take ourselves and our knowing as a territory to be conquered—to overcome the resistance of thinking itself?

Let's come at this from another direction. The earliest Greek ontological or cosmological speculations were often concerned with the question of limits or boundaries. Thus Anaximander claimed that "the Non-Limited is the original material of existing things; further, the source from which exist-ing things derive their existence is also that to which they return at their destruction, according to necessity; for they give justice and make repara-tion to one another for their injustice, according to the arrangement of Time" (Freeman 1978, p. 19). Existing—finite, bounded, or limited—things arise from and return to the Infinite or Non-Limited. They seem to have a built-in tendency toward injustice, that is, encroachment on each other's territory. Boundary violation is punished by the destruction of the offender, and the cosmic balance is restored.

The finite things in Anaximander's cosmology mirror individuals and classes in Greek society. In each instance, injustice involves the transgression of limits, while justice involves observing limits and staying within them—as in our everyday expression of observing the limits of the law. Plato joins the cosmological and social levels in *The Republic*. Thrasymachus in book 1 and Glaucon and Adeimantus in book 2 argue that injustice—overstepping limits and taking that which belongs to another—is to be preferred to justice, so long as one can get away with it. Socrates restores order by placing everything in its proper position. Each individual, as a member of a social class, performs his or her appropriate function, and likewise each faculty of the soul. No individual, class, or mental faculty encroaches on the territory of another. Moreover, dialectical logic obeys the same commands. The laws of logic themselves—Parmenides' great gift of the either/or and its more formal derivatives—determine what something is and what it is not. And, discursively, to define concepts properly is to specify their limits, so that one knows which meanings attach to them and which meanings are to be excluded. Thus, as in the grand schema of the divided line, logic and language insure the rightful division of the world of ideas.

It is evident that my exposition of Nietzsche's perspectivism has been held together by Platonic principles of division. Not only have I placed the components of perspectivism along the divided line (albeit in a critical relationship to it), but I have divided perspectivism into parts, each with its own proper functions. Of course, by arranging the three parts in such a way as to broaden horizons (constrained perspectivism has a broader horizon than the critique of metaphysics, and the perspectival worldview has a broader horizon than constrained perspectivism), I also could claim to have applied a Nietzschean method to Nietzsche. I am not sure that Nietzsche himself would have appreciated such a relatively tidy explication of his position. But whatever he might have thought, this manner of exposition suggests that one can go quite some distance with Nietzsche and still stay within the boundaries of the Western philosophical tradition.

The problem with such an interpretation of perspectivism, even if it were to be Nietzsche's, is that it does not engage the full meaning of the will to power. The will to power is inherently and necessarily boundary violating, even boundary annihilating. In classical Greek terms, it is a principle of ontological injustice. This judgment would hold even for Heraclitus and Empedocles, both of whom bound the creative functions of strife and discord with notions of cosmological law and order. And thus we have another meaning for Nietzsche's assertion that "we must overcome even the Greeks": we must overturn the Greek principle of rightful limits. But in this instance "the Greeks" signify the very idea of a limit or boundary. When, therefore, the Greeks are overcome, so too is Nietzsche's epistemic self-restraint.

Thus perspectivism, driven by the will to power, cannot turn back at the horizon of logic and language. The ceaseless pounding of wave on wave threatens to annihilate the basic categories of thought and plunge us into an abyss of meaninglessness. Nietzsche himself does not quite take this plunge. He looks into the abyss and then looks away again. But he comes close enough to be chilled by the prospect.

In this context, we might consider the famous parable of the madman from *The Gay Science*. The madman announces the death—the murder—of God, with the consequent threat or even necessity of postmetaphysical nihilism. How could this have happened, the madman asks:

> How could we drink up the sea? Who gave us the sponge to wipe away the entire horizon? What were we doing when we unchained this earth from its sun? Whither is it moving now? Whither are we moving? Away from all suns? Are we not plunging continually? Backward, sideward, forward, in all directions? Is there still any up or down? Are we not straying as through an infinite nothing? Do we not feel the breath of empty space? Has it not become colder? Is not night continually closing in on us? (*GS*, p. 181).

The belief in God was the anchor of all valuations, the orienting point for all beliefs. Without God we are lost in space and time. It might even be said that space and time have been lost to us.

Taken straightforwardly, the madman is evoking the crisis in European values attendant on the declining power of Christian faith. If, however, we take "God" as a signifier of the network of metaphysical beliefs—including belief in the metaphysics of language—then the death of God represents a more general collapse of meaning and a fall into the ontological flux that our thinking protectively "falsifies." And from our present position, we can answer the madman's question of how we were able to murder God: the will to power compels us to annihilate the beliefs that give meaning and stability to our existence. We are driven to catch sight of reality, even if it freezes us and drives us mad.

(At this moment, we are reminded of Baubô or perhaps of her horrifying counterpart, the Medusa. Nietzsche might admire the Greek or artistic temperament that can resist the temptation of looking under nature's skirts, but he himself is compelled to look, no matter what the consequences.)

In the next chapter, I will argue that Nietzsche philosophized from the verge of what he experienced as a formless, fascinating, and terrifying feminine or maternal vortex and that the idea of eternal return—his "most abysmal thought," as he himself characterized it (in Strong 1985, p. 327)—was his attempt to conceptualize this situation. But a related idea is more in tune with the present argument. The limit of Nietzsche's philosophy, which he wishes to maintain but is compelled to violate, is logic and language. He treats language as a primitive acquisition of the species, and he argues that logic is embedded in the structure of language itself. He senses, perceives, or intuits processes of transformation beyond this limit, but his own rules, if strictly followed, would forbid him to speak about them. The situation is thoroughly self-contradictory.

Just here we might be tempted to invoke Hegel. Nietzsche's dilemma is that he wishes to be able to conceptualize flux and becoming but believes that language has a built-in tendency toward reification. He therefore is powerless to say what he must also claim to know. By contrast, Hegel goes quite some way, if not all the way, toward the liquefaction of language. He is able to conceptualize both the logic of language and the language of logic as processes, whatever the ultimate absolutizing of his concepts, and by so doing makes transformation comprehensible. Nietzsche, however, never really goes beyond the problematics of Kantian metaphysics. Hence he is vulnerable to the claim that the problem lies not in language and logic as such but only in the logic and language he himself employs.

I will return to these properly philosophical matters in Chapter 6. But as we are about to see, Nietzsche's epistemological limitations can be turned to clinical advantage.

II. Perspectivism in Psychoanalytic Practice

9.

We remember Nietzsche's claim that every philosophy is "the personal confession of its author and a kind of involuntary and unconscious memoir" (*BGE*, p. 13). My conception of psychoanalytic perspectivism partially fits the Nietzschean bill.[7] It is the product of my own psychoanalytic experience and therefore is something of a confession and memoir. So it is best presented autobiographically.

I first entered psychoanalytic training in 1975. Although I had been psychoanalytically oriented from early on in my graduate studies, by the late 1960s and early 1970s my psychoanalytic interests had become subordinated to the concerns of political theory and radicalized politics. Consequently, becoming a psychoanalytic candidate felt like one step forward, two steps back. The step forward was to join practice to theory, in accordance with the value of praxis. The unity of theory and practice was, however, a political value. And from that standpoint, entering a training program meant an unwelcome immersion in alien (bourgeois, privatized) values. That was the first step back. The second was that, in this setting, psychoanalysis was not viewed as a praxis but as a science. With rare exceptions, I found myself in the company of people who believed science was the only epistemological game in town. In this regard, too, I was in alien territory.

I mobilized my philosophical resources to counter these regressive trends. The greatest help came from *The Phenomenology of Spirit*. Hegel's exquisite sensitivity to subject-object (including self-other) interaction and his profound understanding of the creative role played by negation was far in advance of the scientism of the time or even of the then emergent hermeneutic construals of psychoanalysis. And it remains ahead of the inter-subjectivist and social constructionist approaches that only now are finding their way into the field.

The theoretical component of the training program evoked quite a bit of irritation but very little anxiety. The practical component was doubly anxiety-producing: I had no clinical experience and was therefore anxious about my competency; I was exposed to the anxieties of my patients, and these were often indistinguishable from my own. Here again, and with much greater consequence, phenomenological dialectics proved to be invaluable. They provided a structure in and as process that fit the psychoanalytic situation, while the dialectical acceptance of destabilizing transitions from object to subject and subject to object was enormously helpful in enabling me to follow the shifting course of evolving transferences.

Thus (for me) dialectical reason was unifying of the epistemological and practical extremes of the psychoanalytic vocation. There was also guidance to be found at the substantive level, especially in the phenomenology of self-certainty (desire and the battle for recognition; lordship and bondage; Stoicism, skepticism, and the unhappy consciousness), and these concepts too proved to be of clinical value.[8] My experience turned out to be an ironically appropriate confirmation of the second thesis on Feuerbach: the truth and reality of Hegelian phenomenology was demonstrated in practice.

As my clinical experience increased and with Hegel in mind, I worked out a phenomenological model of the psychoanalytic situation (Wolfenstein 1993, chapter 9). Briefly, the individuals constituting the analytic dyad function at the levels of consciousness, work/desire, and sensuousness. As conscious selves, they are capable of both giving and withholding recognition through the medium of language. Mutual recognition is required if any meaningful emotional work is to be performed. But the asymmetry of the relationship mobilizes transferential tendencies in the patient—and countertransferential tendencies in the analyst. These tendencies recurrently disrupt the recognitive frame of the interaction, and it is the interpretation of these disruptions that initiates distinctively psychoanalytic modes of under-standing.

At the level of work/desire, the relationship between analyst and patient is affective and often empathic. Sometimes the affective bond is simply the emotional dimension of consciousness, sometimes it is the source of trans-ferences. But even when these transferences are stormy, they tend to reflect development at the level of the depressive position. They are genuinely interpersonal. They are marked by the patient's concern for the well-being of the analyst, by her or his desire to have needs met without doing injury, hence by the fear that need-fulfillment is injurious to the other. Corre-spondingly, the analyst must be mindful of the emotional vulnerability that accompanies the depressive position and must be prepared to engage in reparative efforts when her or his lack of empathy has been injurious.

The work of interpreting desire mobilizes and brings to the surface mainly preconscious affects and ideas—feelings, wishes, and phantasies that are defended against but not deeply repressed or split off. By contrast, work in the borderlands of sensuousness involves far more primitive states of mind. This is the territory of the deeply unconscious, where mind first emerges from its psychophysiological integument. Here the most common transference phenomena derive from the paranoid-schizoid position, with its characteristic modalities of projection, introjection, projective identifica-tion, splitting, and the like. Because the analyst must offer as little resistance as possible to the deployment of these almost telepathic and sometimes quite pathological processes of communication, boundaries between self and other become difficult to distinguish. Moreover, at times the analytic dyad hangs suspended over an abyss of pre-self levels of functioning, of unmen-talized psychophysiological flows and affective black holes. Yet for many patients, it is necessary to descend into these depths if genuine emotional development is to take place. Thus it is evident that the deeper one goes in analytic work, the more contact one has with intense anxiety and psychic pain. The more this anxiety and pain can be tolerated, the greater the likeli-hood that the analysis will actually prove to be transformational.

This dialectical and phenomenological model of psychoanalytic interac-tion has served me well, and I continue to use it for the theoretical recon-struction of psychoanalytic experience. But, for two reasons, I no longer guide myself by it. First, its synthetical strength can become an analytic weakness—that is, a defense against or resistance to the unstructured and unfilled moments in any thoroughgoing psychoanalysis. It provides too much comfort, too great a confidence that experiences of self-negation and self-dissolution are meaningful, in themselves and as means to affirmative ends. Second, dialectical reason does not solve the psychoanalytic version of the Kantian problem of the thing-in-itself—the problem of gaining knowledge of nonverbal experience. At its neo-Kantian best, it acknowledges this limitation; at its Hegelian worst, it begs the question by identifying knowledge with language. In neither instance does it focus attention on the ways in which both language and logic can function as defenses against and falsifications of nonlinguistic experience. By contrast, Nietzsche's perspectivism enables or forces us to experience the moment at which meaning disappears and we are in danger of falling into a nihilistic void. And it points us toward the realm of nonverbal experience that is developmentally prior to the acquisition of language and is regressively uncovered in the course of psychoanalytic work.

10.

Here, briefly, are three examples of a clinical phenomenon that takes form in a perspectival world beyond the limits of Hegelian phenomenology.

- A clinical associate (psychoanalyst in training) is reporting on a session with a patient to a seminar. I am one of the instructors. As I listen, I feel myself becoming so anxious that I can no longer attend to what is being said. This experience is shared by my co-instructor. The discussion of the reported session becomes fragmented. The group as a whole and the instructors in particular come to recognize that they have been gripped by the patient's psychotic-like anxiety, which had been transmitted to them through the clinical associate.
- A psychoanalyst is describing to me, in a consultation session, an experience with her patient. The patient was describing how she maintained her composure in a very difficult situation. By the time the session ended, the analyst was feeling intensely chilled. As we worked through this experience, it became clear that her body had been the vehicle through which she was containing her patient's terror. The latter's composure had been superficial. Beneath the surface, she was in a panic and this had been projectively communicated to her analyst.
- I am sitting with a patient who is describing with great clarity a feeling of being professionally betwixt and between. This leads back to the time when her parents were divorced and to the experience of being between their two worlds. Then she imaginatively places herself in the apartment she occupied with her mother after the divorce. The mood in the consulting room becomes impenetrably and almost intolerably dark. We mutually acknowledge the darkness—and that the term

"depression" does not even begin to describe it. The hour comes to an end and the patient leaves, feeling quite dazed. I'm left feeling anxious but not disoriented.

The common theme in these vignettes is the communication of intensely painful, nonverbal experience by nonverbal means. I will bypass the question of how such communication is possible. Projective identification names the phenomenon but does not go very far toward explaining it. And, clearly, the reader is entitled to entertain skeptical doubts about the reality of such transferences of affect and sensation. But at a minimum, these experiences call our attention to (a) the paradox of needing to interpret with words experiences that are beyond language and (b) the evident difficulty in bearing this kind of psychic and psychophysiological pain.

As to (a), it is just here that Nietzsche's thought-experiments with the limits of logic and language are clarifying. When he claims that "man could not live" without "accepting the fictions of logic" and that we must recognize "untruth as a condition of life," he is calling our attention to what, in psychoanalytic terms, we identify as the defensive functions of mentation. Not all thinking is defensive, of course. In part it is obedient to the imperatives of communication. We are irreducibly intersubjective creatures. Logic and language serve our need to be known to each other and/or to have our needs known by an other. Which is not to deny that they can also serve us as masks. But partially, and more to the present point, logic and language function as instruments through which we master the powerful flows of sensation and affect in which we are necessarily immersed. Through mentalization, that is, through the creation of meaning, we impose horizons—boundaries and limits—on these premental dimensions of our being.

If this line of reasoning is accepted, we can see the wisdom in Nietzsche's characterization of logic and language as falsifications in the interest of life. Again there are two sides to the story. Through thinking we bring some of the world into ourselves as well as push some of it away. Or, in more narrowly psychoanalytic terms, every defense is simultaneously an expression of what it defends against. The Heraclitean logic of interpenetration expresses this boundary relationship between opposites better than the Parmenidean logic of either/or. But so long as we focus on the defensive functions of mentation, we are in the Parmenidean world that Nietzsche takes as his object of analysis—a world in which interpenetration is denied and the either/or is used to place flux and transformation beyond the limits of possible knowledge.

A further implication of this analysis is that the reality beyond logic and language is not a thing-in-itself, a something about which we can know nothing. Let's think back to the three instances of psychoanalytic experience. In each case, verbal interpretations are offered of nonverbal experience. These interpretations cannot be said to correspond to the experience. It would be better to say that they express it, with all the epistemological ambiguity that a term such as "expression" involves. But there is unmistakably a something there which we know to exist and which our interpretations express. If the interpretation is meaningful to the involved parties, if it provides a common language for the expression of the nonverbal experience, then it has met the epistemological standard of psychoanalytic practice.

The usual epistemological question is, how we can gain valid knowledge of reality? The more usual psychoanalytic question is, why do we prefer to falsify reality rather than to know it? Thus we come to (b): the reality that concerns us psychoanalytically is hard to bear. This "fact" cannot be accounted for in purely Nietzschean terms. It is not adequate to say that we cannot bear being in the world because it is will to power and ceaseless becoming. True enough, as mental beings we are immersed in and emerge (as selves) from a sea of affects and sensations. In this regard, we—Nietzsche, psychoanalysts, and Schopenhauer—are in agreement. But the transition from mental organization to defensive organization, from perspectival knowledge of reality to its falsification, is a function of pain. The greater the pain during the period of self-formation, the narrower the horizons of selfhood will tend to be.

Analysis aims at broadening the horizons of the self—as in Freud's version of the cogito, "where id [it] was, there ego [I] shall be" (1933, p. 80). This means that existing limits and boundaries, the defensive foundations of the self, must be treated as resistances to be overcome. From which it follows that analysis must press the will to power into its service. It must do so, however, in a very specific way: to the extent possible, patient and analyst must use the will to power against the will to power. As redefined, the will to power is the process of overcoming pain to gain pleasure, including the pleasure of overcoming pain. It is essentially active. But analytic work requires that both parties tolerate pain rather than acting to overcome it. They must resist the temptation of playing the *fort! da!* game.

That is not quite accurate. As noted earlier, the roles in the analytic relationship are not symmetrical. For the analysis to proceed, the analyst must have developed the discipline necessary for suspending the will to power. This is required so that the patient has available a space in which habitual defenses, habitual placements of the will to power, can emerge and be interpreted. Thus in the first instance, the analyst's will to power is to be suspended and the patient's will to power is to be activated. But all analysis is ultimately self-analysis. Over time the patient must develop an autonomous capacity for meaningful interpretation. This can happen only if the patient is truly a patient, that is, one who suffers her or his own pain. Eventually, therefore, the aims of patient and analyst converge. Both must learn to tolerate the maximum of anxiety with the minimum of defense.

Although the task of tolerating anxiety is an ongoing aspect of the analytic process, certain moments, such as when patient and analyst confront the not-yet-known, are dread-filled. At these times, it seems that the only alternative to familiar and habitual self-limitations is the madman's plunge into the nihilistic abyss. Yet there is a profound illusion in this experience of dread. Winnicott contends that the breakdown the patient fears in the future has already happened in the past (Winnicott, Shepherd, and Davis 1989, pp. 87–95). The patient dreads the return of "primitive agonies" that could not be assimilated and mastered by the self at the time when they first occurred. They happened but were not experienced because not enough self was there to have the experience. It is necessary, however, to have the experience if it is to be genuinely consigned to the past. Thus the not-yet-known is only partially something that is genuinely new. It is also something only too well "known," but not known mentally.

The fear of breakdown is present in most analyses, but its intensity is highly variable. The more favorable the person's self-formative experience, the less subsequent self-development carries with it the fear of annihilation. I say "person" rather than "patient" because, when the analysis goes deep enough, dread fills the consulting room. Then most of all the analyst must adhere to the rules of the psychoanalytic discipline if an analysis is actually to take place.

11.

So much for conceptualizing a psychoanalytic version of a perspectivist worldview or, more concretely, the perspectivist world of psychoanalytic experience. I come now to the actual process of psychoanalytic interpretation, which, as might have been anticipated, resembles the constrained version of Nietzsche's perspectivism: it is always experimental; each analysis is uniquely shaped by the personalities and personal experiences of the participants; multiple perspectives are always at play; perspectival reversals are required if development is to occur; and the analyst must have the "ability *to control* one's Pro and Con and to dispose of them, so that one knows how to employ a *variety* of perspectives and affective interpretations in the service of knowledge."

There are also differences between Nietzschean and psychoanalytic interpretation. Nietzsche or the Nietzschean philosopher imposes meaning on things. The things are acknowledged to have an independent existence, but their meaning is constructed by the interpreter. Psychoanalysis is not free from such practices of meaning imposition. At a minimum, a whole variety of meanings are embedded in the enterprise itself. But when compared with Nietzsche, the analyst is (or ought to be) a model of restraint, and this in a twofold sense. She or he seeks to offer as little resistance as possible to the patient's own processes of meaning-formation, and she or he attempts to see things from the patient's perspective(s). The analyst must have the capacity to employ a variety of perspectives and affects in forming interpretations but must employ this capacity in an almost inverted fashion, that is, in the suspended manner that we have already specified. This creates the space for the patient's perspectives and affects.

Not much would be gained by attempting a comprehensive enumeration of psychoanalytic perspectives. It is enough to note that patient and analyst see each other from a variety of angles and that neither of them is a simple, unitary self. For example, a woman with a wonderfully vivid imagination and capacity for dramatization experienced herself as two girls who had a relationship to me. One of them was lively, affectionate, and trusting. She viewed me as someone who was or would be her friend. The other girl was angry and mistrustful. She viewed me with suspicion, as someone who would ultimately let her down. So my patient was two people, and I was two people; while these four people could converse with each other, no one of them could be dissolved into the other.

Or consider another instance, one with a certain Foucauldian resonance. A man with a genuinely impressive record of professional achievement combined with equally genuine empathic capacities is perpetually scrutinized by an internal judge and guardian. Hence there is *his* perspective, as the one being judged: anxious, defensive, seldom feeling quite good enough despite his formidable accomplishments. And there is the perspective of the judge, who claims to have the patient's best interests at heart and who was indeed formed (in part) in the interests of his preservation. But the judge has taken on a life of his own. He is cruel, condemning, exacting—as if every moment of decision could be a fatal slip and the undoing of every accomplishment.

In both these examples, we are presented with a divided self. The perspective of the trusting girl is repudiated by the mistrustful one, the self-worth of the achieving self is attacked by the judging one. Intrapsychic life is painfully conflicted. These intrapsychic positions are not quite mutually exclusive, however. Neither side in the struggle seeks the annihilation of the other, and both sides appear within the same psychic territory.

12.

The third component of Nietzsche's perspectivism is the critique of metaphysics. Translated into clinical terms, metaphysics are symbolic precipitants of transferences. Transferences are unconsciously based, affectively charged, intrasubjective and intersubjective configurations. They are lies or falsehoods in the Nietzschean sense, which is also to say they are interpretations and horizons, ways that the patient both experiences "things" and makes sense out of the experience. At the same time, there is a background assumption that the patient might experience things in other ways, some of which might be less painful and/or more productive. Hence the work of the analysis is to permit the emergence of transferences and to analyze them, to evoke and dispel them.

The delicately maintained juxtaposition between the world of transferences and the one in which transferences have been (relatively) dispelled parallels the juxtaposition between the "apparent" and "real" worlds in Nietzsche's critique of metaphysics. The relationship, I believe, is more than analogical. Lived metaphysics, for example, religious beliefs, are among the transferences active in everyday life; clinical transferences (to reverse the perspective) are lived metaphysics. Which does not mean that we either can or should live without transferences and metaphysics.

Although psychoanalytic perspectivism resembles philosophical perspectivism in presupposing and functioning as a critique of metaphysics, the critical function is performed quite differently. The Nietzschean philosopher attempts to live outside metaphysical illusions and to destroy them. Her or his stance is basically polemical and martial. The analyst enters into and even helps to construct a metaphysical world. She or he lives out this peculiar reality with the patient, tolerates its storms and stresses, and (sometimes) watches it dissipate. In other words, the perspectival world of the psychoanalytic situation is simultaneously a metaphysical one. Consequently there is no distinction to be drawn between postmetaphysical and ontological nihilism. Dispelling metaphysical meaning seems to carry with it the threat of complete meaninglessness. Especially with severely disturbed patients, this outcome cannot be ruled out in advance. But in the more usual and fortunate event, the extremes of the unbounded perspectival world and the metaphysical world resolve into a bounded one, in which things can be seen more clearly—and from more points of view—than was formerly the case.

That being said, there is a quite different way in which metaphysics impinges on the psychoanalytic situation. Analytic training equips the analyst with theories of human development and therapeutic technique. These can be maintained dogmatically. Think, for example, of the many years during which American psychoanalysis was held captive by the most rigid interpretation of the Freudian legacy. These dogmatic beliefs permitted analysts to enter the consulting room armed with the Truth. They were in the position of "the one who knows," while the patient was in the position of "the one to be known." Or we could say that the analyst was presumed to have knowledge of the "true world," whereas the patient was trapped in the "apparent world." Both parties could gain metaphysical comfort from this unambiguous, Platonic ordering of reality.

There is also a more subtle—as it were, Kantian rather than Platonic—version of psychoanalytic metaphysics. One might believe it appropriate to use psychoanalytic concepts and categories as instruments for gaining knowledge in the clinical situation. Indeed, how could one believe otherwise? How is one to distinguish between analyst and patient, if not on the basis of this theoretical-cum-instrumental competency? The question is not about knowledge, however, but about its employment. In the Kantian instance, the self is connected to object or other *through* epistemic categories. In the psychoanalytic instance, categories and concepts fall into the background, so that the self of the analyst can play the role of instrument. Or somewhat more precisely, the analyst does not *lack* psychoanalytic knowledge but no longer *needs to remember* it. This is one way of interpreting Bion's technical admonition. When we are confronted by anxiety-producing situations, the "natural" human propensity is to act on or escape from them. Given that the analyst cannot escape from the analysis, she or he is prone to have recourse to the available modes of activity—which, as Bion sees them, are memory, desire, understanding, and sensation. To suppress these modalities is to invert the *fort! da!* game—that is, to turn activity into passivity. Thus one might say that the analyst's stance is not only postmetaphysical but also posttheoretical.

I should add that attempting to practice psychoanalysis in this manner can give rise to an evangelical temptation. I have in mind Nietzsche's stunning interpretation of Jesus Christ or the "Redeemer type" in *The Antichrist*. Nietzsche contends that Christ's "glad tidings" are the abolition of guilt, punishment, reward, sin—indeed of the whole causality of moral relations—and the replacement of these ways of mastery with the simple stance of "not resisting" anything that one encounters (Nietzsche 1888a [hereafter *A*], pp. 606–7). The "kingdom of heaven" is neither some place nor some time but a state of mind and a way of living—living without offering resistance to the impositions on the self of the will to power of the other, be it another self, society, or the cosmos.

I believe Nietzsche is accurately describing a state of mind in which it is possible to have an experience of grace. Psychoanalysis does not generate that state of mind, nor does it provide that experience, but patients may come into analysis as penitents and seekers of salvation. Then the analyst, as a response to the patient's transferential expectation of redemption, may be tempted into a countertransferential enactment of the role of redeemer.

There are gross and subtle forms of this phenomenon. The gross form characteristically involves the (more or less) conscious idea that the analyst can save the patient from himself or herself. This temptation especially accompanies work with self-destructive and suicidal patients. The more subtle form takes shape hour by hour, when the analyst attempts a suspension of will to power beyond her or his capacity. The consequence is emotional damage to the analyst or a spontaneous, vengeful counterattack on the patient or both. Yet developing a greater capacity for analytic restraint requires risking this fall.

13.

Our inquiry began in the political space of our own time and advanced through the transitional spaces of interdisciplinary psychoanalysis and psychoanalytic training. The end of this line is the consulting room, which we are now to enter. That is, I am going to offer a perspectival interpretation of clinical experience. This involves the reporting of clinical facts and the formulation of generalizations based on data. Yet the truth-value of all such reports is highly ambiguous. Bion remarks, in reconsidering his own clinical reporting, that the distortions necessary for protecting a patient's identity are never incidental or innocent. They follow from the "pre-conceptions derived from the experience of psycho-analysing the patient" and so are integral to the "reality" being presented. Consequently, any expectation that such a report "represents what actually took place must be dismissed as vain" (1967, p. 120). He doubts, moreover, whether "a report written within an hour or so of the events it is supposed to describe has a special 'built-in' validity and superiority over the account written many months or even years later." Instead, he supposes that "they are two different accounts of the same event without any implication that one is superior to the other" (ibid.).

It is evident that Bion is unusually sensitive to the perspectival nature of psychoanalytic knowledge. Yet he, like most psychoanalytic writers, leaves out of his account the most obvious perspectivist limitation: clinical accounts are almost always written from the point of view of the analyst. We are not given the patient's experience but at most the analyst's experience of the patient's experience. This means that we should not interpret clinical accounts as factual representations but as reports of the state of mind of the analyst, which may be useful to other people who are interested in learning from analytic experience, whether or not they are analysts. Thus the public presentation of psychoanalytic experience falls within the methodological problematic of constrained perspectivism. Clinical facts are constituted in the process of looking at them; their re-presentation is irreducibly perspectival; and the "actual" events of the analysis must be acknowledged to exist even if they cannot be known "as such."

14.

To suggest the perspectival nature of psychoanalytic experience, I will describe the transference and countertransference dynamics of my relationship with two patients, whom we will call Maya and Anna.

Maya is highly intelligent, creative, aesthetically sensitive, and psychologically minded. She was quite profoundly depressed when the analysis began. There was an immediate empathic connection between us that quickly blossomed into an erotic transference. For quite some time, the analysis was characterized by a combination of erotic tensions and depression. Eventually, a persecutory netherworld became accessible to interpretation and, along with it, fears of annihilation. Thus we can construct a model of the analysis having four levels or modalities: erotic transference, depression, persecution, and fears of annihilation.

Erotic transference. Although the sensual dimension of Maya's relationship to me was palpable, this sensuality was in part misleading. It is better seen as a kind of idealization, in which the patient's desire for sexual union with the analyst approximates to the worshiper's yearning for union with God. Thus Maya believed that I, or my life, contained everything that she lacked. She imagined that sexual consummation would be deeply healing—that anxiety, depression, and feelings of doubt and worthlessness could be cured by a loving, passionate, physical union. Hence it was extremely painful, to say nothing of humiliating, that she was powerless to bring about the desired state of affairs.

There was something resembling a life-historical reality behind this phantasy, but nothing quite so firm as memory. Imagine a baby girl with strong, healthy appetites and a mother who, and whose body, satisfies them.

This experience is internalized and constitutes part of the daughter's inner world. It is transferred into the analytic situation, transforming the analyst into the ultimate object of sensual gratification. I am then the embodiment of Maya's internalized (m)other. The appearance of intersubjectivity, an appearance maintained by the patient's physical location on the couch and the analyst's in a chair across the room, is an illusion. Maya (as self and internalized other) is on both sides of the room, and her desire is the affective link between the polarities.

Seen from this angle, the presumed cause of Maya's suffering—my withholding of sexual gratification—is rather an effect of the transference configuration. But the patient's belief in the possibility of erotic liberation establishes the horizon within which meaningful interaction is possible. In Maya's case, the belief was particularly strong. Hence, initially, there was little to be gained by interpreting her desire as transference. She had to tolerate being rejected, and I had to tolerate her experience of being rejected.

The suffering of the erotic transference did have some compensatory value. Because it provided the occasion for intense, sensual yearnings, it yielded some relief from the deadening effects of Maya's depression. It also gave a degree of meaning to her depression by answering the question, "Why do I suffer?" (*GM*, p. 162). Maya did not believe I caused her depression, but she did see me as tormentingly withholding the cure. This could be viewed as resulting from my cruelty or her unworthiness. But either way, she suffered from unrequited love.

Depression. Maya's erotic transference was driven by the memory of fusion with her mother and the desire to recapture an experience of profound gratification. Her depression, the second perspective constituting the analysis, also originated in her relationship with her mother. It reflected a catastrophic rupture between them and the impossibility of undoing the damage that had been done. And it was fundamental to her view of reality. I might see her depression as a state of mind or a mood. This implied another way of experiencing the reality of the situation. But for Maya, there were no alternatives; the situation simply was as grim as she perceived it to be.

Maya's depression, which felt existential or ontological, is unambiguously an example of perspectival experience. She might have good moods, but they were like time outs from reality. This is the common experience of people who are chronically depressed; good moods seem illusory, like bubbles easily popped. Depression is dark, deep, and substantial. Its weight tells you that it is real, and it seems to have no temporal horizon. Hearing it described as a state of mind feels trivializing and derealizing. But for the person who is not at that moment depressed, it is difficult not to interpret it as a state of mind—if for no other reason than that its weight is so hard to bear.

In addition to its expressive meaning, Maya's depression served to defend her from the anxiety that accompanies hope. From the beginning she had placed her hopes for the future in me. Equally, her relationship with me was hopefully self-affirming, a vote of confidence in her ability to grow. Both these meanings were implicit in the erotic transference. But the life she had led to this point seemed to be evidence for the foreclosure of future development. Hence her hopes for transformation were accompanied by terrible fears of failure.

Depression countered these fears in two ways. First, it was a way of shutting down the psyche—akin to and often edging over into sleep. It absorbed and reduced anxiety, albeit at the expense of reducing liveliness in general. Second, it had the meaning that defeat was inevitable, that there was no chance of escaping the iron cage of the past. The situation was therefore hopeless, but also much less anxiety-provoking. Yet more closely considered, it is not really possible to draw so clear a distinction between past and future. Having hope about the uncertain future, which is anxiety-provoking enough in its own right, almost always brings with it the fear of breakdown. In part, this is because we come into the world hopeful and vulnerable. But a developmental trauma such as the one Maya experienced damages one's hopefulness and trust in the world. A powerful resistance develops to hoping again, for how is one to believe that this time will be different? Moreover, as Winnicott realized, there is a way in which infantile traumas are not experienced. Thus in part the fear is that this time the breakdown will be experienced—and that it will prove to be emotionally fatal.

Persecution. The picture changes as we enter more deeply into Maya's depressed inner world. It is apparent that her erotic yearning was tormenting and that the object of her desire was the tormentor. Increasingly the frustration and rage of the situation came into view. The tormenting object of her love was preserved from attack, however, and her rage was turned back on herself.

In time, an internal persecutor became visible. The internal persecutor was a causal agent or explanation in the Nietzschean sense. At a more basic level than the erotic transference, persecution established responsibility for suffering. In the first instance, the responsible party was Maya herself, who deeply believed she deserved to be prosecuted. In the second instance, prosecution was recognized as persecution, and the persecutor was viewed as maliciously and cruelly punishing her.

This situation of internal persecution may be interpreted in various ways. Its fit with the paranoid-schizoid position is almost self-evident. The paranoid polarity is explicit in Maya's own characterization of her inner world. But as she recognized, her depression functioned as a means of withdrawal. It formed a shell that protected her from the bombardment of excessive external stimulation. Of course, because the persecutor was a figure in her inner world, it was an imperfect defense.

We may also interpret Maya's experience of internalized panopticism from the perspective of the will to power. Assume first, and by contrast, a situation of gratification, as when a mother and baby share a pleasurable experience of nursing. The baby's will to power takes the form of a healthy assertiveness, a hungry, lusty connection to its mother's breast. This, we might say, is the prototypical creative experience. But what if the mother and baby are both anxious? Nursing then becomes painful and torturous. The baby becomes enraged but cannot escape being tortured. Its anxiety leads it to identify with its torturer and channel its rage back against the self. Moreover, it is only a small step from the experience of persecution to the moralization of the persecutor, hence to the full flowering of guilt and self-punishment. Thus—reversing the analytic regress from prosecutor to persecutor—we might view the persecutor as the prototype for "bad conscience" in the Nietzschean sense (*GM*, part 2).

Maya had both gratifying and persecutory experiences, but as her depression testifies, the second displaced the first. Her own creative efforts, including the creativity of the analysis, were constantly under attack. So long as she accepted the legitimacy of the persecutor's moral claims, she was almost powerless to counter the assault. But when the persecutor was stripped of its moralizing disguise, its accusations could be seen as unjustifiable cruelty directed against the self. Then it could be said, "Too long, the earth has been a madhouse!" (p. 93). Then too resistance became possible.

Threat of annihilation. Mad people live inside madhouses, but even sane people may live with madhouses inside of them. Yet madhouses are living spaces too. For Maya, the inner world of persecution and torture was itself a defense against the threat of emotional annihilation.

Like her yearning for sexual redemption, her depression, and the experience of persecution, the threat of annihilation originated in Maya's relationship with her mother. All other meanings and emotional valences converged at this point, because all other meanings and emotional valences grew out of it. Her mother's inner world was filled with terror or, rather, overflowed with it. For reasons of her own, she saw threats to survival everywhere. Her daughter, whose capacity for introjection matched the mother's capacity for projection, became the container of this terror—from which, however, her mother claimed to be the only refuge. Maya was trapped in a metaphysical and maddening world, in which she was supposed to believe that the one who horrified her was her only protection against the horror!

Reverting for a moment to Hegelian terms, we could say that Maya was engaged in a life-and-death struggle for recognition. Her mother, driven by her own anxiety, had the phantasy that her daughter would be safe only when she was entirely under her control—when the mother's will was perfectly controlling, when the daughter's resistance had been totally overcome. With certain confusing exceptions, she waged war on the spontaneously evolving manifestations of Maya's selfhood. Consequently, Maya's selfhood, her capacity for self-filled and self-fulfilling activity, became virtually a thing-in-itself, a will-o'-the-wisp instead of a will to power. The only cognizable meaning of her life and the only stable position within it was the relationship of persecution. Hence her depression, which reflected the hopelessness of this situation. Hence also the erotic transference, which combined the original situation of persecution with the desire for deliverance.

It thus appears that Maya's condition was almost perfectly self-negating. To be herself, the self she might become, she had to destroy herself, the only self she had ever been. To live and to grow meant to be perpetually terrified not only by the threat of persecutory annihilation but also by the dread-filled prospect of annihilating herself. This is one case, however, in which appearances are deceiving. Emotional growth did not involve the risk of annihilation but only, at most, the possibility of experiencing postmetaphysical nihilism. The illusion that becoming autonomous meant self-negation was a recursive reimposition of the ideology of Maya's mother. It was her mother who mesmerized her into believing the nihilistic dogma that to become separate is to die. It would be nearer the truth to say that living in this world meant leaving her mother's "true" world behind.

So much for a perspectivist reconstruction or perhaps phantasy of Maya's inner world; let's turn our attention to the role played by my will to power in its exploration.

Within the flow of the transferences, my more or less stable identities were container of anxiety and embodiment of hope. These are maternal functions in the first ontogenetic instance, but in Maya's case, her mother was in too much pain to perform them adequately.

Each of these transference functions involved a difficulty. As I have previously argued, the patient must have the strength and courage to permit the emergence of whatever is most anxiety-producing, while the analyst must be able to tolerate the anxiety without actively resisting it. The greater the mutual capacity for tolerating anxiety, the deeper the analysis can go, and the greater the patient's chances for transformation. But the persecutory nature of Maya's inner world meant that we were constantly in a state of siege, with attendant feelings of dread. The first difficulty, therefore, was the almost unbearable tension we had to experience to remain in the territory where transformation might occur.

Despite the recurrent feeling of imminent catastrophe, the problem of anxiety had a clear solution: tolerate it. The problem of hope was more complex. On the one hand, it seemed necessary to keep hope alive, which meant lending my own hopefulness to hers. On the other, a stance of hopefulness warded off or functioned as a resistance to the full force of Maya's depression. It involved a kind of interpretive activity that amounted to doing battle with the persecutor—in short, the mobilization of my will to power.

I would like to think that my performance of this antipersecutorial role was necessary to the progress of the analysis and that my efforts were to Maya's advantage. I am aware that this might be wishful thinking. Either way, as time passed Maya and I both recognized the diminishing utility of this stance. She put less pressure on me to confirm or disconfirm her depressed perspective; I did my best not to resist her view of things. And so eventually we reached the point where further growth required that she exert herself against me with the full force of her persecutorial passion. We had contrived to avoid this moment for a very long time, out of fear that we would not survive as an analytic couple. But there was no other way to demonstrate that *her* will to power was not fundamentally destructive.

Let me put this another way. Maya was always concerned for my well-being. She was not developmentally fixated in the paranoid-schizoid position. To the contrary: quite apart from the erotic transference, she had sustained affectionate feelings for me, felt guilty when she was critical of me, was always desirous of repairing any damage to me or to the relationship, and so forth. Her personality was rich in the attributes Melanie Klein assigned to the depressive position. But the persecutor was a split-off container for her rage. To both overcome the split and prove that her rage was not world-destructive, she needed to experience it in the first person and to direct it against the nurturing object or other. She needed some approximation to the experience—missing in her childhood—that Winnicott describes in "The Use of the Object and Relating through Identifications":

"Destructiveness, plus the object's survival of the destruction, places the object outside the area of objects set up by the subject's projective mental mechanisms. In this way a world of shared reality is created which the subject can use and which can feed back other-than-me substance into the subject" (1969, p. 94). I only need add that the subject who can use an object is created at the same time as the object that can be used.

Following this Winnicottian directive, one day Maya began a critical, ruthless dissection of the analysis. Her rage was under control and all the more overwhelming on that account. I did my best not to resist, but I failed. I offered her an interpretation aimed at the communicative function of the assault, something to the effect that I could more nearly understand her experience of being persecuted from the way I was now feeling. But she understood the "real" meaning of my response: please stop attacking me, I can't bear it. She fell silent—angry, defeated, and depressed. I had no doubt about my failure and no doubt that I needed to acknowledge it. The next session began with this acknowledgment. Maya understood what had happened without my saying it, but (at least so it seems to me) my forthrightness substantially restored the recognitive bond between us. This permitted her to take the risk of resuming the attack, which—from my side—it no longer seemed necessary to resist.

This experience has a double implication. On the one hand, it verifies Nietzsche's claim that the "will to power *interprets*." Analytic interpretations are expressions of will to power, variable mixtures of cruelty and creativity. No analysis is possible without them, but the patient is ill-served if the analyst needs to remain ignorant of this meaning of the interpretive act. On the other hand, there is the imperative of not interpreting, of suspending the operation of the will to power—subjecting oneself to Bion's disciplined denial of memory and desire. It is the performance of this negative function that distinguishes clinical psychoanalysis from both philosophy and psychoanalytic publication. The place from which the analyst's will to power has been withdrawn is the place in which the patient's potential for transformation has a chance of being realized.

15.

My experience with Anna—the woman mentioned earlier who experienced aspects of her personality as two little girls, one trusting of me and the other mistrustful—brings us closer to the preverbal depths of the psychoanalytic world. Anna is an imaginative, talented, and successful artist whose personality had been shaped, indeed bent, by parental neglect. At a certain point in the analysis, after a long period of gestation, her psyche underwent one of those profound changes that justify the dialectical notion of the transformation of quantity into quality. For the first time in her life, she was standing outside the inner world formed during her childhood. A third girl appeared—a newborn child with only a shimmering field of anxiety for skin. The trusting little girl, her loving connection to me secure, now slipped into the background and the mistrustful one emerged with great clarity. Scraggly haired, scared, and prone to rage—but neither hateful nor hate-filled—she was charged with the protection of the newborn. For all her volatility, she was easy to like and to respect. And because I made no attempt to persuade her to set aside her anger or lay down her arms, her mistrust, which was her best defense, began to weaken. She could not help but like me, which truly terrified her. In one session, she (the scraggly haired girl) was dancing exuberantly around the room, so glad that I wanted her around. In the next, she sat absolutely still, paralyzed with fear, on the edge of a psychophysiological abyss so deep that words lost their meaning when cast into it. The resultant anxiety was more than she could bear by herself, and so it was my job to help her bear it.

The linked psychoanalytic principles of being able to suspend the will to power and tolerate the maximum of anxiety with the minimum of defense were here put to a rather severe test. To understand why, we must dip for a moment into the ordinary mysteries of psychoanalytic life. In the context of an earlier therapeutic relationship, Anna had had this dream. She is guided to the edge of an abyss by a wolf who stands calmly beside her as she looks down into wildly flowing lava. The wolf then gestures with his head away from the precipice and leads her to a wooded glade. There she sees a man dancing, with African rhythm sticks, and she dances with or perhaps becomes him.

Anna, who quickly settled into calling me "Wolfie," took this dream as prophetic. It was as if she dreamed it in anticipation of her relationship to me. It contained both the terror of self-dissolution (the threat of plunging into the molten lava) and the hope of rebirth (dancing, dancing free). The two sessions noted above expressed this fear and hope in reverse order. But the mystery of the dream is not that it foretold later events in Anna's life. I am the wolf in the dream only by retroactive imposition. Its uncanny quality is rather a reflection of a profound matching between Anna's emotional needs and my capacity to respond to them. It intimates that she was predisposed to bring me entirely into her world and to fill my inner world entirely with hers. Hence the question: was the psychoanalytic space I had developed over years of disciplined practice large enough to hold her? When the time came, could I contain her newborn helplessness, anxiety, and rage—the principal ingredients of panic—and remain the guardian/guiding wolf of her dream?

The answer was yes and no. I was able to be with Anna, to commiserate with her, the way she needed me to be and so to fulfill my moral or ethical obligation as her analyst. But her world did implode disruptively into mine. The implosion itself was not the issue. Like any psychoanalyst who really makes himself or herself available for the patient's emotional development, I had grown accustomed over the years to feeling the presence of my patients inside me even when I was not physically with them. Or, to put the point more cautiously, I would find myself inhabited by a representation of them built around sensuous, affective, and cognitive remnants of current interaction. Sometimes my dreams would contain these remnants as well, and the knowledge gained in this peculiar fashion could be put to good clinical use. All this is an ordinary part of the psychoanalytic life, commonly experienced, if somewhat difficult to explain. But what made these nights different from most other nights was the disruptive impact of the transference/countertransference conjuncture. This is evident in one of my dreams from this period. I am standing in my living room, and suddenly my dog leaps into the room through the screen door that connects the house to the fenced-in backyard. The glass door had been left open, and the screen door is badly damaged, although I know it can be repaired or replaced. My dog, I realize on waking, is also the wolf from Anna's dream, transformed from sacred guardian into primitive, ruthless appetite. This was a part of her as I was experiencing it. But it was my dream, after all, and so the wolf necessarily was also a representation of my own ruthless desire. Either and both ways, the feeling of the screen ripped apart is one of terror—although the house is not destroyed and I maintain my stance of observer, knowing that the screen can be repaired.

Here is a another way of interpreting the dream. We remember (from Chapter 2) Mark Epstein's equating of the therapist's empty and receptive state of mind with sunyata, "a pregnant void, the hollow of a pregnant womb." When properly maintained, the analyst's memory, desire, and will to power are excluded from this uterine space. The analyst is outside it, with the consequence that he or she is, if minimally, protected from the patient's transferential intrusions, and reciprocally, the patient is protected from countertransferential attack. The breaking of the screen door in my dream represents a wounding of this uterine wall, actual damage to my analytic capacity. We might think in this regard of the evangelical temptation noted earlier. Had I attempted a suspension of the will to power beyond my (existing) capacity? No doubt. Did the attempt disrupt my peace of mind, forcing me to confront long-denied aspects of myself? Equally beyond question. Did I have any choice in the matter? Probably not. In any case, the dream reflects the intrusion of Anna's long-repressed desire into her mental space as well as into mine, a double wounding necessary for her emotional development.

Not surprisingly, two days later Anna came in with a dream of being enraged with her father, so angry that she violently shook him. This led to reexperiencing in a more contained fashion a terrible panic state she had fallen into years earlier. She had been ruthlessly and enviously attacked by a coworker, who became identified with her version of an internal persecutor. She was flooded by waves of terror and a concomitant feeling of self-disintegration. While still struggling with this no-longer-repressed trauma, she dreamed of being in a car in a strange, mountainous region. Suddenly huge waves are crashing down on her. But this time she does not panic. She keeps her head and leaves the car at just the right time to fight her way to the surface. She grabs hold of rocks protruding from the waters and climbs to the top of a mountain, above the waves, where she finds herself in the company of another woman with whom she feels a safe and erotic connection.

On the surface, this dream seems to take place within the paranoid-schizoid position. At one extreme, Anna is drowning in intense feelings of panic and persecution; at the other she has risen above the tide and withdrawn into safety. But more closely considered, the dream is about surrendering the defensive security of the paranoid-schizoid position. As Anna remarked, when the dream began she had expected to be able to watch it from the outside, from beyond a window. She was terrified to find herself inside the car with the waves towering above her. The car, we can now see, is a schizoid enclosure. To survive (to grow) she must abandon it at the right time and of her own free will. With her experience of newborn vulnerability in mind, we might also say that she needed to will her own rebirth. This extraordinary exercise of her will to power resulted in a significant strengthening of character and the transformation of prementalized sensations into erotic affect. The gain in both selfhood and eros is represented by her relationship to the woman at the end of the dream. And it was a kind of realization of Anna's "prophetic" wolf dream: she had plunged into lava flows of abject terror and, relying not only on me but also on her own lupine instincts, had survived. Struggling up to higher ground instead of dancing off into the woods, she stood on the edge of self-unification.

16.

I hope these two stories derived from clinical experience make plausible the claim that psychoanalytic inquiry requires of the analyst a perspectival fluidity, a tolerance for barely mentalized states of being, and a disciplined capacity to suspend the will to power that goes beyond the epistemic limits of both commonsense and dialectical reasoning. Still, our focus on the will to power and perspectivism has been aimed at supplementing rather than displacing other ways of interpreting psychoanalytic theory and practice. It is evident, for example, that Hegelian problematics of recognition did not disappear from the clinical picture and that we could reconstruct the progress of Maya's and Anna's analyses in dialectical terms. But the further we travel toward the inward horizon of the psychoanalytic world, the more Nietzschean the scene becomes.

And now it is time to leave our world for his.

4

"The end is in the beginning and lies far ahead"

"I don't know," he said. "I suppose sometimes a man *has* to plunge outside history."

—RALPH ELLISON, *Invisible Man*

1.

To this point we have focused on Nietzschean thoughts but not directly on the man who thought them. We only required sufficient knowledge of Nietzsche himself to avoid or at least minimize errors in conceptual representation. When it comes to eternal return, however, living must be joined to thinking.

Briefly, "eternal return" is the idea that everything that is happening has happened exactly the same way and infinite times in the past and will happen exactly the same way and infinite times in the future. This idea plays a double role for Nietzsche: he suffers it as his most overwhelming, terrifying, or self-annihilating thought, and he affirms it as his greatest self-overcoming and the fullest expression of his will to power. It is the central teaching of *Thus Spoke Zarathustra* and, in his own judgment, the great divide in the history of Western philosophy.

If the world or even, say, critical social theorists agreed with Nietzsche's self-evaluation, biographical considerations might be safely set aside. We could take Nietzsche at his word when he says, "I am one thing, my writings are another matter" (*EH*, p. 259) and simply devote ourselves to learning the great lesson he taught. But time has not been kind to the idea of eternal return. It cannot be validated as a cosmological hypothesis, nor does Nietzsche offer anything remotely resembling satisfactory proofs and argument along these lines; furthermore, attempts to rescue it by begging the empirical question and treating it as a thought-experiment or mental exercise rob it of its import. Nietzsche characterized eternal return as "the greatest weight" (*GS*, p. 273). It would not be nearly so heavy or so deep if it were merely a thought.

Thus eternal return is intrinsically puzzling. Why did Nietzsche value it so highly, when it seems so philosophically insubstantial? Because, I will be answering here, he actually experienced the eternal return of the same. It was more like an incarnation than a scientific experiment or a thought-experiment. Given its insubstantiality—and unlike the will to power and perspectivism—it therefore tells us more about Nietzsche than it does about ourselves.

Yet Nietzsche is a mirror in which we might see ourselves reflected. I do not mean to deprive him of his autonomy by reducing him to this psychological function. Quite the contrary: I hope to grant him a kind of recognition that is frequently denied. Alexander Nehamas, for example, argues that in "engaging with his works, we are not engaging with the miserable little man who wrote them" but with the "magnificent character" Nietzsche created in and as his writings (1985, p. 234). I contend that Nietzsche's misery was not belittling—that it was the very soil in which he planted the "secret garden" of his philosophy.[1] And beyond this, I hope to show that we learn something about ourselves as temporal and gendered beings when we spend time in his company.

As in the clinical exploration of the last chapter, here too I will adopt the stance of constrained perspectivism. I assume a preexisting life-historical reality to which interpretations must in some sense correspond, although the standards of judgment that I seek to satisfy are as much aesthetic and psychological as they are strictly empirical. The aim is to tell a coherent, psychologically plausible story that is at once empirically based and meaningful for us.

The first task will be to expand the horizons of our psychoanalytic perspective, so that room—not quite a consulting room, to be sure—is created for the exploration of time and gender. Then, something like the following tale will unfold: the death of Nietzsche's father when he was not quite five condemned him to living in an unstable transitional space between (to use the appropriately stereotypical terms) the eternal feminine and the historical masculine. Within this space, he recurrently suffered from somatized melancholia and abjection. Eternal return in its negative or nihilistic aspect reflects these cycles of inescapable pain. But living in this precarious fashion also had as its reward an experience of sublimity and elation in which the antipodes of gender seem to be overcome. And here lies the affective basis for the affirmative aspect of eternal return.

I will proceed with the story in straightforward fashion. First I consider Nietzsche's life up to and through the writing of the *Untimely Meditations* of the early 1870s. I argue that, within certain developmental limits, he was able to follow the path of normative masculine development. Correspondingly, in "Uses and Disadvantages of History for Life" he defends (against his own doubts) a masculine conception of the historical. Next I analyze Nietzsche's turning away from the conventional pathways of masculine development and his plunge into the abyss of recurrent and apparently interminable suffering. Here an abjective identification with his mother and a melancholic identification with his father are strikingly in evidence. Finally I take up eternal return itself—first as concept, then as Nietzsche experienced it, and finally as he dramatized it in *Thus Spoke Zarathustra*.

I. Time, Gender, and Transitional Space

2.

The analysis that follows relies on Julia Kristeva's analysis of gendered temporality in "Women's Time" (1979), as well as on her conceptualization of abjection and sublimity in *Powers of Horror* (1982).[2] It presupposes the model of gender development briefly adumbrated in the Chapter 1. And it involves a somewhat unorthodox use of Winnicott's ideas about transitional space (1971).

In "Women's Time," Kristeva begins by distinguishing between "father's time" and "mother's species"—that is, between linear, historical, masculine time and cyclical feminine time. She characterizes the former in standard, modernist terms: "time as project, teleology, linear and prospective unfolding: time as departure, progression and arrival" (1979, p. 192). In psychoanalytic terms, "A psychoanalyst would call this 'obsessional time', recognizing in the mastery of time the true structure of the slave" (ibid.). On the other side of the psychotemporal divide is the "hysteric (either male or female) who suffers from reminiscences" (ibid.) and who parallels the obsessional subject of linear time. More generally, the temporality of female subjectivity "would seem to provide a specific measure that essentially retains *repetition* and *eternity* from among the multiple modalities of time known through the history of civilizations" (p. 191). Thus women's time is characterized by "cycles, gestation, the eternal recurrence of a biological rhythm which conforms to that of nature and imposes a temporality whose stereotyping may shock, but whose regularity and unison with what is experienced as extra-subjective time, cosmic time, occasion vertiginous visions and unnameable *jouissance*" (p. 191).

Kristeva's use of eternal recurrence is textually rather loose, although not entirely off the Nietzschean mark. Similarly, she introduces a conception of "monumental" temporality that is Nietzschean in form but not in content. She uses the term to signify time that virtually subsides into spatiality, time beyond or around history. Thus she identifies linear time in Europe with the experience of nationality, monumental time with the "englobing" of even "supra-national, socio-cultural ensembles within even larger entities" (p. 189). One might also say that, for Kristeva, the monumental is time beyond time: "All-encompassing and infinite like imaginary space, this temporality reminds one of Kronos in Hesiod's mythology, the incestuous son whose massive presence covered all of Gea in order to separate her from Ouranos, the father" (p. 191). Monumental time is thus one or both of two things. It is ur-temporality, a temporality prior to the distinction between feminine and masculine time. On this reading it preserves the developmental dualism of psychoanalysis: immersion in the mother-world, emergence/individuation via the intrusion of the father. Alternatively, it is simply a deepening of women's time, the precyclical matrix of gestational cycles and biological rhythms. As we shall see, neither of these is what Nietzsche had in mind in his own use of the concept. But textual reservations aside, Kristeva usefully links time to gender in a manner at once Nietzschean and psycho-analytic.

3.

"Mother's species" and "father's time" are not only ways in which we gender time; they also correspond to the space of the preoedipal mother-world, on the one side, and the postoedipal patriarchal world, on the other. Hence the concepts themselves raise the question of the transition from one to the other—that is, of the complex processes through which we become male and female, heterosexual and homosexual, and so forth.

The model of human development presented in the first chapter linked individuation and gender formation to the paranoid-schizoid and depressive positions. Let's remind ourselves of the main points and refine the model just a bit.

Briefly, we assume a mother and an infant joined in the processes of nurture and nutrition. Nursing pulls the infant toward or into a fused, identificatory relationship with its mother; the cessation of nursing and the infant's withdrawal toward sleep separate the two. When the process is predominantly pleasurable, the space between the extremes becomes available for object-relating, optimally for a relatively free play of desire and for the creative uses of the will to power. Here we have the origins of transitional space in Winnicott's sense. When, by contrast, the process is predominantly painful, feelings of intense anxiety and rage are provoked. Interaction becomes paranoid and persecutory, withdrawal into proto-individuality becomes an escape from danger, and the space between the extremes becomes marked with an either/or. That is, the extremes are mediated by mechanisms of splitting and projective identification that function as security measures. The emergent self is rigidly armored against possible intrusion and is always already prepared for interaction to be combative. In this situation the will to power takes on the aggressive features that Nietzsche characteristically ascribed to it.

So long as mothers are the primary caregivers, nurture is gendered feminine and maternal. By contrast and biologically speaking, the infant is either male or female. Gender identity is overlaid on this biological substratum, sometimes in ways that seem to fit with the needs of the infant and sometimes in ways that seem to be at odds with them. In the former case gendered self-formation will be less paranoid-schizoid, in the latter case more paranoid-schizoid. But either way, the development of selfhood is concomitant with gaining a gender identity. He becomes a boy, she becomes a girl.

For both boys and girls (according to virtually all versions of psychoanalytic theory), the father plays a vital role in breaking up the mother-infant dyad and in establishing the gendered identity of the child. The boy identifies with the father and thereby disidentifies with the mother—he is not, or is no longer, her, although she remains an object of desire. The girl partially and problematically identifies with the father and, more ambiguously, disidentifies with the mother by becoming her rival for the father's affections. Thus we find ourselves on the borders of the oedipal situation.

In the next chapter, I will attempt to articulate the body language that characterizes the normative masculine passage from the preoedipal into and through the oedipal domain. Of greater present concern, however, is an aspect of the individuation process that can be obscured by the entrance of the father. Stated as a question, what happens to the mother, or to the imago of the mother, as and when the infant—especially but not only the male infant—disidentifies with her?

We might think of two basic possibilities that would, in practice, be varyingly interpenetrated. If the relationship of infant to mother is mainly centered in the depressive position, with its rich array of mutualizing affects and attitudes, the mother would take form as a living (also life-giving) internal object or other. There is then a matrix of the self, the mother-world as an internal environment; the emergent self; and the evolving maternal other, who both personifies and mediates the self's relationship to its inner life-world. No doubt one also finds here the moment of negation, but in this instance, negation plays its classical—that is, ultimately creative—dialectical role.

If, by contrast, disidentification is centered in the paranoid-schizoid position, negation—the categorical either/or of splitting and projective identification—will be the predominant moment in the process. Self-formation becomes a process of defending against the emergence and stabilization of a persecutory internal other. This is the context in which the mother-infant unit must be abjected.

According to Kristeva, "abjection" is a preobjectival process through which we attempt to "release the hold of *maternal* entity even before existing outside of her, thanks to the autonomy of language. It is a violent, clumsy breaking away, with the constant risk of falling back under the sway of a power as securing as it is stifling" (1982, p. 13). The experience has distinctive affective and psychophysiological qualities, of which "food loathing is perhaps [its] most elementary and archaic form" (p. 2):

> When the eyes see or lips touch that skin on the surface of milk—harmless, thin as a sheet of cigarette paper, pitiful as a nail paring—I experience a gagging sensation and, still farther down, spasms in the stomach, the belly; and all the organs shrivel up the body, provoke tears and bile, increase heartbeat, cause forehead and hands to perspire. Along with sight-clouding dizziness, *nausea* makes me balk at that milk cream, separates me from the mother and father who proffer it. "I" want none of that element, sign of their desire; "I" do not want to listen, "I" do not assimilate it, "I" expel it. But since the food is not "other" for "me," who am only their desire, I expel *myself*, I spit *myself* out, I abject *myself* within the same motion through which "I" claim to establish *myself*. . . . During the course in which "I" become, I give birth to myself amid the violence of sobs, of vomit. (Pp. 2–3)

Abjection in this depiction is a paradoxical and self-undermining process of self-formation or self-maintenance. My prior point is that it presupposes an intersubjective field in which the primitive sensations, needs, desires, and affects of the infant are not being adequately processed and contained. In this situation, which I would characterize as paranoid-schizoid, there is an incitement to abjective reactions.

Note, however, that the skin on the milk might have two meanings. At first glance, the emergent self seems to be oppressed and invaded by parental desire. The persecutory quality of the situation, which invokes both terror and disgust, approaches it from the outside. But parental desire is, or is also, a product of infantile projection, the infant's desire writ large. When we change the angle of vision, the persecutory situation is recognized as having its origin in the too great desire of the infant. We now see that the reaction to the skin on the milk is defensive and reaction formative. Disgust is a horizon of a self that is drawn beyond itself into an abyss of unbounded desire.

These two meanings of abjection are complementary rather than mutually exclusive. The infant (or adult) is trapped in a situation of a desire so overwhelming that it induces nausea; he or she restores the fragile boundaries of the self by vomiting out fragments and flows of abjective affect. Or, if the self has a more stabilized paranoid-schizoid configuration, abjection may be joined to formidable, focused, and often coldly malicious processes of destruction. In reality and in phantasy, the corpse, especially the decaying corpse, is then the perfectly perverse embodiment of the abject—the ultimate defilement of the all-too-desired maternal body.

Perhaps the most unsettling perversity of abjection is its intimate relationship to the experience of sublimity. When we come to the experience of eternal return, we will see how the one becomes the other. But we could say that Kristeva has been there before us. Like the abject, she claims, sublimity is not, in any usual sense, a subject-object relationship: "When the starry sky, a vista of open sea or a stained glass window shedding purple beams fascinate me, there is a cluster of meaning, of colors, of words, of caresses, there are light touches, scents, sighs, cadences that arise, shroud me, carry me away, and sweep me beyond the things that I see, hear, or think. The 'sublime' object dissolves in the raptures of bottomless memory." Kristeva goes on to link the advent of sublimity to a moment of naming that brings it to life: "Not at all short of but always with and through perception and words, the sublime is a *something added* that expands us, overstrains us, and causes us to be both *here*, as dejects, and *there*, as others and sparkling. A divergence, an impossible bounding. Everything missed, joy—fascination" (p. 12). Thus the sublime has a palpable quality of terror associated with it. It is not the experience of god's grace—deep, golden, calm, and consoling. It is more nearly related to mania, which is anxiety-driven and not genuinely joyous. Consequently, sublimity—the sublimity joined to abjection—further depletes the self rather than restoring it.

Both abjection and sublimity are possibilities for boys and girls, women and men, and because both experiences originate in the mother-world, they tend to be gendered feminine, or feminine maternal. Masculine gender identity therefore functions as both a defense against abjection and a foreclosing of sublimity. It also means that boys and men tend to experience abjection as a loss of masculinity and sublimity as access to or even fusion with the eternal feminine.

Although abjection is not the only or even the most important path to gendered selfhood and sublimity is not always or only abjection's other side, we will be able to see Nietzsche in Kristeva's mirror.

4.

In the previous section, I touched lightly on the idea that the transitional space of creative desire comes into being between the extremes of the infantile metabolic cycle. Winnicott claims that developmentally this space "is made possible by the mother's special capacity for making adaptation to the needs of her infant, thus allowing the infant the illusion that what the infant creates really exists." But this intersubjective experience becomes intrasubjective as well: "This intermediate area of experience, unchallenged in respect of its belonging to inner or external (shared) reality, constitutes the greater part of the infant's experience, and throughout life is retained in the intense experiencing that belongs to the arts and to religion and to imaginative living, and to creative scientific work" (Winnicott 1971, p. 14). Nietzsche had an unusual capacity for living in this space, where it is neither necessary nor possible to determine what is real or what is not, what is inside or what is outside. We think of his comfort with thought-experiments and recurrent shifts of perspective as well as his interpretation of language as creative falsification. When we come to eternal return, however, we will find that the boundaries of this space were stretched to or even beyond their limits, into an unbounded space of both exhilaration and terror. Nietzsche accurately characterized this as an experience of inspiration (*EH*, pp. 300–301). It is therefore beyond truth and falsehood as we would normally think of them. One can no more question its reality than one could ask for empirical proofs of Apollo's presence in the utterances of the Delphic oracle.

This is not the whole story about transitional space or of Nietzsche's experience in occupying it. Although Winnicott was an extraordinary psychoanalyst and by instinct a dialectical thinker, his presentation of his thoughts was obedient to the laws of Aristotelian logic. Hence it is all too easy in reading him to think in either/or terms: true self or false self, transitional space or pathologizing infringement on transitional space.

Without going too far afield into a dialectical reconstruction of Winnicott's theorizing, we can strengthen our understanding of the transitional if we conceptualize it in temporal as well as spatial terms. We then view it as the time between pre-self and self—that is, as the processes through which the self emerges from its pre-self matrix. Transitional space in Winnicott's sense is then one side—more or less empirically present—in this developmental process. Its other or opposite, with which it is necessarily interpenetrated, is constituted by the kinds of experience signified by such concepts as abjection and sublimity. Thought of this way—which I believe to be Winnicottian in conceptual spirit if not in verbal flesh—the notion of the transitional allows us to think of developmental advance, fixation, or regression simultaneously with assessments of the quality (affective, ideational, and so forth) of experience at any given developmental moment. This will prove to be vital in the analysis of Nietzsche's early life. It will also permit us to grasp something of the complexity of the experience of eternal return—even if we stop short of claiming to explain it.

II. Walking the Line

5.

Human thought and action are permeated with temporality and its denial—ontologically speaking, with the flux of becoming and attempts to escape from it. We cannot think without evoking time, yet time is also notoriously difficult to think about. Hence we usually take linear time as a given, imagining it as a stream that flows in one direction only. We are then free to use the usual interrogatives: who, when, where, what, how, why. This being the path of least resistance, we will follow it here, taking as our guide the autobiographical riddle of *Ecce Homo:* "I am . . . already dead as my father, while as my mother I am still living and becoming old."[3]

6.

It is psychoanalytically appropriate to start with Nietzsche's relationship with his mother—and to place that relationship within the historically appropriate patriarchal frame. Karl Ludwig Nietzsche was a Lutheran pastor and the son of a Lutheran pastor. He had been a tutor in the ducal court at Saxe-Altenburg and his pastorate at Röcken was bestowed on him by King

Friedrich Wilhelm IV of Prussia. He took his pastoral duties most seriously, but besides "being the very model of a loyal, conservative pastor, Ludwig was apparently dandified and histrionic" (Pletsch 1991, p. 20). He married Franziska Oehler on his thirtieth birthday (October 10, 1843), and their first child was born October 15, 1844, which happened to be the birthday of the king. With gratitude and more than a hint of narcissistic grandiosity, he named his son after his benefactor. The son also benefited from the circumstance of his birth: "My birthday was a holiday throughout my childhood" (EH, p. 226).

Nietzsche says of his father that "he was delicate, kind, and morbid, as a being that is destined merely to pass by—more a gracious memory of life than life itself" (p. 222). He was a musician of sorts, skilled at improvising on the piano; his son could be soothed, when in a discontented mood, by listening to his father play. He was also conflict aversive in the extreme. His response to disharmony in the household "was to withdraw to his study, where he stayed, denying himself food, drink, and conversation until harmony was fully restored" (Pletsch 1991, p. 22; see also Förster-Nietzsche 1912, p. 15).[4] He died in July 1849, after injuring his head in a fall the previous year and a subsequent prolonged and painful struggle with "softening of the brain." His symptoms included severe headaches and, eventually, blindness. He was thirty-six years old at the time of his death.

Nietzsche's mother also came from a clerical family. She was seventeen when she married Ludwig and moved into his household, which was presided over by his mother and his two unmarried sisters. She quickly adopted his attitudes, including his too decorous piety, without, however, quite losing herself. Along with Friedrich, she gave birth to Elisabeth (whose full name was Elisabeth Therese Alexandra, after the princesses whom Ludwig had tutored) and Joseph (after the duke of Saxe-Altenburg, the father of the princesses). She was twenty-three when she was widowed. Her younger son Joseph died six months later. After this double bereavement, she and the remaining children continued to live with the older Nietzsche women, who moved from Röcken to Naumburg.

Franziska had only one occupation and that was the care of her children. Her confinement to this role was given a spatial definition after her husband's death: "Franziska and the two children occupied the rooms in the rear of the house, excluded except at mealtimes from the front rooms and social intercourse" (Pletsch 1991, p. 32). The son, it is fair to say, was the center of this little universe, and he was attached to his role within it: Franziska's nephew "recalled her jesting at this time about how she would still be carrying Friedrich to bed when he was an adult if he didn't learn to go by himself soon" (ibid.).[5]

There is an additional interesting fact. Friedrich did not learn to speak until age two and a half, a lag that a local doctor explained on the basis of his having been spoiled: "for since things were given to him virtually before he required them, he had not the need to express himself" (p. 24). This "interpretation" led to unfortunate attempts at forcing the boy to ask for and name things. But that aside, it can be seen as pointing in the right direction. Let's assume that Franziska was exquisitely attuned to her son's needs and desires, indeed that she desired nothing beyond the satisfaction of his needs. Then two things might be true. On the one hand, mother and son were one. On the other, insofar as the son was nonetheless centered in himself, his unspoken wishes—replete with our human, all-too-human sensuality and erotic desire—were her commands. Either way, not only was speaking unnecessary, but to speak was also to break the spell. The use of language both established a degree of individuation and involved a loss of magical power. It separated the son from things-as-such—that is, from the fluid reality of the mother-world.

Yet this would not have been entirely a loss. For if Franziska made her son's needs and desires her own, in the process her needs and desires would have become his. The affective flow would have been in both directions, leaving the son confused as to which feelings were his and which were hers. From this perspective, the use of language would be seen as a much needed boundary between self and (m)other. Thus—to bring these two sides of the analysis together—it might be that language acquired a second-order magicality for Nietzsche. Through its use, he gained the power of creating a semblance of the mother-world that was under his own control.[6]

These partially psychoanalytic and partially Nietzschean speculations fit with Nietzsche's claim that he lives and grows old as his mother. Yet both his autobiographical interpretation and our biographical one seem to be contradicted by a section that was editorially excised from *Ecce Homo*:

> Were I to look for the deepest contradiction to me, I would always find my mother and my sister—to believe myself related to such *canaille* would be a blasphemy on my godliness. The treatment I have experienced from the side of my mother and sister . . . infuses me with an unspeakable horror: here is at work a perfect infernal machine, [one that operates] with an unfailing certainty as to the moment when I can be bloodily wounded—in my highest instances. (Strong 1985, p. 327)

He concludes: "I recognize that the deepest objections to the 'eternal return,' that is, my own most abysmal thought, are always mother and sister" (ibid.). Here Nietzsche seems to be completely repudiating his identification with his mother. But the intensity of the attempted disidentification testifies to the strength of the identification. His evident anger, even rage, might be interpreted as reflecting his frustration at never being able to liberate himself from her. In other words, we might understand him to be saying that *despite* himself he is alive and growing old as his mother.

We might take a step further. When Nietzsche states that his relationship with his mother is a blasphemy on his godliness, he would seem to be saying that it defiles and contaminates him. He is divine, she is vulgar scum—and we have entered the territory of abjection. Given the limitations of the data available to us from his earliest childhood, we are not permitted to go very far in this direction. But we might speculate that there was a latent abjective component in his relationship with his mother, one that might become manifest with the passage of time.

7.

At this juncture in the archetypal course of things, we should come to the oedipal situation and the father's role in liberating his son from his fused and confused relationship to his mother.[7] The son identifies with his father and thereby severs his identificatory bond with his mother. There is always, however, the temptation to regress and transgress—to plunge back into the mother-world and to defy the Law of the Father. Hence in myth, fairy tales, and unconscious phantasy, this temptation is often removed: first the mother dies, and then the son takes up his role in the patriarchal order.

The requirement that the mother die so that the child can be "born" is not limited to male individuation. Kristeva puts it this way:

> For man and woman the loss of the mother is a biological and psychic necessity, the first step on our way to becoming autonomous. Matricide is our vital necessity, the sine-qua-non of our individuation, provided it takes place under optimal circumstances and can be eroticized—whether the lost object is recovered as erotic object (as is the case for male heterosexuality or female homosexuality), or it is transposed by means of an unbelievable symbolic effort, the advent of which one can only admire, which eroticizes the *other* (the other sex, in the case of the heterosexual woman) or transforms cultural constructs into a "sublime" erotic object. (1989, pp. 27–28)

The "death" of the mother as object of desire opens up the field of erotic relationships and even makes possible the emergence of the sublime. If abjection is an affective component of this matricidal process, it would seem to be a prerequisite for the experience of sublimity. But I will suspend this question just for the present.

Kristeva's interpretation of individuation suggests that, in the male instance, the son dies as his mother and lives on as his father. But in Nietzsche's case, the archetypal course of development was reversed. The father literally died, and the mother survived. This set up the second of his identificatory relationships—I am already dead as my father—which by its very nature was *melancholic*.

The symbolic moment in the formation of this melancholic identification, whether as fact or phantasy, is described by Elisabeth Förster-Nietzsche:

> Toward the beginning of April we left Röcken; the day of our departure and our journey made an ineffaceable impression upon Fritz. He got up in the night, dressed himself, and went into the courtyard where the heavily laden carriage stood waiting with its shining red lamps. The wind set up a powerful dirge, the faithful dog howled in heartrending and gruesome tones, and the moon, pallid and cold, shot her rays over the low roofs of the neighbouring buildings into the great courtyard with its ghastly lights and all its mournful echoes. (1912, pp. 18–19)

As we will see, this scene is reproduced in *Thus Spoke Zarathustra*. It is the memory to which Zarathustra returns in telling his parable of eternal return. It is the memory, I suggest, to which Nietzsche returns, just because it symbolizes an interminable process of mourning the loss of his father. Or to put it in terms of self-formation: Nietzsche identifies with the dying father, not the living one, and therefore experiences his masculine self as moribund. Hence he remains perpetually on the edge of self-dissolution— of plunging back into the mother-world from which he had only partially emerged.

The evidence for the hypothesis that Nietzsche was bound up in a melancholic identification with his father is rather substantial. First, and as if designed to gratify the psychoanalyst's desire, there is a dream. Nietzsche describes it in a precocious autobiography written when he was fourteen:

> On this occasion [several months after the father's death] I dreamt I heard the sound of the church organ playing a requiem. When I looked to see what the cause of it was, a grave suddenly opened and my father in his shroud arose out of it. He hurried into the church and in a moment or two reappeared with a small child in his arms. The grave opened, he stepped

into it and the gravestones fell once more over the opening. The sound of
the organ immediately ceased and I awoke. (Ibid., p. 18)

Because this dream was quickly followed by the sudden death of Joseph, who
was buried alongside his father, the family treated it as prophetic. It might
also be interpreted as the product of sibling rivalry. Pletsch argues convincingly, however, that the small child is best interpreted as Nietzsche himself,
whose desire to be reunited with his father is joined to the fear of being
dragged into the grave with him (1991, pp. 27–28). And if we interpret the
grave as an opening into the maternal body (mother earth), then union with
his father plunges the son into the womb as tomb. In any case, whether or
not the grave is gendered feminine, Nietzsche's identificatory relationship
with his father leads down into an eternal night rather than up into the daylight.

In addition to confirmation derived from the interpretation of this dream,
there is also evidence of Nietzsche's melancholic identification with his
father in his everyday life and pathology. His close friend Wilhelm Pinder
wrote of him, "His fundamental character trait was a certain melancholy,
which was apparent in his whole being" (in Hayman 1980, p. 21). He identified with his father's clerical role to such an extent that he was sometimes
called the "little pastor" (Pletsch 1991, p. 34). In exaggerated imitation of his
father, he was gravely proper in his comportment and rule-abiding to an
extreme. And, like his father, he retreated from conflict rather than engaging in it. Förster-Nietzsche reports:

[My brother] was exceedingly strong, and, as a child, very hot tempered—
a characteristic which he did not like to hear mentioned in later years,
because, in accordance with the family tradition of the Nietzsches, he
soon learned to control himself. When he was older, if ever he did anything
awkward, or broke something, for which he had to be scolded, he would
grow very red, say nothing, and withdraw silently into solitude. After a
while he would reappear with modest dignity, and would either beg for for-
givness, if he had convinced himself of his fault, or else say nothing. (1912,
pp. 12–13)

She neglects to add that he would also walk away from *her*, sometimes in
contempt for her "willful ignorance" and sometimes to escape from her
"violent fits of temper" (Peters 1962, pp. 10–11).

Withdrawal into solitude was Nietzsche's lifelong response not only to
conflict but also to the stress of everyday intimacy. As is clear in this depiction, his narcissistic vulnerability was an important component of his inabil-

ity to sustain intimate relationships on a day-to-day basis. Also evident here is Nietzsche's formidable self-discipline. This self-overcoming would seem to have a double aspect. As Förster-Nietzsche claims, he did internalize parental and especially paternal authority. To use the conventional terms, this is the process of superego formation, here intensely moralized by the ministerial connection. In addition, one cannot help but be struck by the self-will in his self-discipline. Taking both aspects together, Nietzsche is the prototype of the guilty individual he himself analyzes in *On the Genealogy of Morals:*

> The man who, from lack of external enemies and resistances and forcibly confined to the oppressive narrowness and punctiliousness of custom, impatiently lacerated, persecuted, gnawed at, assaulted, and maltreated himself; this animal that rubbed itself raw against the bars of its cage as one tried to "tame" it; this deprived creature, racked with homesickness for the wild, who had to turn himself into an adventure, a torture chamber, an uncertain and dangerous wilderness—this fool, this yearning and desperate prisoner became the inventor of "bad conscience." (P. 85)

Bad conscience is the product of the will to power turned against the self. The self's own natural inclinations constitute the resistance that must be overcome. The result is "the gravest and uncanniest illness" (ibid.), man's suffering of himself—Nietzsche's suffering of himself.

Given the evidence adduced thus far, one might think that this Nietzschean interpretation of Nietzsche goes too far. But consider the following midadolescent incident. One day "he became involved in an argument about Gaius Mucius Scaevola, the Roman soldier who, failing to kill Porsenna, put his hand into a fire to prove his indifference to pain. Taking a handful of matches, Nietzsche set them alight and held them unflinchingly in the palm of his outstretched hand until a prefect knocked them to the ground" (Hayman 1980, p. 28). Hayman interprets this enactment as sadomasochistic. It can also be seen as a symbolic autocastration, a suitable punishment for the imaginary crimes of the flesh. Neither interpretation precludes us from viewing the incident as an instance of the cruelty of self-overcoming.

Despite such heroic efforts, Nietzsche's melancholic identification with his father could not be overcome. Even earlier than the incident just considered, he began suffering from intense headaches and other symptoms of his father's fatal illness (ibid., p. 24). Importantly, he interpreted these symptoms in terms of his relationship with his father. When he was a student at Schulpforta and suffering variously from catarrh, "rheumatism," and wandering headaches, the school physician noted that the elder Nietzsche died from softening of the brain and that "the son is of the age at which his father was already ill" (Pletsch 1991, p. 54). Pletsch comments: "It is . . . particularly striking that Friedrich should have told doctor Zimmerman about his father's death and especially that he was of an age at which his father was already ill (which of course he was not). He apparently associated his suffering with his father's, and feared he was fated to die in the same fashion" (p. 55). And years later Nietzsche made a point of this connection: "My father died at the age of thirty-six. . . . In the same year in which his life went downward, mine, too, went downward: at thirty-six, I reached the lowest point of my vitality" (*EH*, p. 222). In 1879, he suffered through one hundred and eighteen days of intense migraine attacks accompanied by nausea, as well as recurrent bouts of near blindness. Between Christmas and the new year he fell into a coma and, when he recovered consciousness, alternately longed for death and believed it to be near (Hayman 1980, p. ?19). He was ill and depressed through a good part of 1880, and that year for "the first time in his life, he forgot his birthday, his thirty-sixth" (p. 227). One does not have to be a Freudian to see this forgetfulness as symptomatic of Nietzsche's conflicted relationship with his father.[8]

Although the direct relationship between Nietzsche's symptoms and his father's illness is impossible to overlook, there is another, not incompatible, way of viewing them: "Wherever the will to power declines in any form, there is invariably also a physiological retrogression, decadence. The deity of decadence, gelded in his most virile virtues and instincts, becomes of necessity the god of the physiologically retrograde, of the weak" (*A*, pp. 583–84). Here Nietzsche, in characteristic fashion, equates feminization and decadence. Hence his decadence might be seen as a "feminine" attribute, despite its more obviously masculine / paternal derivation. And from this perspective, his prolonged struggle with illness and especially with nausea might be seen as abjective, as a recurrent attempt to disgorge a feminine identity that unmanned him.

The abjection of the feminine can also be seen in a well-known incident from Nietzsche's university days. Somehow he found himself in a brothel. As he described it to a friend, "I suddenly saw myself surrounded by half-a-dozen apparitions in tinsel and gauze, who looked at me expectantly. I stood for a moment speechless. Then I made instinctively for a piano in the room as to the only living thing in that company and struck several chords. They broke the spell and I hurried away" (in Hollingdale 1965, p. 36). The women in this depiction are mesmerizing ghosts. They are like the sirens in *The Odyssey* who lure men to their doom. Nietzsche's horrified response no doubt signifies castration anxiety—not merely the loss of the phallus, however, but also the loss of the phallic self. Hence he strikes the keys of the piano, which in this context represents his connection to his father. His masculine identity is thereby restored, and the women are abjected. They are not even living things.

In sum, it can be plausibly argued that Nietzsche was trapped in a transitional developmental space between an abjective, preoedipal identification with his mother and a melancholic (and guilty) oedipal identification with his father. The result, along with his recurrent illness, was an inhibition of both sexuality and aggressivity (the latter manifested in the use of withdrawal as a technique of conflict avoidance). Hence we might see him as someone who failed to advance into the normative heterosexuality of his time.

8.

There is another side to the developmental story. The transitional space of self-formation is also a transitional space in the Winnicottian sense. This space was created for Nietzsche intersubjectively and by him intrasubjectively. In the former regard, his parental generation—the Nietzsche women, his maternal grandfather, and the fathers of his closest friends—not only made allowance for but also actively supported childhood fantasy, play, and display. For example, his mother, sensitive to his love of music, both bought him a piano and took lessons herself so that she could teach him the rudiments of playing.[9] Herr Pinder, the father of Nietzsche's good friend Wilhelm, was willing to take part in a play about the Greek gods written by the two boys (Hayman 1980, pp. 22–23). In the latter regard, Nietzsche demonstrated from early on a formidable capacity for, especially, aesthetic creativity. He organized elaborate games with his sister and friends; wrote, directed, and acted in dramatic productions (such as the one just noted); wrote a great deal of poetry (sometimes as birthday gifts for his mother); and composed music, all by the age of ten. He could improvise freely on the piano, a talent that he inherited from his father. He was an exceptionally good student whose scholarship won him admission to the highly esteemed school for boys at Pforta. And while he was shy and did not make friends easily, the friendships that he did make were both intense and long-lasting. From this perspective, therefore, he stands before us as a talented and promising young man.

During his early manhood, there were ample signs that this promise would be fulfilled. By his early twenties, Nietzsche had outgrown the orthodox Protestant piety of his family and his youth, and he was proving himself to be a brilliant student of philology. At the same time, he became a convert to Schopenhauer's philosophy. Because his philological talent served to open the door to an academic career, in the short run he chose to place his philosophical interests in the background. But in the somewhat longer run, university life did not preclude functioning as what we now term a "public intellectual," a role in which he could give full expression to his philosophical side. Thus as he entered adulthood, Nietzsche seemed to have found his own pathway into the patriarchal order.

Here is a related way of looking at this phase of Nietzsche's life. In an autobiographical fragment dated 1868–69, he wrote, "My father, a Protestant clergyman in Thuringia, died all too soon; I missed the strict and superior guidance of a male intellect." He goes on to say that at Schulpforta "I found only a surrogate for a father's education, the uniformizing discipline of an orderly school." This initially created a split in him between outward discipline and inward aesthetic rebellion. But the split was seemingly mended by classical philology. Inspired by the example of his philological teachers, "men with open and energetic minds, who were in part also personally sympathetic" (Middleton 1969, p. 47), he attempted to bend his will to the service of their gods.

We know, and Nietzsche soon learned, that this approach to self-unification was not adequate. His philosophical and aesthetic side could not be expressed within the narrow boundaries of philological science. Once he entered the university, however, he was more successful in replacing the missing father of his childhood. The teachers at Schulpforta were followed by the philologist Friedrich Wilhelm Ritschl and the philosophy of Arthur Schopenhauer. The former—"Father Ritschl," as Nietzsche sometimes termed him (ibid., p. 24)—recognized his unusual talent and was responsible for his appointment to a professorship at the University of Basel at the tender age of twenty-four. The latter was even more of an internal paternal presence. Literally dead like Nietzsche's father but literarily alive in his writing, in tune with Nietzsche's underlying melancholy by virtue of his pessimism and sensitivity to suffering, Schopenhauer slipped without resistance into Nietzsche's paternal pantheon. Thus we find him writing to his friend Erwin Rohde, during his brief period of military service in 1868: "Sometimes hidden under the horse's belly I murmur, 'Schopenhauer, help!'; and if I come home exhausted and covered with sweat, then a glance at the picture [of Schopenhauer] on my desk soothes me" (p. 27).[10] Philosophy here performs the defensive, ascetic functions Nietzsche was later to analyze and criticize.

Nietzsche took one final step forward along the path of normative masculine development in his relationship with Richard and Cosima Wagner. He first met "the Master," whose music he already knew well and admired, in 1868. He was immediately captured by the man, as he had been by the philosophy in the case of Schopenhauer. He became an intimate of the Wagners at their home in Tribschen and an ardent advocate of Wagner's music and projects.

Psychologically speaking, this relationship accomplished three things at once. First, Ludwig Nietzsche, the pious minister who could improvise on the piano, was succeeded or perhaps partially replaced by Richard Wagner, in Nietzsche's view the foremost musician of the age. Second, Franziska Nietzsche, his simple and relatively uncultured mother, was succeeded by the cultured and captivating Cosima. And, third, Nietzsche became the beloved son of these almost divine parents and the leader of a band of loyal brothers (the friends he enthusiastically recruited to the Wagnerian cause).[11]

Nietzsche wrote *The Birth of Tragedy* in this context and as a grand attempt at self-unification. The book had a philological core set against the background of Schopenhauer's philosophy and celebrated Wagner's music as a rebirth of tragedy in the modern age. The Wagners were understandably gratified by this homage to the Master but Ritschl was disapprovingly silent. Thus Nietzsche became something of an outlaw to the philological community and correspondingly somewhat alienated from academic life.

At least some of the projects with which Nietzsche next concerned himself reflected this altered situation. He delivered a set of lectures on the reform of educational institutions and began work on the *Untimely Meditations*. In both instances, he appears in the guise of critical theorist, but the critique—of the academy in particular and contemporary culture more generally—is developed along fairly conventional lines and within the parameters set by his loyalty to Schopenhauer and Wagner. Thus in one of the most notable of these critical efforts, "On the Uses and Disadvantages of History for Life," the masculine linearity of time is presupposed. Because this temporal linearity is contrasted with notions of time that would later come together in the concept of eternal return, I will discuss it in some detail.

Nietzsche begins by asking us to consider cattle. They are not tormented by memories; they are forgetful, unhistorical, and for that reason happy. "Man," by contrast, "cannot learn to forget but clings relentlessly to the past; however far and fast he may run, this chain runs with him" (*UM*, p. 61). To live well, therefore, one must forget much, if not quite so much as contented cows. If this proposition seems at all doubtful:

Imagine the extremist possible example of a man who did not possess the power of forgetting at all and who was thus condemned to see everywhere a state of becoming: such a man would no longer believe in his own being, would no longer believe in himself, would see everything flowing asunder in moving points and would lose himself in this stream of becoming: like a true pupil of Heraclitus, he would in the end hardly dare to raise his finger. (P. 62)

Although without the power of forgetting the self would dissolve into a chaos of becomings, the extent of forgetfulness necessary for self-maintenance varies. Nietzsche measures both individuals and cultures by the weight of existence they are capable of bearing. The more powerful the self, the broader the horizon:

> The stronger the innermost roots of a man's nature, the more readily will he be able to assimilate and appropriate the things of the past; and the most powerful and tremendous nature would be characterized by the fact that it would know no boundary at all at which the historical sense began to over-whelm it; it would draw into itself and incorporate into itself all the past, its own and that most foreign to it, and as it were transform it into blood. (Ibid.)

Yet even the most powerful nature has some need to forget and to ignore. Cheerfulness and the capacity for action require an appropriate ignorance as well as an appropriate knowledge.

As opposed to the active men of both ordinary and extraordinary horizons, there are those who achieve a "*suprahistorical* vantage point" (p. 65). In a sense their horizons are broad, their memories expansive. But these are the ones who have seen it all before. For them "the past and the present are one, that is to say, with all their diversity identical in all that is typical and, as the omniscience of imperishable types, a motionless structure of value that cannot alter and a significance that is always the same" (p. 66). Living therefore becomes meaningless, "for how should the unending superfluity of events not reduce him to satiety, over-satiety and finally to nausea!" (ibid.).[12]

Thus we are brought back to Nietzsche's basic distinction: suprahistorical men are the ultimate exemplars of those who study life for the sake of history (for the sake of knowledge); historical men (be their horizons narrow or broad) study history for the sake of life. The former step out of historical time. Abstraction and world-weariness are their defenses against the Heraclitean flux, nausea is the symptom of their inability to digest life. The latter use history to live; how they live determines how they use history:

> If the man who wants to do something great has a need of the past at all, he appropriates it by means of monumental history; he, on the other hand,

who likes to persist in the familiar and the revered of old, tends the past as an antiquarian historian; and only he who is oppressed by a present need, and who wants to throw off this burden at any cost, has need of critical history, that is to say a history that judges and condemns. (P. 72)

Kristeva, as previously noted, identifies monumental history with either the suprahistorical or women's time. But nothing could be more historical and masculine than the monumentalist's striving after greatness.

Still, Nietzsche has difficulty maintaining his distinction between life for history and history for life. Antiquarians are turned against life's transformations; critical historians slide toward the suprahistorical vantage point. Even the monumental man, primed for action, has trouble making sense of time. He looks to the great deeds of the past to inspire great deeds in the present. But at bottom "that which was once possible could present itself as a possibility for a second time only if the Pythagoreans were right in believing that when the constellation of the heavenly bodies is repeated the same things, down to the smallest event, must also be repeated on earth" (p. 70). Such a literal return of the same is not to be expected until "the astronomers have again become astrologers." Failing that eventuality, the aspirants to greatness must be content with approximations to reality and a tenuous relationship to real historical causes and effects—"which, fully understood, would only demonstrate that the dice-game of chance and the future could never again produce anything exactly similar to what it produced in the past" (ibid.).

Here, again, we have the ambiguity that is constitutive of Nietzsche's perspectivism. Both action and knowledge require the maintenance of horizons, but horizons separate us from our own life process. To live we must be partially turned away from life, and so the aim of using historical knowledge for life can never be fully realized.

Despite these ambiguities, there is a discernible difference between engaging life and retreating from it. Nietzsche's complaint against the historical sciences of his own time anticipates his later critique of metaphysics. As an end in itself, as knowing that aspires to a disinterested objectivity, history inhibits action and robs life of meaning. It is suitable for and practiced only by those who have been emasculated:

This is a race of eunuchs, and to a eunuch one woman is like another, simply a woman, woman in herself, the eternally unapproachable—and it is thus a matter of indifference what they do so long as history itself is kept nice and 'objective', bearing in mind that those who want it so are for ever incapable of making history themselves. And since the eternal womanly will never draw you upward, you draw it down to you and, being neuters, take history too for a neuter. But so that it shall not be thought that I am seriously comparing history with the eternally womanly, I should make it clear that, on the contrary, I regard it rather as the eternally manly. (P. 86)

Making history is a masculine enterprise into which women figure appropriately as objects, not subjects. When, for example, a man has a "vehement passion for a woman or for a great idea," he creates "a little vortex of life in a dead sea of darkness and oblivion" and can be moved to great and / or terrible deeds (p. 64). Women themselves are acted on rather than active, while men who refuse the active life, who retreat from making history to dispassionately studying it, are self-neutering.

Nietzsche's rather too emphatic affirmation of the masculinity of history suggests that this way of viewing things is a horizon—that history thus conceived wards off another, feminine experience of time. By contrast, the concept of eternal return was born out of Nietzsche's surrender to the feminine (that is, the masculine experience of the feminine). In parallel fashion, he now pushes away the problem of time as he would later conceptualize it. Late in the essay, to add one more instance, he parodies Eduard von Hartmann's *Philosophy of the Unconscious* by pretending that Hartmann himself is the parodist:

'The concept of evolution is not compatible with ascribing to the world-process an infinite duration in the past, since then every conceivable evolution must have already been run through, which is not the case (oh rogue!); so likewise we cannot concede to the process an infinite duration in the future; both would annul the concept of evolution toward a goal (rogue again!) and would make the world-process resemble the Danaides' water jugs. The complete victory of the logical over the illogical (oh rogue of rogues!) must, however, coincide with the temporal end of the world-process, the Last Day.' (P. 111)

Here Nietzsche presents in the form of parody a vital element of what he would later proclaim as the "fundamental conception" of Zarathustra and the "highest formula of affirmation that is attainable" (*EH*, p. 295).

To sum up, "Uses and Disadvantages" contains pieces of eternal return, separated from each other spatially and rhetorically and rejected in favor of a proto-existential but still linear and masculine history. When we gather together these rejected and varyingly unhistorical moments, we have a Heraclitean flux of memories that undermines any and all self-sameness; a suprahistorical perspective from which one sees only a meaningless and nausea-inducing sameness within the flux; a Pythagorean return of the same, which is contradicted by the contingency and novelty of actual history; and an infinite past and future extension of time, parodied in relation to evolution and teleology. There are hints that these temporal modalities are gendered feminine. By contrast, history itself is generated out of vehement masculine passion, and its course (we might infer) is marked by those exceptional men who are strong enough to push back the horizon and sail on the broadest of historical seas. Thus we have, as Kristeva puts it, mother's species and father's time, the familiar juxtaposition and opposition of feminine circle and masculine line.

9.

When we review our interpretation of Nietzsche's childhood and early adulthood, it is evident that we are seeing him from two quite different angles. Viewed one way he is trapped between abjection and morbidity. Viewed another, he is creative and lively. How are we to reconcile these two interpretations of his developing character?

In his own terms, for a start. Nietzsche saw his life as a struggle or oscillation between health and decadence. He also saw his decadence—his illness—as essential to his creativity. "Only great pain," he says in the 1887 preface to *The Gay Science*, "the long, slow pain that takes its time—on which we are burned, as it were, with green wood—compels us philosophers to descend to our ultimate depths" (p. 36). This ability to use one's pain productively presupposes that one is healthy "at bottom": "A typically morbid being cannot become healthy, much less make itself healthy. For a typically healthy person, conversely, being sick can even become an energetic *stimulus* for life, for living *more*" (*EH*, p. 224). Hence, albeit without his permission, we might interpret Nietzsche's development dialectically: his illness is the middle term, the immanent negativity and dynamus, of the self-developmental process.

We might also invert this dialectical perspective. We could grant that Nietzsche's development was dialectical so long as it was held together by the masculine *Weltgeist*, but we would remind ourselves that Nietzsche's ultimate affirmation of his illness in *Ecce Homo* was written as he was hovering on the brink of madness. The proof that he was not healthy "at bottom" lay just ahead. From this standpoint, the dialectic would have to be interpreted negatively—that is, as a process of dissolution in which decadence (illness, self-negation) is the dominant aspect. But again—and this is the tantalizing paradox of Nietzsche's life—short of his final insanity his illness does seem to have been a necessary condition of his creativity. For it is only during the years following his more normatively masculine period, as illness imposed itself on his life or, as may also be the case, he imposed illness on his life, that he became involved in the thought-experiments that constitute the better part of his philosophical legacy.

The paradox can be partially resolved if we look at Nietzsche from the perspective of the will to power. In his use of the term, his healthy creativity would be an unambiguous instance of will to power in the mode of affirmation. His illness would seem to be the basis for a reactive (envious, resentful) mobilization of the will to power. But Nietzsche claimed, and with considerable justification, that he did not go down this path. To the contrary, he would have us believe that he affirmed his illness by not resisting it—that he accepted it with "*Russian fatalism*, that fatalism without revolt which is exemplified by a Russian soldier who, finding a campaign too strenuous, finally lies down in the snow." Only for Nietzsche, fatalism was not a dying but a slowing down of metabolism, "a kind of will to hibernate" (*EH*, p. 230). Thus we have two, mutually constitutive modalities of the will to power: *amor fati*, "love of fate," and Russian fatalism, not resisting one's own fatality.

We shall see that Nietzsche spent a considerable time struggling against his fate, a struggle that is reflected in *Thus Spoke Zarathustra*. His illness was not only a stimulus to his creativity but also painful and debilitating. We grasp the two sides of his development more firmly, therefore, if we take pain into account and interpret the will to power in our own fashion. We then would say that Nietzsche was confronted with the necessity of coping with an enormous amount of pain, if he were to preserve the possibility of creative pleasure. Hence he was forced to center himself in the will to power, understood as overcoming pain to gain pleasure, including the pleasure of overcoming pain. Indeed the derivative position—gaining pleasure from overcoming pain—became his driving force and the source of his deepest, most philosophical, self-expression.

III. The Abyss

10.

We come now to Nietzsche's plunge out of history—his illness or "decadence" during the late 1870s and early 1880s, the period of truly abysmal pain which gave rise to eternal return, his most abysmal thought.[13] We must be careful not to treat his condition in a medically reductive fashion. This is especially important given his eventual insanity and the fairly substantial indications that the disease was syphilitic in origin, conceivably even congenital. But no matter what the organic basis of the illness, Nietzsche struggled with and found meaning in it. Moreover, from early on his symptoms were responsive to his moods. To take just one quite unambiguous example, in 1875 one of his closest friends left Basel with the intention of becoming a Catholic priest: "Nietzsche was so upset by this departure that he had to spend the next day in bed with a headache lasting for thirty hours, and frequent vomiting" (Middleton 1969, p. 132 n). This pattern was typical. Although his attacks of illness frequently came on without specific external inducement, interpersonal and other stresses would almost invariably produce them. And increasingly, from the mid-1870s through the early 1880s, anything more than the most superficial interactions with other people were liable to result in an attack.

Thus Nietzsche's symptoms were, at least in part, psychogenic. But even if this had not been the case, they would still have psychological meaning, for us as well as for him. We have already seen that he believed his life reached its lowest ebb when he approached the age of his father's death. This was also the period when he was breaking away from both his filial devotion to Wagner and his academic career. So we are free to interpret his intense suffering during this period as symptomatic of oedipal rebellion: the son desires to replace or surpass the father and is punished for this ambition. From this perspective, Nietzsche's symptoms betray his guilty intentions, in a specifically hysterical form: "You wish to displace your father, to kill him and take his place with your mother? Well, then, you may be just like him— moribund!" Here we have the madness that follows the murder of God— that is, Nietzsche's melancholic identification with his dead father.

Yet Nietzsche's illness was not just symptomatic of an unsuccessful oedipal rebellion. The territory he was coming to occupy was outside—perhaps beneath, perhaps beyond—the historical, masculine world as he himself had defined it in "On the Uses and Disadvantages of History for Life." We might think of it this way. Throughout his childhood, adolescence, and early adulthood, Nietzsche was predominantly healthy and able to function well both professionally and socially. His bouts of illness interrupted or punctuated his life, but they did not define it. During the time period under consideration here, the relationship was reversed. Illness became the rule and healthy periods the exception. This descending spiral of well-being can be traced in his correspondence:

- To Carl von Gersdorff, December 13, 1875: "Unfortunately, there is added to [intellectual joys of various kinds] my chronic misery, which seizes me for almost two whole days every two weeks, and sometimes for longer periods—well, that ought to end one day" (Middleton 1969, p. 140).

- To his sister, August 1, 1876: "Continuous headache, though not of the worst kind, and lassitude. Yesterday I was able to listen to *Die Walküre*, but only in a dark room—to use my eyes is impossible" (p. 146).

- To Wagner, September 12, 1876: "This neuralgia goes to work so thoroughly, so scientifically, that it literally probes me to find out how much pain I can endure, and each investigation lasts for thirty hours. I have to count on this study's recurring every four to seven days" (p. 148).

- To his sister, April 25, 1877: "I was so unwell! Out of fourteen days, I spent six in bed with six major attacks, the last one quite desperate" (p. 156).

- To Erwin Rohde, March 24, 1881: "For you would not believe *how many days* and how many *hours* even on tolerable days have just to be *endured*, to say the least" (p. 175).

- To Franz Overbeck, July 30, 1881: "Beyond that, my health is not as I had hoped. Exceptional weather here too. Continuous change of atmospheric conditions—it will force me to leave Europe. I must have *clear* sky for months on end, or I shall never make any progress. Six bad attacks already, lasting two or three days!" (p. 177).

- To Franz Overbeck, September 18, 1881: "I am desperate. Pain is vanquishing my life and my will. What months, what a summer I have had! My physical agonies were as many and various as the changes I have seen in the sky. In every cloud there is some form of electric charge which grips me suddenly and reduces me to complete misery. Five times I have called Doctor Death, and yesterday I hoped it was the end—in vain. Where is there on earth perpetually serene sky, which is my sky?" (p. 179).

We can read this series of reports from the perspective of time and gender. In the first letter linear, masculine time is presupposed. Nietzsche is moving forward in his life, although his progress is periodically interrupted. Then, in the letter to Wagner and the second letter to his sister, it is the disease that is progressing, so that time is becoming circular: periods of health alternate with periods of illness. Following Kristeva, this circularity would have to be gendered feminine, and so we would characterize Nietzsche as regressing from masculinity to femininity. This might seem arbitrary or even misguided. What, after all, is feminine about incapacitation? But it must be remembered that we are describing stereotypes, specifically the stereotypes that crystallize within the male imaginary. From this perspective, illness is a loss of manly vigor and health. It is both feminizing and infantilizing. Finally, in the two letters to Overbeck, even the circularity of time is barely maintained. Nature itself is attacking Nietzsche, incessantly and unpredictably (with every even minor change in the weather). His misery bespeaks his abjective fusion with the world, his mother.

It is not just a metaphor to say that Nietzsche had descended into a malignant version of the mother-world. We are, beneath it all, psychophysiological organisms who experience our earliest nurturing environment sensuously—not yet mentally *or* physically. The internalization of the mother-world (assuming the mother or women as primary caregivers) forms the matrix of the self. In adult life, we may or may not interact with others directly at this level, but we invariably have a psychophysiological relationship to what is sometimes termed our "life-world"—including the places we live, the homes we make for ourselves, or the natural environment. Here the process of self-formation is reversed. Via projection and other primitive mental processes, the life-world becomes the external or externalized matrix of the self.

By the late 1870s, Nietzsche's life-world had become cancerous—hostile and persecutory. He was no longer comfortable anywhere. He moved restlessly from place to place, from health spa to health spa, from doctor to doctor. He followed one diet and prescription after another, with at best only temporary positive results. When he was ill, he was tormented by migraine headaches, nausea, and fits of convulsive vomiting. His eyes caused him such pain that it often hurt to see, much less to read. He spent prolonged periods in darkened rooms, nearly blind and in abject misery. Sometimes, especially early on in his endless odyssey, he had people to read to and write for him. Other times and increasingly, he attempted to minister to himself, withdrawn from any intimate contact with other people (except via correspondence). Eventually he was reduced to such a state of psychophysiological irritability that he resembled one of those little particles of emerging life depicted by Freud in *Beyond the Pleasure Principle*—an organism lacking adequate contact barriers, unable to put up resistance to bombardment by overwhelming, and overwhelmingly painful, natural stimuli.

In short, the world of Nietzsche's illness was a precise inversion of the apparent world of his earliest childhood, the one in which his mother, as if by magic, anticipated and gratified his every desire. From this perspective—that is, in retrospect—it is plausible to hypothesize that the later condition was latent in the earlier one. And if this interpretation is accepted, then we would see in his suffering a return of the abjected mother-world.

Abjection, as discussed above, is a process of individuation that operates by rejecting and defiling the pre-self involvement with the mother. The result of the process is a narcissistic self that must be constantly defended from invasion by the abject. Normative masculinity can function as just such a defense. But for Nietzsche, the pathway into and through the oedipal situation had been blocked off, and he was unable to avail himself, in any sustained fashion, of the adult equivalent of preoedipal nurture. After reading his friend Malwida von Meysenbug's *Memoires of an Idealist*, for example, he wrote to her, on April 14, 1876: "One of the highest themes, of which you have first given me an inkling, is the theme of motherly love without the physical bond of mother and child; it is one of the most glorious revelations of *caritas*. Give me something of this love, *meine hochverehrte Freundin*, and look upon me as one who, as a son, needs such a mother, needs her so much!" (Hollingdale 1965, p. 142). Nietzsche actually spent several months with von Meysenbug late that year and during early 1877. His health improved somewhat with her care. But by late spring he was off again, none the better overall. Thus he was condemned to relying on his own emotional resources. As he wrote to Rohde in the letter cited above: "Ah, my friend, so I have to go on living off 'my own fat,' or, as everyone knows who has really tried this, drink my own blood. It is important not to lose the thirst for oneself, and just as important not to drink oneself dry" (Middleton 1969, p. 175). This is a striking metaphor coming from a man who was the constant victim of nausea and vomiting. It suggests that he could not tolerate the ingestion of his own "fat" and "blood," that it was disgusting or even poisonous—as I have been contending, abject.

We may also specify, or perhaps simply speculate on, the affective aspects of this recurrent return of the abjected mother-world. Both Nietzsche's nausea and his hysterical sensitivity to climatic variation suggest intense anxiety, while his migraine headaches suggest rage as well as anxiety. One imagines a vicious psychophysiological circle in which locked-up affects become physical symptoms that in turn stimulate these very same affects. It's as if he were a victim of the ascetic priests he portrays in *On the Genealogy of Morals*, who tend their charges by medicating—poisoning—them with "orgies of feeling" (*GM*, p. 139).

Thus the same emotional elements we preliminarily identified in Nietzsche's early life are dramatically present during this time of increasing illness and isolation. In both instances, there are signs of his melancholic identification with his father and his abjective identification with his mother. But the two periods are mirror images of each other. In the one health predominates, and in the other, decadence; in the one there is, to all appearances, nurture and maternal solicitude, and in the other we see a persecutory mother-world from which no escape seems possible. If the paranoid-schizoid position is the fundamental horizon of selfhood, here we see it nearly shattered by the experience of abjection.

And yet Nietzsche's regression into abjection was neither meaningless nor, ultimately, a defeat. As he stated, it is "the long, slow pain that takes its time—on which we are burned, as it were, with green wood—compels us philosophers to descend to our ultimate depths." It was in and through his suffering that he came to have a mind of his own. Looking back on this period, he wrote to von Gersdorff (on June 28, 1883): "The past six years have been in *this* respect the years of my greatest self-conquest—which is leaving out of account my rising above such matters as health, solitude, incomprehension and execration" (Middleton 1969, p. 213). Or, as he wrote two years later to von Meysenbug (March 13, 1885): "I am by far my best doctor. And the positive side of it—that I can endure it and assert my will against so much resistance—is my proof of that" (p. 236).

I find Nietzsche's "proof" irresistible, and for just this reason I resist Nehamas's judgment that, when we read his works, "we are not engaging with the miserable little man who wrote them but with the philosopher who emerges from them." This judgment seems to me doubly wrong. The man is in the works, abject misery and all, and viewing Nietzsche as just a "miserable little man" devalues a struggle that is more appropriately viewed as heroic.

IV. You Can't Run Away from Yourself

11.

This period of Nietzsche's life includes his "discovery" of both eternal return and the will to power. When he writes to von Gersdorff in June 1883, this achievement is presupposed; when he writes to von Meysenbug in March 1885, he interprets himself from the perspective of the will to power. Hence, as a biographical matter, we must see how these concepts emerge from his abjection and melancholia. Because we have not yet represented the idea of eternal return, however, we will begin with it. Next comes its biographical emergence and, finally, its dramatic deployment in *Thus Spoke Zarathustra*.

Nietzsche initially articulated the idea of eternal return in the penulti-mate section of the fourth book of *The Gay Science*. The passage and the concept constitute the break and the bridge between the Greeks, whose pes-simism must be overcome, and Zarathustra, the greater affirmer of life, overman or near-overman, who overcomes it:

The greatest weight.—What if, in some day or night a demon were to steal after you into your loneliest loneliness and say to you: "This life as you now live it and have lived it, you will have to live it once more and innumerable times more; and there will be nothing new in it, but every pain and every joy and every thought and sigh and everything unutterably small and great in your life will return to you, all in the same succession and sequence— even this spider and this moonlight between the trees, and even this moment and I myself. The eternal hour glass of existence is turned upside down again and again, and you with it, speck of dust!"

Would you not throw yourself down and gnash your teeth and curse the demon who spoke thus? Or have you experienced a tremendous moment when you would have answered: "You are a god and never have I heard anything more divine." If this thought gained possession of you, it would change you as you are, or perhaps crush you. The question in each and every thing, "Do you desire this once more and innumerable times more?" would lie upon your actions as the greatest weight. Or how well disposed would you have to become to yourself and to life *to crave nothing more fervently* than this ultimate eternal confirmation and seal? (*GS*, pp. 273–74)

Here we have a hypothesis concerning matters of fact and a psychological question posed in relation to it. The plain meaning of the hypothesis is that all events in our lives, down to the smallest detail, have occurred and will recur an infinite number of times. The question becomes, can we affirm our life just as it is, or do we recoil in horror at the thought of having to live it over and over again, through all eternity?

We are entitled to raise a prior question: what rational or evidential grounds do we have for believing that things recur eternally? Nietzsche does not provide us with much of an answer. To the contrary, the lines of argument he tentatively explores in the notebooks and that he puts into the mouth of Zarathustra are all quite obviously flawed.[14] Yet in the absence of supporting evidence and argument, there is no way of even assigning a probability to the idea. And I, at least, do not find it intuitively plausible. The most that can be said in its favor is that it cannot be ruled out. But this is to say that its truth-value can at best be weakly affirmed. And this being the case, it is hard to see the concept as the "greatest weight." To pursue the notion further, therefore, we must permit ourselves a willing suspension of disbelief and ask, what conception of time does eternal return imply or require, and what philosophical problem(s) does it solve?

Nietzsche constructs his basic model of time, in both *Thus Spoke Zarathustra* and the notebooks, from the perspective of any given present moment. Time stretches infinitely forward and backward from this point. It has no beginning and no end. With respect to human events, it both is and is not linear. In any one lifetime, events unfold unidirectionally, but each life line returns eternally. In defiance of ordinary experience, the past already contains all future events, and the future consists of events that have already taken place in the past. Hence it might appear as if time is a circle. But by definition a circle is closed or finite. One can go around it an infinite number of times, but the circle itself is bounded. In any case, Nietzsche is not saying that the past loops around on itself and becomes the future, while the future loops around itself and becomes the past. He is contending, rather, that the same linear sequence of events happened exactly the same way an infinite number of times in the past and will happen that same way an infinite number of times in the future. It would seem to follow that any present moment is being infinitely repeated at that very moment—that if we could break the barriers that limit us to experiencing only this moment in this life, *déjà vu* would be the rule and not the exception.[15] Consequently, there is absolutely no way in which we can run away from ourselves. Because our lives are infinitely repeated, we are who we are once and for all.

It is evident that eternal return cannot be identified with the stereotypes of *either* masculine *or* feminine temporality. Although it is linear and historical, each line of time is trapped in a recursive loop. Yet the loopiness of linear time has little in common with the natural, organic cycles of the mother-world. We might better say that it is both and neither: linear, masculine time recurs in infinite feminine circles, while the infinite, feminine circularity of time consists only of masculine lines. And we shall see in the following sections that affirming eternal return can give rise to an experience of sublimity in which the distinction between having the mother and being her is overcome. Hence we might see Nietzsche as attempting to sublate—to supersede dialectically—the distinction between mother's species and father's time.

"Perhaps so," a Hegelian might respond. "But leaving aside the issue of gender, Nietzsche's conception of time is precisely *not* dialectical. He sets up his thought-experiment in such a way that the presumed infinity of the past is rather finite, since it begins at the finite point of the present moment, and likewise the infinity of the future. This is precisely a 'spurious infinity,' i.e., a finite concept of the infinite (Hegel 1969, pp. 138–42). Nietzsche is merely stumbling around in the dark, without the lantern of dialectical reason that uniquely permits one to reconcile infinite past with infinite future."

Although this judgment is quite correct from a Hegelian perspective, Nietzsche is entitled to reply that the Hegelian dialectic is an horizon, a perpetual going beyond and ipso facto a nihilistic defense against living in the present moment.[16] Present life is judged as lacking, either intrinsically or in comparison with an imagined future moment of fulfillment. By contrast, the idea of eternal return presupposes life as a Dionysian plentitude—not the Dionysian of *The Birth of Tragedy*, with its Schopenhauerian resonances, but rather the Dionysian redefined as a superabundant self-overcoming, lacking nothing and including nothing needlessly. In this Dionysian world, no moment is ever surpassed or superseded. We are not on the road to a better place and time, and there is no possible redemption of the present through the future. All escape routes from life as it is being lived have been cut off. Hence the challenge of eternal return: is your will to power strong enough, healthy enough, to affirm the eternal recurrence of every moment of your life? Or do you lack this strength? Would you turn away from your life— would you need to change it, subtract something from it, or add something to it? In other words, do you view your life as lacking in one or more respects? If you do, then you have taken a step down the nihilistic path and have, to just that extent, demonstrated that you are not capable of bearing the weight of your own existence.

It might seem that, if all things return eternally, choice becomes meaningless. The future is already past and cannot be changed in any respect. Why bother to try? But this world-weary question quite misses the point. Properly seen, each moment we live and each choice we make is eternally determining. You will have to experience the consequences of your decisions again and again. Each choice is therefore meaningful in the extreme, perhaps overwhelmingly so. But this is only to say that the stress of making decisions in the face of their eternal consequences is another resistance to be overcome, another test of the will to power.[17]

Once we come to the making of choices, including the possible choice of affirming eternal return, we enter the field of moral and other valuations. I will postpone a substantive exploration of this area until Chapter 6. It is evident, however, that the affirmation of eternal return really does amount to a transvaluation of our conventional moral values—that it is a form of valuing that goes beyond the distinctions (good/bad, good/evil) that structure moral codes. It also would seem to preclude an important derivative of moral judging—that is, the belief that good times compensate for bad or that pain can be justified by the pleasures that result from enduring it. If, for example, we are engaging in a struggle, we can no longer comfort ourselves with the idea that it will be over and we will be free to reap its benefits. The struggle itself will come again, along with whatever has been, in the usual sense, gained from it. Hence if we are really to affirm eternal return, we must affirm the means along with the ends, or treat the means as an end. We can truly affirm eternal return only if we experience the overcoming of resistance as an end in itself. From this perspective, will to power and eternal return completely converge. Eternal return conceptualizes the greatest resistance to and the ultimate test of our capacity for self-overcoming.

12.

Here is a thought-experiment or perhaps a pragmatic objection. Let's grant that all things return eternally. Still, we live but one life at a time. The recursive duplication of moments does not change the moments themselves and their meaning for us. What does concern us are repetitive patterns in the life we are living now. And even these patterns do not necessarily give rise to concern. Picture, for example, an individual whose life has been what she or he would have wished it to be. Such a person is confronted with eternal return, either as Nietzsche articulates it or in the more commonsensical version of repetitive cycles within a lifetime. Would the mere fact of life repeating itself be burdensome?

The point of this hypothetical example is obvious. Whether or not repeated experience is hard to bear depends on the nature of the experience. The thought of eternal return would hold no terror for someone whose life was not only bearable but deeply fulfilling. Indeed, no thought could be lighter or more delightful. The further one's life departs from this fortunate condition, however, the more terrible the idea of eternal return would become. So it cannot be asserted as a general principle that eternal return is the greatest weight. Rather, its weight varies, depending on the life that has been and is being lived.

This refinement of the notion is beside the biographical point. Nietzsche, who was recurrently reduced to the most abject misery, did find the idea genuinely terrifying. Thus the manner in which he communicated it to Lou Salomé: "Unforgettable for me are those hours in which he first confided to me his secret, whose inevitable fulfillment and validation he anticipated with shudders. Only with a quiet voice and with all signs of deepest horror did he speak about this secret. Life, in fact, produced such suffering in him that the certainty of an eternal return of life had to mean something horrifying to him" (Salomé 1988, p. 130). He had, in short, all the reason in the world to curse the demon who forced the idea of eternal return on him.

This is not the whole story. In the summer of 1881, in Sils-Maria, "6000 feet beyond man and time," Nietzsche also experienced the "tremendous moment" referred to in "The Greatest Weight," the moment in which the idea seemed "divine" (*EH*, p. 295). On August 14 he wrote to Peter Gast:

The August sun is overhead, the year passes on, the mountains and the forests become more quiet and peaceful. On my horizon, thoughts have arisen such as I have never seen before—I will not speak of them, but will keep my unshakable peace. I really shall have to live a few more years! Ah, my friend, sometimes the idea runs through my head that I am living an extremely dangerous life, for I am one of those machines which can explode. The intensities of my feeling make me shudder and laugh; several times I could not leave my room for the ridiculous reason that my eyes were inflamed—from what? Each time, I had wept too much on my previous day's walk, not sentimental tears but tears of joy; I sang and talked nonsense, filled with a glimpse of things which put me in advance of all other men. (Middleton 1969, p. 178)

Here we have a report of eternal return, as it is being lived for the first time.

As we know from the letters to Overbeck of July 30 and September 18, Nietzsche's initial experience of eternal return was a short-lived ecstasy bounded by intense suffering and even despair. Nietzsche affirms his life absolutely in August and calls for Doctor Death in September. We are reminded of organically based manic-depressive cycles, an interpretation that could be strengthened by tracking the succession of elevated moods alternating with melancholic ones that characterize this period. But even if we put purely psychiatric considerations to one side, we still might see Nietzsche's elevated moods as an anxiety-driven defense against or escape from depression and pain. This interpretation fits with his sense that he might explode from the intensity of his emotions, as well as with Salomé's view that the "quintessence of the teaching of eternal recurrence, later constructed by Nietzsche as a shining apotheosis to life, formed such a deep contrast to his own painful feelings about life that it gives us intimations of being an uncanny mask" (1988, p. 130).

Leaving aside Salomé's mistaken belief that Nietzsche's affirmation of eternal return came later than his initial conception of it, I think such psychiatric and diagnostic interpretations, whatever their plausibility, are relatively empty. They stay outside Nietzsche's experience while claiming to explain it and displace his self-understanding rather than engaging it. So let's step back and see if we can come closer to the experience itself.

Nietzsche contextualizes the advent of eternal return this way:

If I reckon back a few months from this day, I find as an omen a sudden and profoundly decisive change in my taste, especially in music. Perhaps the whole of *Zarathustra* may be reckoned as music; certainly a rebirth of the art of *hearing* was among its preconditions. . . . But if I reckon forward from that day to the sudden birth [part 1 of *Thus Spoke Zarathustra*] that occurred in February 1883 under the most improbable circumstances—the finale from which I have quoted a few sentences in the Preface was finished exactly in that sacred hour when Richard Wagner died in Venice—we get eighteen months for the pregnancy. This figure of precisely eighteen months might suggest, at least to Buddhists, that I am really a female elephant. (*EH*, p. 295)

It seems permissible to read this passage as having the death of Wagner on both sides and the gestation of Zarathustra in the middle. This was the period during which Nietzsche rejected Wagner's music in favor of music by Bellini, Bizet, and his friend Peter Gast, while Wagner himself dies as Zarathustra is born. In between, we have Zarathustra's conception and gestation.

This reading barely goes beyond the text itself. We may take another, modest step by recalling that Wagner was the successor to Nietzsche's father, that during the preceding period Nietzsche had been struggling to free himself from his filial obligations—and that he had been afraid that he, like his father, would die at age thirty-six. Yet he had outlived Ludwig Nietzsche and outgrown Wagner. At least during those "tremendous moments," he was living outside his melancholic identification with his father. He was the successful murderer of God—not a nihilistic madman but rather the father himself, now capable of creating a son in his own image. On April 6, 1883, he wrote to Gast: "You would not believe, dear friend, what an abundance of suffering life has unloaded on me, at all times, from *early* childhood on. But I am a soldier—and this soldier, in the end, did become the father of Zarathustra" (Middleton 1969, p. 211). And as with God the Father and God the Son, here too there are two forms but one essence. Nietzsche and Zarathustra are conjointly the teachers of eternal return, the doctrine that constitutes the foundation of the great transvaluation of all (especially Christian) values.

There is also room for the Holy Spirit. Nietzsche does not experience himself solely as Zarathustra's father. He characterizes the birth of Zarathustra in maternal terms, even if he needs his elephant joke to make good on the simile. And prankishness aside, I think Nietzsche intends to be taken seriously in the claim that his generative powers are maternal as well as paternal. Here is his description of the inspiration that breathed life into Zarathustra:

If one has the slightest residue of superstition left in one's system, one could hardly reject the idea that one is merely incarnation, merely mouthpiece, merely medium of overpowering forces. . . .

A rapture whose tremendous tension occasionally discharges itself in a flood of tears—now the pace quickens involuntarily, now it becomes slow; one is altogether beside oneself, with the distinct consciousness of subtle shudders and of one's skin creeping down to one's toes; a depth of happiness in which even what is most painful and gloomy does not seem opposite but rather conditioned, provoked, a *necessary* color in such a superabundance of light. . . .

Everything happens involuntarily to the highest degree but as a gale of a feeling of freedom, of absoluteness, of power, of divinity.—The involuntariness of image and metaphor is strangest of all; one no longer has any notion of what is image or metaphor: everything offers itself as the nearest, most obvious, simplest expression. (*EH*, pp. 300–301)

I would argue that this depiction of inspiration gives us the affective content that goes with the maternal form and that we may interpret Nietzsche's experience as a *return of the maternal sublime*. Outliving his father was a necessary condition for this state of being. He had triumphed over his morbidity. In these tremendous moments, neither his identification nor his oedipal rivalry with his father cut off access to the mother-world. And stripped of these defensive prohibitions, the abjective identification with his mother also broke down, or was broken through. Nietzsche was flooded with pent-up, split-off, and highly sensualized feelings of being at one with the world. He was caught up on a Dionysian tide that swept away all the usual boundaries, limits, or horizons of individuality. Remarkably, he did not go mad.

Here's the picture of eternal return that seems to be emerging. On the one side, we see Nietzsche trapped in cycles of recurrent pain that result from his melancholic identification with his father and his abjective identification with his mother—cycles of pain from which he cannot hope to escape and which at their worst leave him at the mercy of malign, persecutory natural forces. On the other side, we witness a breaking of identificatory bonds and a dissolution of gender distinctions, a floodtide of sublime feelings (both affects and sensations) and an effortless soaring of thought, an ecstatic union with the world itself.

This depiction of eternal return suggests a primal splitting, a division of the mother-world into spheres of the abject and the sublime. But the experience of eternal return is not merely a replication of a primal either/or. A mediating link exists between the two sides. In "The Greatest Weight," the demon might be interpreted as telling Nietzsche that he will be in the future what he was in the past—abjectly wretched. The question is then, can he affirm this fate? Can he *will* it? Can he experience his wretchedness as a stimulus to his will to power, as a resistance to be overcome? Confronted with this question, Nietzsche answers, "yes!" The consequence of this affirmation is the enormous release of energy that made possible the creation of *Thus Spoke Zarathustra*. And just this experience of creative overflow is the model for the concept of the will to power itself, or at least for its affirmative incarnation.[18]

The willing of eternal return is not just the experience of a dam bursting, with the resultant flood of creative energy. It is overcoming resistance of whatever kind, including the *rancune* (rancor) of what is great: "Everything great—a work, a deed, turns *against* the man who did it. . . . Something one was never permitted to will lies *behind* one, something in which the knot in the destiny of humanity is tied—and now one labors *under* it!" Thus "the years during and above all *after* my *Zarathustra* were marked by distress without equal. One pays dearly for immortality: one has to die several times while still alive" (EH, p. 303). The affirmation of eternal return requires not merely the ability to suffer through dark times but rather the strength to will the suffering itself.

The rancune of what is great has another implication. Eternal return is "something one was never permitted to will." Affirming it is a transgression; Nietzsche's subsequent suffering is punishment for his crime. The laws of the old order reimpose themselves, and ecstasy gives way to melancholy and sublimity to abjection. One thinks of the "pale criminal" from the first part of *Thus Spoke Zarathustra* who was "equal to his deed when he did it" but "could not bear its image after it was done" (*TSZ*, p. 150). He was undone by his guilt, the image of his deed. In like fashion, we might interpret Nietzsche's suffering in more or less classical Freudian terms, namely, as the manifestation of unconscious guilt, retribution for appropriating the procreative powers of both mother and father.

There is also a less classically Freudian way of interpreting the lived reality of eternal return. Nietzsche claimed for himself a dual experience: "looking from the perspective of the sick toward *healthier* concepts and values and, conversely, looking again from the fullness and self-assurance of a *rich* life down into the secret work of the instinct of decadence" (EH, p. 223). Eternal return contains both perspectives, the abject misery of decadence and the great ecstasy of the sublime (if not really of health). It could be argued, however, that the two perspectives are not of equal interpretive value. Nietzsche writes to Overbeck on March 24, 1883:

I no longer see *why* I should live for another six months—everything is boring, painful, *dégoûtant*. I forego and suffer too much, and have come to comprehend, beyond all comprehension, the deficiency, the mistakes, and the real disasters of my whole past intellectual life. It is too late to make things good now; I shall never do anything that is good any more. What is the point of doing anything?

This reminds me of my latest folly—I mean *Zarathustra* (can you read my handwriting? I am writing like a pig). Every few days I forget it. (Middleton 1969, p. 210)

Here we have the rancune of what is great: the sublime object and its creator have become abject. Yet this is not, at least for now, how the story ends. Nietzsche may have been punished for his transgressions, but to a quite extraordinary extent he was able to will not only his deed but its afterimage.[19] He made himself into an experiment, testing how much recurrent suffering could be not only accepted but affirmed as well. This might be viewed, á la Freud in *Beyond the Pleasure Principle*, as turning passivity into activity. But short of his insanity, the perspective of the will to power trumps all other interpretations. Nietzsche could truly claim to be the master in gaining pleasure from overcoming pain.

13.

As noted above, inspired states might be seen as the limit-experience of transitional space, once the terror of the transitional is admitted into the concept. These are states of mind in which the distinction between what is real and what is not is suspended, in which thoughts are omnipotent and scarcely distinguishable from deeds, and in which one risks becoming lost in the madman's infinity. This is the psychic location of eternal return, within which *Thus Spoke Zarathustra* was created and which we, the readers, are invited to share.

The text consists of four parts that fit together in the manner of tragic trilogy and satyr play. In the first part, Zarathustra proclaims the overman: "*I teach you the overman*. Man is something that shall be overcome" (*TSZ*, p. 124). In the second part, the principle of overcoming, that is, the will to power, is articulated: life confides to Zarathustra that it is "*that which must always overcome itself*" (p. 227). And in the third part, we are confronted by eternal return—that which must be affirmed if the human, all-too-human is to be overcome. The fourth part, although it does contain one additional attempt to articulate the affirmative experience of eternal return, is largely parodic.

We shall pass by part 1 and most of part 2, in which Zarathustra appears as a would-be philosophical leader of men. To some extent, he succeeds. He has disciples, who are struggling to free themselves from conventional beliefs—although they have a tendency to idealize rather than to understand him. Indeed, from beginning to end Zarathustra is ill-understood, and not only by his disciples. Thus he mirrors Nietzsche, who attempted to play the role of philosophical leader in his youth and whose subsequent writings were not only misunderstood but also largely ignored.

The turning point in the drama of eternal return takes place in the transition between the last sections of part 2 and the first sections of part 3. Hence interpreting them is our present concern.

"*The Soothsayer.*" The barrier that Zarathustra confronts at the end of part 2 is not the inadequacy of his followers but rather his own. Although he is unwilling to embrace the truth of eternal return, he cannot ignore it. We see him struggling, unsuccessfully, to carry its weight.

A soothsayer appears, proclaiming one of the implications of eternal return: "All is empty, all is the same, all has been. . . . We are still waking and living on—in tombs" (*TSZ*, p. 245). Zarathustra takes in his words and "walked about sad and weary." He is oppressed by what Nietzsche had earlier termed the suprahistorical perspective, or—to vary the metaphor—he is infected with the mood of the Preacher in Jerusalem: "The thing that hath been, it *is that* which shall be; and that which is done *is* that which shall be done: and *there is* no new *thing* under the sun" (Eccl. 1:9).

In this melancholy mood, Zarathustra falls asleep. When he awakens, he tells his disciples his dream, which he challenges them to interpret. He had become "a guardian of tombs upon the lonely mountain of death." Alone at midnight he found himself holding a rusty key and standing before great, creaking gates. Time became distorted. It "passed and crawled, if time still existed—how should I know?" He tried to open the gate with the key and failed, but "a roaring wind tore its wings apart; whistling, shrilling and piercing, it cast up a black coffin before me." Then: "And amid the roaring and whistling and shrilling the coffin burst and spewed out a thousandfold laughter. And from a thousand grimaces of children, angels, owls, fools, and butterflies as big as children, it laughed and mocked and roared at me. Then I was terribly frightened; it threw me to the ground. And I cried in horror as I have never cried" (*TSZ*, p. 247). Zarathustra's most beloved disciple offers the interpretation that he, Zarathustra, is the strong wind, who brings new life into the soothsayer's world of melancholy. This is clearly incorrect. The disciple completely fails to grasp the horror of the dream. It's as if he were seeing the rose on the cross but not the suffering of the God-forsaken Christ.

Later, Zarathustra offers a partial interpretation of both the soothsayer's world-weary wisdom and the dream. He was reluctant to leave his disciples, but "the longest boredom" urged him to go (p. 274). As he hesitated, his "past burst its tombs; many a pain that had been buried alive, awoke, having merely slept, hidden in burial shrouds." Or, to restate the point in our terms: on the surface Zarathustra is oppressed by the repetitive monotony of everyday life. His depression is a function of the same things happening over and over again, of there being nothing new under the sun. But his world-weariness is also a defense against powerfully disturbing memories that lurk, repressed, beneath the surface of consciousness and that break through in dreams. Then the gates of memory are flung open, and he is overwhelmed by the return of repressed pain. Yet the depression that functions repressively and the repressed itself are joined at the root; the tomb is the signifier of the one as of the other. And so it is easy to guess which memory of Nietzsche's is here haunting Zarathustra, for we remember the childhood dream in which "a grave suddenly opened and my father in his shroud arose out of it." Thus Zarathustra's experience provides proof of the proposition Nietzsche put forward in "On the Uses and Disadvantages of History for Life," namely, that "man cannot learn to forget but clings relentlessly to the past; however far and fast he may run, this chain runs with him" (*UM*, p. 61).

"*On Redemption.*" When we see Zarathustra or Nietzsche—it makes little difference which—struggling to overcome the irrepressible pain of his past, we gain a deeper appreciation of what appears in the text as the problem of redemption. Having recovered from the experience of his dream, Zarathustra comes to a bridge, where he is surrounded by cripples. A hunchback asks him to follow in Christ's footsteps and perform miracles. Zarathustra refuses. He is concerned with the crippling of the human spirit, not with physical deformity: "Verily, my friends, I walk among man as among the fragments and limbs of men. This is what is terrible to my eyes, that I find man in ruins and scattered as over a battlefield or a butcherfield. And when my eyes flee from the now to the past, they always find the same: fragments and limbs and dreadful accidents—but no human beings" (*TSZ*, p. 250). And fragments they ever shall be: "Every prisoner becomes a fool; and the imprisoned will redeems himself foolishly. That time does not run backwards, that is his wrath; 'that which was' is the name of the stone he cannot move" (p. 251).

This brings us to a second implication of eternal return. Whether construed psychologically or cosmologically, it tells us that the past will come again. Just because it is the past, however, it cannot be changed. What is done cannot be undone, despite the fact that we cannot be done with it. We therefore would seem to be powerless with respect to it. The act of willing is creative and redemptive, but it seems impossible to will what already has been: "'It was'—that is the name of the will's gnashing of teeth and most secret melancholy. Powerless against what has been done, he is an angry spectator of the past. The will cannot will backwards; and that he cannot break time and time's covetousness, that is the will's loneliest melancholy" (p. 251).

The apparent impossibility of willing backward might be viewed simply as a narcissistic affront. Indeed, there is ample textual evidence to support this interpretation. Zarathustra continually strives to be godlike; he wants to bend all things to his will. The past cannot be changed and therefore cannot be creatively redeemed. Again, however, we may ask the particularizing question: godlike ambitions aside, when does the past require redemption? Only, we might reply, when it is somehow lacking or deficient, so that we would change it if we could. The lack might be of various kinds, including too little that is heroic and too much that is mediocre. And if the deficiency is great enough, it might well give rise—as Zarathustra would have it—to the spirit of revenge, "the will's ill will against time and its 'it was'" (p. 252). But here the anger and desire for revenge result from *what* took place and not from the mere fact of its occurrence. Conversely, if the past is not deficient, if it is what we would have wished it to have been, wouldn't we accept it with gratitude and view our memories as a blessing? And might we not be glad to experience the moment again, just as it was?

In other words, I contend that ill will toward the past results at least as much from its experiential content as from its temporal form. *Zarathustra's* past is horrifying to him. When it is recalled, coffins split open and he is overwhelmed by the return of buried pain; and because the return is eternal, he cannot escape from it. Hence the issue becomes, will Zarathustra fall victim to the spirit of revenge by turning angrily against the past and condemning it, or will he be able to affirm the past—to will the return of everything that terrifies and disgusts him?

"The Stillest Hour." Zarathustra cannot resolve the dilemma. He will not give in to the spirit of revenge, but neither can he affirm the eternal return of the same. As he begins his retreat into his final solitude, he tells his disciples about the internal conflict of his "stillest hour": "Do you know the

fright of him who falls asleep? He is frightened down to his very toes because the ground gives under him and the dream begins. . . . Yesterday, in the stillest hour, the ground gave under me, the dream began. The hand moved, the clock of my life drew a breath; never had I heard such stillness around me; my heart took fright" (p. 257). The silence of the hour, which he characterizes as his "angry" and "awesome mistress," communicates with him voicelessly. It challenges him to speak the thought of eternal return. He acknowledges that he knows it, but he cannot, or will not, speak it:

> Thus everything called out to me in signs: "It is time!" But I did not hear, until at last my abyss stirred and my thought bit me. Alas, abysmal thought that is *my* thought, when shall I find the strength to hear you burrowing, without trembling any more? My heart pounds to my very throat whenever I hear you burrowing. Even your silence wants to choke me, you who are so abysmally silent. As yet I have never dared to summon you; it was enough that I carried you with me. (P. 274)

Here we have the heart of Zarathustra's dilemma. He can redeem the past only by willing that it come again, but the thought of things returning eternally is abysmal, both infinitely deep and dreadful. He chokes on it and still will not say it.

It is notable that Zarathustra's stillest hour is gendered feminine. It is his angry and awesome mistress. She is like an angry mother who commands her child to speak. And in this context, we might recall that Nietzsche did not learn to speak until he was two and one-half, that his parents were worried by this lag in development, and that—following medical advice—his mother forced him to name things that previously had come to him as if by magic. In this situation, it would make no difference whether the anger originated with him or with his "awesome mistress." Either way, learning to speak might be indistinguishable from choking on one's words. And, it might be wondered, would one of those first words have been "mother"? If so, we might view Zarathustra's mistress as demanding he name *her*. Eternal return would then be the name of the abysmal mother as well as of the erupting grave of the dead father.

"*On the Vision and the Riddle.*" This section, in which the concept and the experience of eternal return are brought together, is our principal concern.

Just as Zarathustra in part 1 mirrors the young Nietzsche who aspired to be a philosophical leader of men, so Zarathustra in part 2 mirrors, in the end, the Nietzsche whose melancholic and abject identifications drove him off the path of normative masculine achievement and ever more deeply into the internal abyss of eternal return. As the third part begins, the question becomes, can he bear the weight of the recurrent past?

Zarathustra is aboard a ship, on his way back to his mountain solitude. He tells the sailors ("bold searchers, researchers, and whoever embarks with cunning sails on terrible seas"—likewise those who prefer to "guess" rather than to "deduce") a vision and challenges them to interpret it.[20]

In his dream-vision, he is ascending a mountain path, carrying and burdened by a dwarflike spirit of gravity. The dwarf mockingly tells him that his attempt at overcoming and self-overcoming will come to nothing— metaphorically, that the stone he throws up high will fall on him: "You threw yourself up so high; but every stone that is thrown must fall. [You are] sentenced to yourself and your own stoning" (p. 268).

The dwarf is a kindred spirit to the soothsayer, at once cynical and nihilistic. He is an embodiment of Zarathustra's self-doubts or even despair, and so he speaks the malicious and bitter self-reproaches of despondency: "It is hopeless," he is saying. "You will be crushed by your own attempts to go beyond yourself. Give it up." Yet Zarathustra struggles on, until at last he gains the courage to face the dwarf—the same courage that "slays even death itself, for it says: 'Was *that* life? Well then! Once more!'" (*TSZ*, p. 269). This is his first step toward the affirmation of eternal return. Instead of letting his dwarfish thoughts of life's burdens defeat him, he turns the tables: "You think I am condemned to self-stoning? Well, you don't know the half of it: 'you do not know my abysmal thought. *That* you could not bear!' (p. 269)."

A kind of battle of wits has now been joined. Zarathustra and the dwarf stand at the gateway, "Moment"—the present moment. It faces two ways, and an eternity stretches out in either direction. There is therefore a contradiction, and Zarathustra asks, "But whoever would follow one of them, on and on, farther and farther—do you believe, dwarf, that these paths contradict each other eternally?" (p. 270). The dwarf, like one of the proud Athenians interrogated by Socrates, thinks he knows the answer and murmurs contemptuously: "All truth is crooked; time itself is a circle." He correctly understands that time is not simply linear, which he supposes Zarathustra to be presupposing, but he does not understand that it is not simply circular. "Do not make things too easy for yourself," Zarathustra responds, angered by the dwarf's trivialization of the self-contradiction of temporality. He offers a quite different answer to the question:

"Behold," I continued, "this moment! From this gateway, Moment, a long, eternal lane leads *backward:* behind us lies an eternity. Must not whatever *can* walk have walked on this lane before? Must not whatever *can* happen have happened, have been done, have passed by before? And if everything has been there before—what do you think, dwarf, of this moment? Must not this gateway too have been there before? And are not all things knotted together so firmly that this moment draws after it *all* that is to come? Therefore—itself too? For whatever *can* walk—in this long lane out *there* too, it *must* walk once more.

"And this slow spider, which crawls in the moonlight, and this moonlight itself, and you and I in the gateway, whispering together, whispering of eternal things—must not all of us have been there before? And return and walk in that other lane, out there, before us, in this long dreadful lane— must not we eternally return?" (P. 270)

Thus we have Zarathustra's second step toward affirming eternal return, as well as a further dramatization and argumentative elaboration of "The Greatest Weight."[21] The emphasis is placed on the present moment. This moment has happened before in the infinity of the past. It is, however, also happening now. The moment has been doubled; it is equally and indistinguishably past and present. Moreover, just because the present moment has already been in the past, its present occurrence is the future of its own past. Looking forward, therefore, the present moment always has itself in front of itself. It is always the past of some future recurrence and equally the future occurrence itself. Thus the present moment is infinitely multiplied or deepened. It has become abysmal.

As Zarathustra predicted, the thought of eternal return is unbearable for the dwarf, who vanishes from the scene. Or as we would view it psychoanalytically, the dwarf's cynicism is a resistance to experiencing the full horror of eternal return. Zarathustra's argumentative presentation of eternal return is akin to the successful analysis of a defense. It overcomes a resistance, perhaps even the resistance of ratiocinative argumentation itself. When the dwarf disappears, the scene has been set for the experience of eternal return rather than arguments about it.

Zarathustra, who has become lost in his own thoughts, suddenly hears a dog howl: "Had I ever heard a dog howl like this? My thoughts raced back. Yes, when I was a child, in the most distant childhood: then I heard a dog howl like this. And I saw him, too, bristling, his head up, trembling, in the stillest moonlight when even dogs believe in ghosts" (p. 271). The moonlight links present and past—that past *is* this present. The childhood is, of course, Nietzsche's. The memory is of leaving Röcken, the event that symbolizes the death of his father. We recall Elisabeth's depiction of the moment: "[Fritz] got up in the night, dressed himself, and went into the courtyard where the heavily laden carriage stood waiting with its shining red lamps. The wind set up a powerful dirge, the faithful dog howled in heartrending and gruesome tones, and the moon, pallid and cold, shot her rays over the low roofs of the neighbouring buildings into the great court-yard with its ghastly lights and all its mournful echoes." Fate and fatality are here wrapped together. The son is condemned to return again and again to the moment of the father's death.[22] The past can never be laid to rest.

The distinction between Nietzsche and Zarathustra is never very clear, but here it has almost disappeared. The death of Nietzsche's father consti-tuted a fixation point, a limit he could not go beyond. It stands in the posi-tion of cause, with melancholia and abjection as its effect. This inverse developmental causality is recapitulated in the present text. Zarathustra's memory of the tragedy of Nietzsche's childhood is followed by his con-frontation with melancholia, abjection, and the sublime.

Zarathustra awakens himself from his reverie, and the remembrance of things past gives way to the perception of things present. He is alone among wild cliffs in the bleakest moonlight. This is the eerie, isolated landscape or dreamscape of the paranoid-schizoid position. In another time and place, Zarathustra might be "the man with no name," as he is played by Clint East-wood in *Hang 'Em High*. But in this instance, it is redemption from revenge, and not revenge, that is the issue.[23]

Nietzsche says elsewhere, "I have given a name to my pain and call it 'dog'" (*GS*, p. 249). The dog in the vision relocates the pain from the past to the present. Zarathustra now recognizes that the dog is not merely howl-ing but is rather crying for help. There on the ground lies a young shep-herd, "writhing, gagging, in spasms, his face distorted, and a heavy black snake hung out of his mouth" (*TSZ*, p. 271).[24] The snake seems to have crawled into the young man's mouth while he was asleep and has bitten itself fast into his throat. He is overcome with nausea and pale dread. Zarathustra is impelled to help. He attempts to pull the snake out, but in vain.

In part 1 Zarathustra had identified himself with the eagle and the ser-pent, the proudest of animals and the wisest of animals, respectively. Here the serpent has become the eternal return of the same disgust and the same pain, the abysmal causality that underlies the world-weary wisdom of the soothsayer and the dwarf, or (to use an earlier reference) the nauseating wisdom of the suprahistorical perspective. The shepherd is not Christ, the Good Shepherd, but closer to the antichrist, and in any case Zarathustra's alterego. He is choking on the thought, or even the knowledge, that everything mediocre will recur eternally. As Zarathustra says later, "My sighing sat on all human tombs and could no longer get up; my sighing and questioning croaked and gagged and gnawed and wailed by day and night: 'Alas, man recurs eternally! The small man recurs eternally!'" (p. 331).

This much is largely given in the text. We advance beyond it if we see the small man, the mediocre human being, as a rejected part of Nietzsche himself—invalid (ill) or invalid (not valid), not manly, rather the "miserable little man" that is concealed by his narcissistic grandiosity. Zarathustra is then choking on the humiliating thought or sense of his impotence. We go deeper, however, when we see the snake as symbolizing melancholia and abjection, the self-identifications that, in their recurrence, induced Nietzsche's nausea and pale dread. And we provide a psychic location for this experience if we take its orality seriously. The shepherd then would be seen as a nursling in an abjective and persecutory relationship to the breast (symbolized by the snake) that nurses him. He is small, weak, dependent, and envious of the one who has what he lacks. His rage and envy—his ressentiment and his rancune—are projected into the nurturing breast. It is filled with the defiled, perhaps excretory, parts of himself and becomes overwhelmingly disgusting and dangerous. In this way, the tables have been turned—his desire to bite it has become its biting into him. He is being strangled and suffocated.[25]

To put this more concisely, my basic intuition about the interaction of the shepherd and the snake is that it symbolizes abjection as a paranoid phenomenon. And viewed this way, the problem itself suggests the solution: splitting, breaking off contact with the persecutory and abjected breast. Because this is the structurally given—that is, schizoid—solution, pulling the snake out must necessarily be ineffectual. To detach the snake without injury to either party would be a process of working things out, and the either/or structure of the paranoid-schizoid position precludes this kind of emotional development. Instead, there must be a clean break: "Then it cried out of me: 'Bite! Bite its head off! Bite!' Thus it cried out of me—my dread, my hatred, my nausea, my pity, all that is good and wicked in me cried out of me with a single cry" (p. 271). The original situation of the infant who wants enviously to bite the breast is now restored. Activity that became passivity has again become activity. The snake is to be killed, beheaded (castrated if one prefers to gender the snake as masculine), and the infant is to be liberated—manically freed from its infantile dependency.

And yet, as always with such purely psychoanalytic interpretations, there is another perspective. In Nietzsche's terms, pulling the snake out is an attempt to deny what the snake means. The snake is the eternal return of the same. Once the thought has "gained possession of you" (*GS*, p. 274), it cannot be made to go away. It must be engaged, indeed embraced. One must affirm life just as it is, without the desire to change anything in it. For desiring to change what has been and what therefore will be again is a craving for revenge. One judges and condemns one's life—it is not what it ought to have been. But it is precisely *this* desire, this human, all-too-human response to suffering, that condemns one eternally to melancholia and abjection. Driven by it, one is precisely a small man, mediocre and miserable, too weak to take in and digest what life serves up. Hence the only solution to the problem of eternal return is to bite into it—to mobilize one's will to power to say "yes" even to the nausea of the encounter itself. (And it is Zarathustra's will to power that speaks through him, not his rational mind that tells the shepherd what to do.) And so "the shepherd . . . bit as my cry counseled him; he bit with a good bite. Far away he spewed the head of the snake—and he jumped up. No longer shepherd, no longer human—one changed, radiant, *laughing!* Never yet on earth has a human being laughed as he laughed!" (*TSZ*, p. 272). Transparently, this is Nietzsche's own experience of the sublimity of eternal return. He affirms eternal return, overcoming the last resistance to life's suffering. He has access to all of life and triumphantly experiences the maternal sublime.

There is, however, a problem with this reading. Let's grant that the snake cannot be harmlessly released—that is, that freeing both snake and shepherd would be an avoidance of eternal return. Still, in what sense is biting off the head of the snake and spewing it out an affirmation? This seems rather like the abjective act itself, with a manic version of the sublime as its consequence. Hence the shepherd's sublime laughter (Nietzsche's own laughter)—indeed, in its very sublimity—is precisely human, all-too-human. It is a mood or state of mind which passes away and which, as Kristeva says, overstrains the human organism that has been possessed by it. The price of sublimity is recurrent abjection. The interpretation of the parable calls its intended meaning into question, a question that is not just psychoanalytic. Rather, the act of biting off the snake's head is problematic in Nietzsche's own terms. One might even see the situation that he presents as aporetic. Because the snake has bitten into his throat, the shepherd cannot swallow it and truly allow it to enter him—which is what amor fati and the real acceptance of eternal return would seem to demand. But biting off the head, while indubitably an overcoming of disgust and a kind of self-affirmation, is not an affirmation of the nausea itself.

There is, within certain limits, a psychoanalytic way of solving this problem. For the difficulty arises only when the idea of recurrence is dread-filled, which is to say, when the pain of living, then or now, drags one—for defensive reasons—into the paranoid-schizoid position. In this psychic situation, there are a limited number of options. Overcoming terror and disgust, biting into one's own abjection and melancholia, is a formidable demonstration of the will to power, in either Nietzsche's sense or our own. Well might we ask ourselves, would we be able to do the same?

14.

Not a fair question? Here's a true story. A friend of mine had been a Marine in his youth. In boot camp, one of his fellow recruits had a horror of snakes. The drill sergeant captured a snake (a rattlesnake, I believe) and held it, one hand behind the head and the other near the tail, in front of the young man. He moved it up and down, up and down, hypnotically, and then barked out the command, "Bite!" The recruit bit the snake in half and, in that action, conquered his fear—and not only of snakes.

15.

In "On the Vision and the Riddle," Zarathustra has articulated but not fully accepted eternal return. He has distanced himself from it by encapsulating it within a kind of dream and by embodying the experience of it in the shepherd. It is not yet his own. It is not until we are close to the end, in the section "The Convalescent," that he first summons it as his own most abysmal thought. This action quite overwhelms him, and he has to recover from it (hence the title of the section). He has left the world of men behind and is surrounded by his animals. They speak to him comfortingly of eternal return, paralleling in this regard the beloved disciple at the end of part 2. He characterizes their telling of the tale a "hurdy-gurdy song," not because they misrepresent the thought but because they—as animals—cannot grasp its human, all-too-human gravity. He retreats inside himself and into a space that becomes increasingly erotic. The stark, paranoid-schizoid setting of "On the Vision and the Riddle" gives way to Zarathustra's Bacchic pursuit of "life," who is figured as a maenad. When he catches her, or she catches him, he whispers the secret of eternal return in her ear, surrendering his wisdom to her and himself to eternal return. Then "life was dearer to me than all my wisdom ever was" and with successive strokes of a cosmic clock, we rise orgasmically into "The Yes and Amen Song":

> Oh, how should I not lust after eternity and the nuptial ring of rings, the ring of recurrence.
> Never yet have I found the woman from whom I wanted children, unless it be this woman whom I love: for I love you, O eternity.
> For I love you, O eternity! (P. 340)

By the time we reach Zarathustra's supreme moment, eternal recurrence has been gendered feminine. Zarathustra is a lover, ecstatically united with his beloved. "Eternity" has lapsed back into Goethe's "Eternal-Feminine," which draws the soul heavenward. Where once eternal return posed the *problem* of the abject and the sublime, now its own becoming has disappeared into the sublime itself. Momentarily, it approximates to Kristeva's notion of women's time as the "eternal recurrence of a biological rhythm which conforms to that of nature and imposes a temporality whose stereotyping may shock, but whose regularity and unison with what is experienced as extra-subjective time, cosmic time, occasion vertiginous visions and unnameable *jouissance*." But only momentarily, because for Nietzsche if not Zarathustra, vertiginous visions and unnamable jouissance passed once more into melancholia and abjection. Hence—Kristeva aside—we join in the hurdy-gurdy song of Zarathustra's animals when we interpret the eternal return of the same as an "eternal recurrence of a biological rhythm." We come closer to the mark when we recognize that its abysmal meaning reflects a profound disruption of precisely those rhythms.

5

Only the Lonely/
"Woman as Such"

Then Agave cried out: "Maenads, make a circle
about the trunk and grip it with your hands.
Unless we take this climbing beast, he will reveal
the secrets of the god." With that, thousands of hands
tore the fir tree from the earth, and down, down
from his high perch fell Pentheus, tumbling
to the ground, sobbing and screaming as he fell,
for he knew his end was near. His own mother,
like a priestess with her victim, fell upon him
first.

—Euripides, *The Bacchae*

1.

I come now—appropriately enough, given my interpretation of eternal
return—to Nietzsche's engagement with the feminine. As in the last chapter, I begin by creating a conceptual space for the exploration. The investigation then proceeds from cultural surface to personal depth, taking up in
turn the intertextual evolution of Nietzsche's thinking about women and
femininity, Zarathustra's internalization of the feminine in *Thus Spoke
Zarathustra*, and finally Nietzsche's actual relationship with women. In the
latter regard, the focus will be on his short-lived and ill-fated relationship

with Lou Salomé—the decisive breaking point in his relationship with women and his construction of the feminine.[1]

I. Body Language

2.

In the last chapter, we were primarily concerned with abjection and melancholy and their related opposites, sublimity and mania. Here the focus is more on the development of sexual difference. Like the problem of gender formation in general, this is a complicated and much controverted area. It is even misleading to speak of a "moment" or single period in which gender is fixed or consolidated. Gender emerges, is formed and reformed, from birth through adolescence and beyond. For present purposes, however, we will collapse time into a hypothetical moment and limit the discussion to themes of especial relevance to Nietzsche.

The recognition of sexual difference occurs in the language of bodies and is accompanied by intense anxiety. Within the emergent masculine imaginary and from the masculine perspective, maleness is identified with possession of a penis, femaleness with its absence. The vagina signifies the reality of castration. It is the horrifying proof that the boy can be unmanned.

Castration anxiety is not the whole story. As Karen Horney argued early on (1933), neither female identity nor feminine anxieties can be contained within the masculine model (see also Bernstein 1990; Tyson 1994; Dorsey 1996; and Richards 1996). Even for little boys, the vagina is not just an absence covering over a wound. It is also, if paradoxically, an object of desire—that is, an object of the very desire for sexual union with the mother that carries with it the threat of castration. And at a deeper, sensuously encoded level, it is "known" to be the entrance to the womb. In this regard it is the dangerous passageway into the magical, (re-)generative, and self-destroying interior of the mother's body. In multiple respects, then, the vagina is in the position of the negative in the male imaginary: it signifies the not-yet-self (the mother-world from which the masculine self emerges), the not-self (the feminine other), and the no-longer-self (castration as loss of masculine identity).

Let's be just a bit more systematic. Here is one version of the prehistory of masculine phantasy:

- The interior of the mother's body. There is a sensuously encoded memory of intrauterine existence, along with the birth process that brings it to an end. The interior of the mother's body, later identified as her womb, figures in phantasy as a domain of infinite riches and gratification (Aladdin's or Sinbad's cave), on the one hand, and as a horrifying, "fathomless" depth or void—infinite, empty space—on the other. It can also be figured as limitation and suffocation when it becomes fused with the birth process. In the latter regard, passage into and out of the body becomes associated with intense, self-shattering anxiety. Consequently the passageway itself, eventually understood to be the vaginal canal, is magically enticing or just as magically terrifying.

- The neonatal relationship. The child is only partially differentiated from the mother. He *is* her as much as, or more than, he *has* her. The mother is experienced as environment or world, not yet as a self. This does not mean she lacks intention, but her intentions are the creation of infantile projection. Hence she/it can be experienced as enraged, devouring, intensely desiring, and so forth—not as a self, however, but as a force of nature.[2]

- The son is not the mother. To become himself, as male, he must be not-her, as female. He must split off, perhaps by abjective means, the part of himself that is her in order to have her. The penis begins to take on its meaning as signifier of sexual difference. It then determines or plays its part in relation to the mother, who is now beginning to be a woman:

  - The penis is identified with the self. Phantasies of entrance via the vagina into the mother's body carry with them the threat of self-dissolution.

  - The penis is taken to be a part of the son's body. Phantasies of using it to penetrate the mother's vagina are associated with fears that it will be lost there, absorbed, bitten off, cut off. Because the father does not figure into this phantasy, we might view this as a preoedipal form of castration anxiety.[3]

  - The vagina is not a penis or is the absence of a penis. It is a castrated male genital. Hence it must be disavowed. Veiling the pudendum is one form of disavowal; phallicizing the woman's genitals is another. The phallic mother is not the original maternal or sexual incarnation but rather a defense against the terrible temptation of attempted entry into the maternal/feminine orifice. The phallus is the mother's flaming sword, which cuts off access to the Garden of Eden.

- As noted, the father does not figure into these phantasies. But after the initial stages of the process, he is more excluded than absent. The mother's phallus is displaced from the father as much as it is projected from the son. When it is replaced as paternal attribute, it is the phallus proper, the almighty aegis / the aegis of the Almighty, signifier of the Law. The threat of castration now proceeds from oedipal rivalry in the proper sense. God the Father drives Adam from the Garden of Eden, and he places the flaming sword at its entrance. And so the son, guiltily identified with the father, passes into the world of men.

3.

Like his psychoanalytic successors, Nietzsche too spoke body language. He had, in fact, an unusual philosophical interest in female genitals.

Consider Sarah Kofman's approach to this subject in her provocative "Baubô: Theological Perversion and Fetishism" (1988).[4] Kofman begins from the question of Nietzsche's purported misogyny: "Does Nietzsche not himself repeat the ancient theological misogyny that woman is the locus and source of all evil? . . . Or should this famous misogyny not itself be rethought and reevaluated from a standpoint that would differentiate it into types?" (p. 177). She observes, as do many other writers, that for Nietzsche "woman is a surface that mimes depth" (p. 191). Female "modesty appears as a beguilement that permits the male to desire a woman without being petrified (*médusé*); it is a veil which avoids male homosexuality, a spontaneous defense against the horrific sight of female genitalia, and the opportunity for life to perpetuate itself" (ibid.). This view fits with the preceding remarks, linking them, appropriately, to misogyny.

In contrast to this masculine horror of the female genitals, Kofman focuses on Nietzsche's invoking of the figure of Baubô in the 1886 preface to *The Gay Science*. As we remember, Baubô makes Demeter laugh by lifting her skirts and exposing her belly and genitals. Her iconic representation emphasizes her vulva. She is unveiled, fecund, and bawdy female sexuality. Kofman links her to Dionysus and considers them both to be names for "protean life" (p. 198).

How to reconcile these two images, Medusa and Baubô? Kofman claims, plausibly enough, that Nietzsche's feelings for women were shaped by his profoundly ambivalent relationship to his mother. And so the "maxims and arrows Nietzsche directs toward women: Is not their very severity the mark of this ambivalence? Are they not symptomatic of a deep love for women, all of whom had abandoned him, when they might have served him as a lightning rod?" (p. 199).

Kofman's argument usefully draws our attention to women's bodies, sexuality, and Nietzsche's mother. (We'll bypass the odd, or in light of our preceding comments perhaps not so odd, figuration of woman as lightning rod.) It is notably empathic, especially in its claim that Nietzsche was abandoned by women that he loved. If Nietzsche were Kofman's patient, this might well have been his self-presentation. But with the exception of Lou Salomé and, more ambiguously, his sister, Nietzsche was not abandoned by women—rather he abandoned them, preferring or needing his solitude. As for his mother and his sister, recall the excised text from *Ecce Homo* cited in the last chapter:

> Were I to look for the deepest contradiction to me, I would always find my mother and my sister—to believe myself related to such *canaille* would be a blasphemy on my godliness. The treatment I have experienced from the side of my mother and sister . . . infuses me with an unspeakable horror: here is at work a perfect infernal machine, [one that operates] with an unfailing certainty as to the moment when I can be bloodily wounded—in my highest instances. (Strong 1985, p. 327)

As we know, this passage does not tell the whole story. Nietzsche's actual relationships with his mother and sister do demonstrate considerable ambivalence. And I would certainly grant Kofman that misogyny is complex and in need of subtle psychoanalytic investigation. But subtlety should not be used to cover over Nietzsche's evident hostility toward the women who were closest to him. Moreover, the reference to Baubô is not so affirmative as Kofman seems to claim. It is indecent, Nietzsche implies, to look too closely at the truth. One should rather respect the "bashfulness" of nature. For perhaps "truth is a woman who has reasons for not letting us see her reasons? Perhaps her name is—to speak Greek—*Baubô?*" (*GS*, p. 38). Truth = woman, reasons = vulva. But what are the real reasons for not looking? Indeed, are we (male philosophers) to look or not look? Kelly Oliver suggests that "Baubô lifting her skirts . . . may also threaten castration" (1995, p. 117). A good reason, then, for not looking. Elsewhere in *The Gay Science*, Nietzsche claims that old women are more skeptical than men: "They consider the superficiality of existence its essence and all virtue and profundity is to them merely a veil over this 'truth,' a very welcome veil over a pudendum—in other words, a matter of decency and shame, and no more than that" (*GS*, p. 125). This sounds to me like the phobic male conception of the vagina as an absence, a no-thing covering over a missing thing. And even if the vagina signifies everything, a plenum and an infinite richness, it is still nothing more than a space filled with masculine phantasies of an eternal feminine.

Let's take a step back. We human beings are embedded in complex webs of social and cultural relationships that markedly influence how we see the world. Sexuality and gender are among the most basic of these relationships, hence also among the most basic loci of the will to knowledge. This does not mean that all knowing is structured by sexuality and gender, although some contend that it is. But human knowledge is more structured by sexuality and gender than we (men especially) have been willing to admit.

It cannot be said that Nietzsche was a protofeminist who subjected the stereotypes of gender to critical scrutiny or who breached the sexual divide, in an attempt to see things from women's perspectives. Yet he does take sexuality and gender seriously. He creates a discursive space where these issues can be contested, even if we find ourselves contesting these issues with him. And this is a gain in comparison with philosophizing that denies the significance of sexuality and gender altogether—that insists on the nonperspectival neutrality or objectivity of human knowledge.

Nietzsche regularly wrote about men and women, but of greater present concern is the way in which he inflected apparently nongendered concepts with gendered meaning. Thus in the passages cited above, truth is a woman or a woman's genitals. And we remember that in *Thus Spoke Zarathustra* the search for knowledge is metaphorically presented as a sexual contest: "Brave, unconcerned, mocking, violent—thus wisdom wants *us*; she is a woman and loves only a warrior" (*TSZ*, p. 153). Wisdom is a woman who wishes to be overpowered; seekers of wisdom are warriors who violently overcome her resistance. The will to power here functions in characteristically masculine fashion.

Perhaps because they are both stereotypical and demeaning of women, we might be inclined to disregard this gendering of epistemic relationships. One strategy for so doing is to split off Nietzsche's metaphors from his concepts. This is the procedure I followed in my psychoanalytic appropriation of the will to power—a legitimate procedure, I would argue, so long as we are concerned with our own theorizing. But when we are concerned with the interpretation rather than the appropriation of Nietzsche's thinking, such an approach must be rejected. For Nietzsche persistently crosses the line between concept and metaphor and, by so doing, denies us the right of ignoring the gendering of his worldview.

Here we touch on an issue that was largely avoided in Chapter 3. In the usual order of epistemic things, concepts are associated with philosophical truth and metaphors with artistic illusion. There is also a tendency to align the one with processes of discovery and the other with processes of creation. This is not to say that, in actual practice, the realms of philosophy and poetry can be so neatly differentiated. Witness Plato's *Republic*, in which these divisions are simultaneously proclaimed and dramatically disregarded. One could even characterize the history of philosophy in the West as a succession of failed attempts at either establishing the relationship or maintaining the distinction between the categories. But we nonetheless tend to differentiate between facts and fancies in our everyday ordering of experience.

Nietzsche boldly disregards these boundary markers. Wherever it goes, the will to power overcomes resistance. It imposes form and creates meaning. We are not speaking here of a creation ex nihilo. A reality of some kind, a world of raw material, is presupposed. But truth and beauty are equally impositions on reality. No fundamental distinction can be maintained between philosophical "truthification" and artistic falsification.

The will to power provides a common ground for concept and metaphor, and in *Thus Spoke Zarathustra*, the difference between the two can scarcely be maintained. But even before his discovery or invention of the will to power, Nietzsche did not accept the order of epistemic things. This comes through most clearly in the relatively polished although not published essay of 1873, "On Truth and Lies in a Nonmoral Sense." Here he argues, as he does later on, that words are inherently falsifying, that they impose equivalences that do not really exist. But he pushes the argument further. Metaphors are given epistemological priority; they are the original creative falsifiers of reality. The concept is "merely the *residue of a metaphor*," the product of forgetfulness:

> Only by forgetting . . . [the] primitive world of metaphor can one live with any repose, security, and consistency: only by means of the petrification and coagulation of a mass of images which originally streamed from the primal faculty of human imagination like a fiery liquid, only in the invincible faith that *this* sun, *this* window, *this* table is a truth in itself, in short, only by forgetting that he himself is an *artistically creating* subject, does man live with any repose, security, and consistency. (In Breazeale 1990, p. 86)

In this aestheticized epistemology, metaphors are horizons, and concepts are narrower horizons. To separate concepts from their metaphorical origins is to reify and deaden the artistically created world.

Thus the younger Nietzsche reduces concepts to metaphors, while the older one effects a glissade between the two.[5] Either way, a different light is shed on his perspectivist practices. The reality of ordinary things does not disappear, nor does the background issue of reality itself. But if there is only a relative difference between concept and metaphor, only a difference of accent or emphasis, so to speak, and not a difference of essence, then no clear line may be drawn between historical and fictional narratives. Hence when we read Nietzsche's more historical works, such as *On the Genealogy of*

Morals and *The Antichrist*, we find plausible empirical interpretations freely mixed together with a priori constructions and willful impositions of meaning.

At least during the great moments in which he conceived and gave birth to Zarathustra, Nietzsche occupied a transitional space in which the distinction between what is real and what is not, hence also between concept and metaphor, was held in abeyance. We could even say that, when he was possessed by his most abysmal thought, his words were merely surface expressions of a preverbal maternal depth. This is not to reintroduce outworn ideas about masculine intellect and feminine aesthetic, with concepts pointing in one direction and metaphors in the other. It is to suggest that fluidity in gender identity might have something to do with the magic of transitional spaces and secret gardens—even or especially when they have to be created in utter solitude.

II. From "Woman and Child" to "Woman as Such"

4.

It is always hazardous to impose a trajectory on a philosopher's work. What if, for example, Nietzsche had died just after the publication of *Human, All Too Human?* If we read him at all, we would note his advance from the Wagnerian, Schopenhauerian, and quite German romantic / metaphysical stance of *The Birth of Tragedy* to a position much closer to Enlightenment skepticism and rationality. The *Untimely Meditations* would be seen as transitional works of self-liberation. But Nietzsche did not die at that time, thus the trajectory lengthens. *Human, All Too Human* itself appears as transitional, a means and not an end. And what if Nietzsche had not become insane in 1889? Might not the body of work extending from *Thus Spoke Zarathustra* to the texts of 1888 be seen as a transition to yet another philosophical orientation (assuming, that is, that Nietzsche did not simply work within a circle of consolidation but continued to open up new interpretive ground)?

Put otherwise, all philosophy should be viewed as work in progress, as a process of becoming, and, to the extent possible, from within the process and progress of the author's thinking. Yet each of us passes beyond becoming into being or (as Hegel might say) into the identity of being and nothing. That is, we die. Death imposes a certain finality on the work we have done. Although substituting a philosophical corpus for the philosopher's ongoing self-activity opens the door to metaphysics, essentialism, and all the otherworldly escapes from the anxious contingency of this-worldly life, retrospect too has its place. Looking backward, we can see patterns that are meaningful to us, whatever they might mean to the author.

In the Nietzschean instance, it does not violate his self-understanding to see his philosophizing as leading into and out of *Zarathustra*.[6] First comes *The Birth of Tragedy* (1872), which might be seen as a prelude, a preliminary orchestration of themes or the embryonic form of Nietzsche's subsequent philosophizing. Then comes a series of works which have a primarily critical quality and which are characterized by a kind of restraint. Next we have *Zarathustra*, with its dramatic casting away of restraints, opening up of new stylistic possibilities, and articulation of affirmative doctrines. Finally, on the other side of *Zarathustra*, Nietzsche works through his Zarathustrian experience.

As already noted, Nietzsche's philosophizing about women and his figuration of the feminine fits within this trajectory.

5.

Virtually the first words of *The Birth of Tragedy* sexualize its subject matter: artistic development is bound up with the duality of the Apollonian and Dionysian, "just as procreation depends upon the duality of the sexes, involving perpetual strife with only periodically intervening reconciliations" (Nietzsche 1872 [hereafter *BT*], p. 33). Moreover, the Dionysian is articulated in the (masculine language) of the feminine; it is formless, "nonvisual," rapturous, torrential, akin to intoxication: "In Dionysian art and its tragic symbolism . . . nature cries to us with its true, undissembled voice: 'Be as I am! Amid the ceaseless flux of phenomena I am the eternally creative primordial mother, eternally impelling to existence, eternally finding satisfaction in this change of phenomena!'" (p. 104). The Apollonian, in contrast to the primordial mother of the Dionysian, is masculine: formed and formal, disciplined, self-contained, and individual—also imitative and illusory.

Unlike the preoedipal mother of much psychoanalytic theory, who is benignly containing and undesiring, the Dionysian mother-world is intensely, violently sexual. Dionysian festivals "centered on extravagant sexual licentiousness, whose waves overwhelmed all family life and its venerable traditions; the most savage natural instincts were unleashed, including even that horrible mixture of sensuality and cruelty which has always seemed to me to be the real 'witches' brew'" (p. 39). Not surprisingly, therefore, descent into the Dionysian dissolves the Apollonian *principium individ-uationis*. Perhaps a bit more surprisingly, emergence from the Dionysian induces nausea:

> For the rapture of the Dionysian state with its annihilation of the ordinary bounds and limits of experience contains, while it lasts, a *lethargic* element in which all personal experiences of the past become immersed. This chasm of oblivion separates the worlds of everyday reality and of Dionysian real-ity. But as soon as this everyday reality re-enters consciousness, it is expe-rienced as such, with nausea: an ascetic, will-negating mood is the fruit of these states. (P. 60)

The will is sickened and paralyzed by immersion in the Dionysian; only artistry, the Apollonian capacity to impose form on the formless and re-create illusion as a defense against the experience of disillusionment, reme-dies the disease. Or, to recur to the earlier analysis, the Dionysian experi-ence must be abjected.

From more than one perspective we can say, *hic Rhodus, hic saltus:* here is the problem that Nietzsche had to solve. It would not be stretching the point to say that his subsequent philosophizing was a kind of Apollonian wrestling with the Dionysian, the product of a desperately maintained masculine individuality contending with the allure of submersion in a destructive/erotic mother-world. But his self-experimentation is equally a Dionysian assault on the Apollonian, a partially willed, partially involuntary attempt to lose himself in the selfsame mother-world.

If we read him with some interpretive license, we may define Nietzsche's Rhodes somewhat more precisely. Anticipating and in some ways going beyond Freud, he poses this question:

> Oedipus, the murderer of his father, the husband of his mother, the solver of the riddle of the Sphinx! What does the mysterious triad of these fateful deeds tell us?
>
> There is a tremendously old popular belief, especially in Persia, that a wise magus can be born only from incest. With the riddle-solving and mother-marrying Oedipus in mind, we must immediately interpret this to mean that where prophetic and magical powers have broken the spell of present and future, the rigid law of individuation, and the real magic of nature, some enormously unnatural event—such as incest—must have occurred earlier, as a cause. How else could one compel nature to surren-der her secrets if not by triumphantly resisting her, that is, by means of

something unnatural. It is this insight that I find expressed in that horrible triad of Oedipus' destinies: the same man who solves the riddle of nature—that Sphinx of two natures—must also break the most sacred natural orders by murdering his father and marrying his mother. Indeed, the myth seems to wish to whisper to us that wisdom, and particularly Dionysian wisdom, is an unnatural abomination; that he who by means of his knowledge plunges nature into the abyss of destruction must also suffer the dissolution of nature in his own person. (P. 68)

Where Freud views Oedipus as violating the Law of the Father, Nietzsche views him as desecrating the primordial, Dionysian mother. This reminds us of how preoedipal the oedipal really is, how rooted it is in the hungry, ruthless prehistory of (in this case) the male individual. When we join these two developmental dramas and bring them together in one moment of experience, we have the gateway of masculine individuation. And from this perspective Nietzsche's own fate seems genuinely uncanny. Driven to pursue Dionysian wisdom, symbolically and epistemologically violating the oedipal and preoedipal order, he did in fact "suffer the dissolution of nature in his own person."

6.

The portentous gendering of philosophical and aesthetic experience in *The Birth of Tragedy*, so plainly visible to us, was less visible to Nietzsche himself. He concocted his Dionysian witches' brew out of a combination of Schopenhauer, Wagner, and an ingenuous reading of the Greek tragic tradition. It would take time before a metaphysics (or depth psychology, if you prefer) of the masculine and feminine took root and grew in him. The work is, in every sense, anticipatory.

By the time we reach *Human, All Too Human*, Nietzsche is more clearly speaking in his own voice. And here, in the section entitled "Woman and Child," we find his first attempts at characterizing women and sexual relations. The title largely tells the tale: women enter the field of psychological and cultural analysis in the company of children, from whom they are little differentiated. Women are assigned to their conventional social location, and the core gendered value—the superiority of men to women—is maintained. Thus, "all society that does not elevate one draws one down, and conversely; that is why men usually sink a little when they take wives, while their wives are elevated a little" (Nietzsche 1878–80; 1886 [hereafter *HH*],

p. 151).[7] In other words, the actual sexual relations of Nietzsche's society are clearly visible in his commentary, even if they are shorn of their sentimentality and sanctity.

Amid or underlying the fragmentary, aphoristic form of this section, we find a coherent story. The basic theme is that men and women are able to abide each other only with considerable difficulty. Free spirits—men with a mission or a capacity for greatness . . . men, in short, like Nietzsche—view women as snares and marriage as captivity. "Will free spirits live with women? In general I believe that, like the prophetic birds of antiquity, as present-day representatives of true thinking and truth-telling they must prefer *to fly alone*" (p. 426). The section ends by excluding women altogether: "'O Criton, do tell someone to take these women away!', Socrates finally said" (p. 160).

Although Nietzsche had not yet reconciled himself to his solitude, we see him already valorizing and allegorizing his future condition. We can also interpret him as commenting on his past: "Everyone bears within him a picture of women derived from his mother: it is this which determines whether, in his dealings with women, he respects them or despises them or is in general indifferent to them" (p. 150). Moreover, every man will find a mother in his wife, whether or not he desires one: "In every kind of womanly love there also appears something of motherly love" (p. 151). And this mother-love will prove suffocating for the free spirit:

> *The golden cradle.*—The free spirit will breathe a sigh of relief when he has finally resolved to shake off that motherly watching and warding with which women govern him. For what harm is there in the raw air that has so anxiously been kept from him, what does one real disadvantage, loss, mischance, sickness, debt, befooling more or less in life mean, compared to the unfreedom of the golden cradle, peacock-tail fan and the oppressive feeling that he must in addition be grateful because he is waited on and spoiled like a child? That is why the milk offered him by the women who surrounded him can so easily turn to gall. (P. 426)

Surely we hear echoes of Nietzsche's relationship with his mother—which, true to his own dictum, was the foundation of his later attitude toward women.[8] And it might well be the case that other men in his culture (and ours) would share this view.

Thus far we have Nietzsche commenting primarily on men's experience of women in their maternal function. He has not yet appropriated and transformed that function into masculine generativity. Meanwhile, he offers us an enduringly "Nietzschean" portrayal of sexual relations as a kind of masquerade, in which the participants play different roles in relation to one another. In one instance marriage is a kind of mutual blindness. Women possess reason, men passion, although the latter use their reason more effectively because they are driven to do so by their passion. If, therefore, in marriage women seek intellectual brilliance and men seek emotional depth, "it is clear that at bottom man is seeking an idealized man, the woman an idealized woman" (p. 153). This is marriage depicted as disguised, mutual narcissistic object choice. But rather more conventionally, it is men who fall victim to feminine deceits: "There are women who, however you may search them, prove to have no content but are purely masks. The man who associates with such almost spectral, necessarily unsatisfied beings is to be commiserated with, yet it is precisely they who are able to arouse the desire of the man most strongly: he seeks for her soul—and goes on seeking" (p. 152). Yet the deceiver may be self-deceived. Women invented the idolization of love because it "enhances their power and makes them seem ever more desirable in the eyes of men." But they have forgotten its origins and have become "entangled in their own net." Now they are more deceived than the men and "consequently suffer more from the disillusionment that is almost certain to come into the life of every woman—insofar as she has sufficient intelligence and imagination to be deceived and disillusioned at all" (p. 154).

Substantively, Nietzsche portrays women as "much more personal than objective" (p. 155), as desiring "a quiet, calm, happily harmonious existence" (p. 159), but as more dangerous than men "in a state of hatred" because then they are unhampered by "considerations of fairness" and because "they are practiced in discovering the wounded places everyone, every party possesses and striking at them: to which end their dagger-pointed intellect renders them excellent service" (p. 154). Women, martially as well as maritally, are a threat to men's virility and freedom. The sexual masquerade is also a power struggle.

Although the characters and relationships we find in "Woman and Child" certainly reappear in Nietzsche's later writing, *Human, All Too Human* and the works that immediately followed it—*Assorted Maxims and Opinions* (1879), *The Wanderer and His Shadow* (1880), and *Daybreak* (1881) constitute a distinct phase in Nietzsche's thinking in general and his thinking about women and sexual relations in particular.[9] To put it no doubt too simply, Nietzsche is here an Enlightenment thinker. Where *The Birth of Tragedy* begins with a preface to Richard Wagner, *Human, All Too Human* is dedicated to Voltaire.[10] Moreover, with its relatively dry, matter-of-fact style and skeptical and ironic attitude, *Human, All Too Human* betrays a markedly Enlightenment sensibility. Thus we find a kind of clarity and amused dispassion in the depiction of sexual roles, rather than the strident and defensive insistence on them that typifies the later works. Even the emancipation of women (for example, *HH*, section nos. 416, 425) is treated in a somewhat restrained and thoughtful manner; later, Nietzsche's approach is strongly polemical. At the same time, these writings largely lack the use of women as metaphor, the theme of male pregnancy, and the general stylistic eroticism that emerges with *The Gay Science*.[11] In short, Nietzsche is here more conventionally masculine in perspective and style than he would later become.

7.

Relatively speaking, in *Human, All Too Human* Nietzsche is working close to the social surface. By the time he writes *The Gay Science*, the psychic location has begun to change. The sharp break of *Zarathustra* lies just ahead, but Nietzsche's style has already become more distinctive, self-assured, playful, and poetic. We can begin to see the outlines of an aestheticized and eroticized inner world.

In *The Gay Science* the free spirit still views women from a distance, but he also has begun to fall in love with the image of them he has created. Further, women are no longer confined to the social space (signified by a separate textual section) of woman and child, and the figurative use of the feminine has been dramatically expanded. Nietzsche's eroticized inner world is simultaneously gendered.[12]

For example, in a section on the cultural role of discontent, Nietzsche claims that the "weak and quasi feminine type of the dissatisfied has a strong sensitivity for making life more beautiful and profound; the strong and masculine type, to stick to this metaphor, has a sensitivity for making life better and safer" (*GS*, p. 98). Stereotypical enough, to be sure, as is the identification of the feminine with decadence:

> The former type manifests its weakness and femininity by gladly being deceived occasionally and settling for a little intoxication and effusive enthusiasm, although it can never be satisfied altogether and suffers from the incurability of its dissatisfaction. Moreover, this type promotes all those who know how to provide opiates and narcotic consolations, and it resents all who esteem physicians above priests: thus it assures the *continuation* of real misery. (P. 99)

Nietzsche's ostensible concern is with European misery, thus it might seem desirable to rid Europe of its feminine tendency. But this is not his conclusion: "Europe is sick but owes the utmost gratitude to her incurability and to the eternal changes in her affliction: these constantly new conditions and these no less constantly new dangers, pains and media of information have finally generated an intellectual irritability that almost amounts to genius and is in any case the mother of all genius" (ibid.). Here we have gender detached from men and women and transformed into a trope for cultural tendencies. Gender stereotypy has been preserved and, if anything, intensified. Femininity is a disease. But life (change) ceases without illness; decadence is generative.

This passage does not tell us very much about Europe or about femininity and masculinity (whatever these might be). But it speaks eloquently about Nietzsche, whose suffering and need for opiation during the immediately preceding period was, as we know, especially intense. It testifies to the creative use to which he put his suffering and to the identification of his illness with femininity. This personal experience is projected outward. Nietzsche's inner world appears in the guise of the outer one.

Nietzsche would not accept this confident differentiation of inner and outer worlds, but he would certainly acknowledge more free play in his use of gender categories. Toward the end of book 4, just before his first statement of eternal return and first evocation of Zarathustra, there is his first unequivocal feminization of life: "perhaps this is the most powerful magic of life: it is covered by a veil interwoven with gold, a veil of beautiful possibilities, sparkling with promise, resistance, bashfulness, mockery, pity, and seduction. Yes, life is a woman" (p. 272). It need hardly be added that life is a woman for a man. (Or perhaps that woman is life for a man.)

Within the space created by the projection of gender categories, Nietzsche makes important analogical use of women. In adjoining sections of book 2, he uses men's love of women as a metaphor for the artist's love of his object and a sailboat seen from shore as a metaphor for women seen at a distance.[13] The latter passage reduces to a rather simple and familiar meaning. Women are magical beings who evoke for men their better selves—but only so long as one is not close to them. Here again we have the free spirit who cannot tolerate intimacy, only now he is drawn to women as he imagines them to be.

The former passage is, if somewhat ambiguously, more revealing. "When we [men] love a woman, we easily conceive a hatred for nature on account of all the repulsive natural functions to which every woman is subject" (p. 122). These "repulsive natural functions" stand for everything in nature that men cannot bear and against which they defend themselves by the creation of artistic dream worlds. "We artists," as he puts it, are "somnambulants of the day" (p. 123). Thus, on the one hand, Nietzsche analyzes the defensive functions of artistic idealization; on the other, he identifies himself as an artist. Either way, the starting point is repulsion at women's bodily functions. In the ideal artistic world, as when women are seen at a distance, these can be veiled and perfumed. Likewise women's genitals. Recall the passage on skeptical old women, for whom truth is "a veil over a pudendum." Again there is an ambiguity. Nietzsche, after all, chooses to compare truth to a pudendum and thus calls attention to women's genitals. But this "truth" is properly obscured. Now you see it, now you don't.[14]

Perhaps menstruation is the link between men's repulsion at women's bodily functions and the need to occlude the vagina. If so, it signifies both abjection and castration anxiety. This provides us, preliminarily, with one of the reasons for Nietzsche's personal and philosophical self-enclosure. Still, if life is a woman, a man cannot do without her, and so Nietzsche re-creates women as internal objects and dream images.

The women we find within this deepening philosophical space continue to be defined in relation to men: "Will is the manner of men; willingness that of women—truly, a hard law for women" (p. 126), but a law nonetheless. And, as if to bring to light the consequences of this law, in the next section Nietzsche discusses the "capacity for revenge": "Would a woman be able to hold us (or, as they say, 'enthrall' us) if we did not consider it quite possible that under certain circumstances she could wield a dagger (any kind of dagger) *against* us? Or against herself—which in certain cases would be a crueler revenge (Chinese revenge)" (ibid.). In his inner world, Nietzsche is fascinated by women's capacity for revenge, but not (one would infer) in the outer one.

We might also read Nietzsche as providing women with an additional incitement to vengeance. In a section on "female chastity," he notes that upper-class women "are to be brought up as ignorant as possible about erotic matters," into which they are then plunged abruptly: "And then to be hurled, as by a gruesome lightning bolt, into reality and knowledge, by marriage—precisely by the man they love and esteem most! To catch love and shame in a contradiction and to be forced to experience at the same time delight, surrender, duty, pity, terror, and who knows what else, in the face of the unexpected neighborliness of god and beast!" (pp. 127–28). The "ultimate philosophy and skepsis of woman casts anchor at this point," Nietzsche continues. Afterward she drops a "deep silence" around the experience and "closes her eyes to herself." As a consequence, women "easily experience their husbands as a question mark and their children as an apology or atonement" (p. 128). And might another consequence be a willingness to wield a dagger against men, their children, and themselves?

Thus Nietzsche reverses perspective in quite an interesting fashion. Woman as internal object is also a subject; men and women appear as mirror images of each other. The veil over the pudendum—women's superficiality and silence—that shields men from castration anxiety simultaneously occludes the experience of defloration. Assuming that menstruation is one of women's "repulsive natural functions," it seems to signify castration on the one side and sexual violation on the other. The relationship of men and women is, so to speak, consanguine.

These passages are followed by sections on mothers who "find in their children satisfaction for their desire to dominate" and on "misshapen" infants whom it is cruel to let live. Not a happy tale, to be sure. Still, mother love "is to be compared with an artist's love for his work": "Pregnancy has made woman kinder, more patient, more timid, more pleased to submit; and just so does spiritual pregnancy produce the character of the contemplative type, which is closely related to the feminine character: it consists of male mothers.—Among animals the male sex is considered the beautiful sex" (p. 129). Here we approach the state of mind in which Nietzsche gave birth to Zarathustra. It has little to do, I think, with a woman's experience of pregnancy, but it does reflect with some accuracy widespread male phantasies about pregnancy. And it speaks to one of the major motives for men's artistic creativity, namely, envy of women's capacity to give birth to children. Artistic creation in men is often stimulated by and a simulation of impregnation, pregnancy, and childbirth. This does not make of spiritual pregnancy a maternal experience, however, except in the sense that men associate kindness, patience, timidity, and submissiveness—in other words, passivity and receptivity—with maternity.

We see, then, that the story of sexual relations told in *The Gay Science* has recognizable antecedents in *Human, All Too Human*. There is still a battle of the sexes, a fear of marital and maternal engulfment, a sensitivity to masks and masquerades, and so on. But—at least so it seems to me—the story has become more subtle and is told with considerably more artistic grace. It is also more interesting. It takes place in an eroticized, feminized, and masculinized field, constructed figuratively rather than demarcated socially. The violence of sexual desire is sometimes alluded to, sometimes directly invoked. And at another level, gender roles and sexual identities have become more fluid. One might even argue that the gaiety of *The Gay Science* results from Nietzsche's ability to tap his own erotic wellsprings; if this view is accepted, one might read the text as spreading outward from a core of sexual phantasy.

8.

By the time Nietzsche writes *Beyond Good and Evil*, the joyfulness has gone out of his relationship with women and femininity. We begin on a familiar note: "Supposing truth is a woman—what then? Are there not grounds for the suspicion that all philosophers, insofar as they were dogmatists, have been very inexpert about women?" (*BGE*, p. 2). The text goes a considerable way toward justifying the implicit claim that Nietzsche can more successfully woo the truth than can the dogmatists, but it does not support the other implicit claim that he is an expert when it comes to women. To the contrary, he now sounds more like a rejected suitor than a charming seducer.

There are substantive continuities in Nietzsche's conception of women and sexual relations. Sexual relations continue to be exercises in misrecognition ("The sexes deceive themselves about each other—because at bottom they honor and love only themselves" [p. 87]; "The same affects in man and woman are yet different in *tempo:* therefore man and woman do not cease to misunderstand each other" [p. 82]); women remain dangerous ("In revenge and in love woman is more barbarous than man" [p. 88]); and the truth remains veiled by women's modesty ("Science offends the modesty of real women. It makes them feel as if one wanted to peep under their skin—yet worse, under their dress and finery" [p. 87]). But a different kind of sexual violence has entered the picture: "From old Florentine novels; also—from life: *'Buono femmina e mala femmina vuol bastone [Good women and bad women want a stick].' Scchetti, Nov. 86*" (p. 89).

When he comes to his more sustained discussion of men and women, Nietzsche puts perspectivist brackets around his opinions: "about man and woman . . . a thinker cannot relearn but only finish learning—only discover ultimately how this is 'settled for him'" (p. 162). It is for this reason that his comments on "woman as such" are only his truths. In the present context, however, we need not return to questions about how seriously he intends us to take his substantive positions or the general status of truth-claims in his philosophy. More germane is the sense of something finished and settled— also fundamental and foolish: the convictions involved in such things as sexual relations lead us to "the great stupidity we are, to our spiritual *fatum*, to what is *unteachable* very 'deep down'" (ibid.). This tone of self-mockery and epistemological modesty seems intended to soften somewhat the harshness of the forthcoming comments about women. It also refers obliquely to painful lessons learned and simultaneously places Nietzsche's gay and experimental exploration of the feminine in the past tense.

The term "woman as such" refers to claims put forward by women about women, in an effort to enlighten men: "Woman wants to become self-reliant—and for that reason is beginning to enlighten men about 'woman as such'" (ibid.). This forsaking of feminine modesty, superficiality, and deceitfulness is "one of the worst developments in the general *uglification* of Europe." For woman "has much reason for shame," much that was "repressed and kept under control by *fear* of man" (p. 163). Now women "threaten with medical explicitness what woman *wants* from man." Yet men may wonder "whether woman really *wants* enlightenment about herself, whether she *can* will it" when her "great art is the lie, her highest concern mere appearance and beauty" (ibid.). And so the man who is a friend to women counsels them to stop compromising themselves through enlightenment. His advice? "*mulier tacit de muliere:* woman should be silent about woman" (p. 164).

Postmodern feminists have rightly emphasized the ways in which modernist discourse silences women. If we align Nietzsche with postmodernism, we'd have to add, "Not only modernist discourse."

In any case, the section on "woman as such" is a diatribe against both emergent feminism and the Enlightenment. The irony and detachment of the free spirit has given way to a sarcastic, mocking, and hyperbolic anti-modernism. Modernity has corrupted woman and upset the proper balance between the sexes. There is "the most abysmal antagonism" and "an eternally hostile tension" between men and women (p. 166). Women appropriately feared men, a fear that anchored their "most womanly instincts" (p. 167). But now women have unlearned fear and have simultaneously deprived themselves of their "proper weapons" in the sexual wars (p. 169). Thus modernity has unarmed as well as unanchored women, and it has made them ill: "Almost everywhere one ruins her nerves with the most pathological and dangerous kind of music (our most recent German music) and makes her more hysterical by the day and more incapable of her first and last profession—to give birth to strong children" (p. 169).

In this depiction of women's decadence, we recognize Nietzsche himself. After all, he is the one with the ruined nerves, a hypersensitivity to German (Wagnerian) music, and a style that has become hysterical. The light touch and fluidity of *The Gay Science* have been replaced by a strident insistence on woman's proper place and function. Nietzsche is no longer willing to listen to what women say, with their "medical explicitness," about what they want from men. Consequently, he has nothing very revealing to say about them. Instead, his "great stupidity" about women truly has been revealed. Stripped of its earlier veils and metaphorical charm, it is shown to be the age-old masculine essentialism, in which men are to be feared, women as well as children are to be seen and not heard (spare the rod and spoil the . . .), and women's only vocation is childbirth. In the end, the section on "woman as such" amounts to the self-disclosure of an anti-Enlightenment man rather than a critical exposure of enlightened women.

III. "For I love you, O eternity"

9.

The darkened vision and increased stereotypy of *Beyond Good and Evil*, when compared with *The Gay Science*, leads us to ask, what happened to Nietzsche between the writing of the one and the writing of the other? A fair question but one that ignores a gap in my textual presentation of Nietzsche and the feminine, namely, *Thus Spoke Zarathustra*. So I turn to the dreamscape of *Zarathustra*, reading it now from the perspective of its protagonist's relationship to women, the feminine, and the maternal.[15] I will then provide an answer to the biographical question.

When he was thirty years old, Zarathustra left his home and retired to the mountains. Ten years later he is overflowing with wisdom: "I am weary of my wisdom, like a bee that has gathered too much honey; I need hands outstretched to receive it" (*TSZ*, p. 122). And so he goes under—descends to the society of men.

The plain meaning of this passage is that Zarathustra has filled himself or has been filled with new ideas, and he is just bursting to tell someone about them. This can be interpreted as male pregnancy and the need to give birth or, even more easily, as a buildup of sexual tension that demands release in and through an other. He needs to plant his seed. We shall see, however, that we needn't choose between these interpretations. One of the more interesting features of Zarathustra's experience is the elision of the distinction between these two demands.

Zarathustra's first teaching is the overman. The overman represents the project of overcoming existing human valuations, hence also a perspective from which to evaluate them. Overcoming existing values requires knowing and experiencing them—that is, going under. Going under is not only Zarathustra's way of giving others the gift of his wisdom but also the path and process through which he overcomes the human, all-too-human in himself. This overcoming is not gender neutral. The man who would be (wills himself to be) overman treats wisdom as a warrior treats a woman. He takes her, conquers her, overcomes her resistance, bends her to his will. The woman who is wisdom loves the man, and only the man, who can overpower her.[16]

In Zarathustra's teachings, sexual violation is not merely a trope. At sundown, with night coming on, a "little old woman" (not quite materialized—she talks not to him but to his soul) asks him to speak about women. He resists: "About woman one should speak only to men." Women should not know the truth about women. The little old woman persuades him that she will not betray his secret: "Speak to me too of woman; I am old enough to forget it immediately" (p. 177). "I am beyond the age of sexual desire," we might hear her saying, "and therefore pose no threat to you."

Zarathustra's wisdom about women preserves the atmosphere of sexual violence we found in *The Gay Science* but anticipates the essentialism of *Beyond Good and Evil*:

> "Everything about woman is a riddle, and everything about woman has one solution: that is pregnancy. Man is for woman a means: the end is always the child. But what is woman for man?
>
> "A real man wants two things: danger and play. Therefore he wants woman as the most dangerous plaything. Man should be educated for war, and woman for the recreation of the warrior; all else is folly." (P. 178)

It might seem that sexual relations are misalliances and mutual misunderstandings, as they were in *Human, All Too Human*. Women want children, men want a plaything. Their goals seem disjunctive. But while woman "understands children better than man does," man "is more childlike than woman." In a "real man a child is hidden." The child wants to play. Woman releases the child in man by being his plaything. And even her desire for a child merges with the imperative of his will: "Let your hope be: May I give birth to the overman!" (ibid.). Thus men and women fit together: "The happiness of man is: I will. The happiness of woman is: he wills" (p. 179). One might even build a marriage on this foundation. "Marriage," Zarathustra later proclaims, "thus I name the will of two to create the one that is more than those who created it. Reverence for each other, as for those willing with such a will, is what I name marriage" (p. 182).

The little old woman is appreciative of Zarathustra's wisdom. So in gratitude she gives him a "little truth," which is figured as an infant. Hence this truth can be seen as a product of her union with him. It is, "You are going to women? Do not forget the whip!" (ibid.).

A famous photograph shows Nietzsche and Paul Rée in the position of horses pulling a cart, while Lou Salomé rides in the cart, threatening them with a flowered whip. Hence there is a biographical irony concealed in

Zarathustra's teaching. Using it as one's interpretive perspective, one might read the present text as pretext or as parody and pathos. But not much in the text itself suggests the legitimacy of such a subversive interpretation. The little old woman concludes without contradicting Zarathustra's own wisdom about women. She is also the woman who, as the figuration of wisdom, loves only a warrior. Moreover, "On Little Old and Young Women" is preceded by a section on friendship, of which women are deemed incapable: "Woman is not yet capable of friendship: women are still cats and birds. Or at best, cows." Woman knows only love, not friendship, and "even in the knowing love of a woman there is still assault and lightning and night along side light" (p. 169). In their own way, women do get to fight back. But for the most part, when combat ends and married life begins, they drag men down to their level. Although Zarathustra may articulate the ideal of a creative marriage, when he turns to the actual institution he characterizes it as a "long stupidity" in which "two beasts find each other" (p. 183).

We see, then, that Zarathustra's conception of sexual relations in part 1 is of a piece with Nietzsche's general characterization of them, on the one hand, and with the later darkening of his sexual vision, on the other.

10.

Zarathustra's mood changes significantly in the second part. He continues to teach but in a new voice—more poetic, reflective, internal, and sometimes rhapsodic. Substantively, the will to power takes center stage: "Where I found the living, there I found will to power" (p. 226). It does not simply accompany life, as we know, but is life itself: "And life itself confided this secret to me: 'Behold,' it said, 'I am *that which must always overcome itself*'" (p. 227). The overman slips into the background, although he does not quite disappear. He, of all men, embodies an affirmative will to power and enacts the imperative of self-overcoming. Thus the shift from the overman to will to power is a movement from living individual to life process—a kind of deindividuation, or a sliding of the Apollonian into the Dionysian.

The first part ends and the second part begins with Zarathustra retreating from human company: "Then Zarathustra returned again to the mountains and the solitude of his cave and withdrew from men, waiting like a sower who has scattered his seed" (p. 195). But with the passage of time "his wisdom grew and caused him pain." Sexual tension and pregnancy have become less distinguishable. He continues in a phallic (or perhaps urinary) mode: "Mouth have I become through and through, and the roaring of a stream from towering cliffs: I want to plunge my speech down into the valleys. Let the river of my love plunge where there is no way" (p. 196). But he characterizes the "wild wisdom" which has grown within him and which demands release as a "lioness" and as a woman: "My wild wisdom became pregnant on lonely mountains; on rough stones she gave birth to her young, her youngest. Now she runs foolishly through the harsh desert and seeks gentle turf—my old wild wisdom. Upon your hearts' gentle turf, my friends, upon your love she would bed her most dearly beloved" (p. 197). The boundaries of self and other, male and female, pregnancy and sexual interaction, are disappearing. One could see Zarathustra as impregnating his wild wisdom and, through this union, bringing forth a new doctrine. But he also has been impregnated by or with her. She is in him, so that he is pregnant with her pregnancy and gives birth to her child who is also his child. S/he then wants to bed her beloved child in the love of his friends. They are to be impregnated in their turn.

In this transformed space, Zarathustra's encounter with the feminine is less sadistic, more erotic, and more melancholy. In "The Night Song" he presents himself as an unrequited lover or as an infant yearning to be nursed. Night has come, the songs of lovers awaken, and a craving for love is within him: "Light am I; ah, that I were night! But this is my loneliness that I am girt with light. Ah, that I were dark and nocturnal! How I would suck at the breasts of light!" (p. 217). Light and dark are metaphors for those who give and those who receive. Zarathustra gives and does not receive. He envies those to whom he gives for their capacity to receive: "Oh, it is only you, you dark ones, you nocturnal ones, who create warmth out of that which shines. It is only you who drink milk and refreshment out of the udders of light." Thus night confronts him with his loneliness: "Night has come: alas, that I must be light! And thirst for the nocturnal! And loneliness!" (p. 219).

As if in response to his song of longing, in the next section ("The Dancing Song") Zarathustra encounters girls dancing in a forest.[17] We are reminded of Pentheus in *The Bacchae*, who spied on the maenads and was torn to pieces as punishment for his impiety. This time, however, no violence occurs. Zarathustra sings a song, to which the girls and Cupid dance. The song doubles the scene, for its theme is a kind of dance between Zarathustra and "life," who is characterized as "changeable and wild and a woman in every way" (p. 220). She is virtually indistinguishable from his wild wisdom. Each is seductively feminine, and each is equipped with a little "golden fishing rod" with which she pulls men out of the "unfathomable" womanly depths (ibid.).

What are we to make of this golden fishing rod, which reminds us of Kofman's lightning rod? In the symbolism of *The Birth of Tragedy*, it would represent an element of Apollonian, masculine individuality preserved within the Dionysian, feminine abyss. It also seems to be Zarathustra's phallic or umbilical link to a maternal version of the feminine—a link that, at the same time, safeguards him against sinking into the fathomless interior of the mother's body. It prevents the dissolution of his individuality in the preoedipal mother-world. But it is her phallus, not his—his genitals projectively identified as hers. Life/woman/wisdom is the phallicized mother, woman with her genitals fetishistically transformed so that the terror of castration need not be confronted by the man. Comforted by the sight of her phallus, he need not fear the loss of his own.

And so Zarathustra is saved. But the song and dance ends, and the girls depart.

The "dancing song" is Zarathustra's second and last encounter with women who are not internal objects, as well as a moment in which they are more deeply internalized. At this point, however, he gains only cold comfort from their presence within him. He is left chilled and sad, surprised to find that he is still alive when the song has ended.

The mood of loneliness and intimation of death bring us to the "Tomb Song." The tombs contain the visions of Zarathustra's youth. The song is in part a mourning for their passing:

> O you visions and apparitions of my youth! O all you glances of love, you divine moments! How quickly you died. Today I recall you like dead friends. From you, my dearest friends among the dead, a sweet scent comes to me, loosening heart and tears. Verily, it perturbs and loosens the heart of the lonely seafarer. I am still the richest and most enviable—I, the loneliest! For once I possessed you, and you still possess me: say, to whom fell, as to me, such rose apples from the bough? I am still the heir of your love and its soil, flowering in remembrance of you with its motley virtues, O you most loved ones. (P. 222)

Zarathustra continues in a far more bitter vein, angrily denouncing those who sullied and attempted to strangle the "songbirds of my hopes" (p. 223). Thus when we combine the three songs, we have a tale of loveless love. Zarathustra yearns for love in the "Night Song," cannot touch (and is abandoned by) the girls of the "Dancing Song," and is both melancholy and bitterly angry in the "Tomb Song." From this perspective, it is easy to comprehend the sadomasochistic portrayal of sexual relations in the first part of the text, and we are prepared for Zarathustra's increasing isolation in the third. But they also tell a tale of self-preservation: Zarathustra survives the shattering of his hopes by keeping his songbirds alive in the garden of his memory. And how is he able to do this? How did his "soul rise again out of such tombs?" He answers: "Indeed, in me there is something invulnerable and unburiable, something that explodes rocks: that is *my will*. Silent and unchanged it strides through the years." His will enabled him to "get over and overcome" his wounds (p. 224). And so the "Tomb Song" is followed by "On Self-Overcoming," in which the truth of the will to power is finally proclaimed.

11.

The second part ends with Zarathustra again driven away from human company, this time by his inability to face and speak eternal return, the final part of his wisdom. The third part of the text depicts his journey back to his mountain, in the course of which he faces his final trial—will he overcome or be overcome by his most abysmal thought?

I need not repeat the analysis of eternal return as Zarathustra articulates it in "On the Vision and the Riddle." It clearly marks an important moment in his struggle to give voice to the truth that he carries inside himself. The reward for his courage is a shift in mood. In the following section ("On Involuntary Bliss"), he is again alone and grateful for his solitude. Late afternoon finds him feeling happy but anticipating the return of his unhappiness. Afternoon passes into evening and evening into night, and his melancholy does not reappear. Rather, as morning breaks, "happiness itself came closer and closer to him." Then Zarathustra says to himself: "Happiness runs after me. That is because I do not run after women. For happiness is a woman" (p. 275). Here it is quite explicit that surrender of blissful (erotic) interaction with women is a precondition for Zarathustra's experience of blissful feelings within himself.

Zarathustra travels once more through the world of men, but it disgusts him. Glad to leave it behind, he reaches his home: "O solitude! O my home, solitude! Too long have I lived wildly in wild strange places not to return home to you in tears. Now you may threaten me with your finger, as mothers threaten; now you may smile at me, as mothers smile" (p. 295). His mother, solitude, speaks to him, gently chiding him for the enthusiastic hopes with which he went forth into the world, sympathizing with his experience of being forsaken, and reassuring him that here, with her, he may speak his mind without reserve. In this way Zarathustra's isolation is transformed into a maternal space resembling the "good enough" (Winnicott 1971, p. 11) or emotionally containing (Bion 1962, pp. 90–91) mother we find in psychoanalytic object relations theory. His solitude alone—the establishment or reestablishment of this maternal mental space—will make it possible for him to bear the weight of eternal return.

Next comes a leave-taking. "On the New and Old Tablets" is a grand summation of Zarathustra's teaching, directed backward toward the world of men. In "The Convalescent" his animals speak in their way the truth he is struggling to speak in his own. When he falls silent, they steal away. Zarathustra, now and finally alone with his soul, bids it sing, and we have "The Other Dancing Song."

Life, here unmistakably a maenad, leads Zarathustra in a wild bacchic pursuit. Catching up with her and weary of being her "sheepish shepherd," he chants to her:

> You witch, if *I* have so far sung to you, now you shall cry.
> Keeping time with my whip, you shall dance and cry!
> Or have I forgotten the whip? Not I! (*TSZ*, p. 338)

Zarathustra has taken the little old woman's wisdom to heart, and we would seem to be headed for a climax of sexual violation. But life is unintimidated: "O Zarathustra, don't crack your whip so frighteningly! After all, you know that noise murders thought—and just now such tender thoughts are coming to me" (p. 338). She would be reconciled with him, and he accepts her offer of peace. She knows he is tempted to abandon her; he whispers something in her ear that the reader does not hear but knows to be the secret of eternal return. They weep together, and "then life was dearer to me than all my wisdom ever was" (p. 339). His painful knowledge of eternal return has joined him to life rather than separated him from "her," and we have the ecstatic union of "The Seven Seals"—Zarathustra's ultimate affirmation of eternal return, hence also the final refutation of the spirit of gravity from "On the Vision and the Riddle" and the final transmutation of the parable of the madman who announced the death of God:

> If ever I spread tranquil skies over myself and soared on my own wings into my own skies; if ever I swam playfully in the deep light-distances, and the bird-wisdom of my freedom came—but bird-wisdom speaks thus: "Behold, there is no above, no below! Throw yourself around, out, back, you who are light! Sing! Speak no more! Are not all words made for the grave and heavy? Are not all words lies to those who are light? Sing! Speak no more!" Oh, how should I not lust after eternity and the nuptial ring of rings, the ring of recurrence.

Never yet have I found the woman from whom I wanted children, unless it be this woman whom I love: for I love you, O eternity.

For I love you, O eternity! (P. 340)

The Apollonian has been merged with the Dionysian, all is plentitude, and all values have been transvalued. Zarathustra experiences the truth of the world that words cannot express, the truth beyond or before there was speech. He has simultaneously fallen and risen into the maternal sublime. The madman's cold and disorienting infinite space has become the eternal feminine. At the same time, the experience is intensely erotic. The eternal feminine is the ultimate object of desire. Zarathustra, immersed in her, experiences what amounts to a spiritual orgasm. Castration anxiety has been vanquished, and at this moment, he is supremely procreative.

But if—no doubt more vulgarly—we take the sexual theme quite literally, then the final sexual union is masturbatory. Zarathustra, in his solitude, makes love only to himself.

12.

In sum, *Thus Spoke Zarathustra* depicts its protagonist's appropriation and internalization of the feminine. Through a process of autogestation, in which he is both male and female, impregnator and impregnated, he re-creates his mind (his solitude) as a maternal space. Within this space and, as it were, in the second generation, he stages a drama of seduction and sexual union in which there is—but only apparently—a feminine other to his masculine self.

Zarathustra's ultimate triumph is also his ultimate defeat. In the end as in the beginning, he is alone. His attempt to find a place in the outer world for himself and his teachings has been a failure. The world of women and men is noxious and nauseating to him. It fills him with a great disgust, and it has caused him great pain. He is better off without it, at one with *his* eternal feminine.

With this picture of Zarathustra in my mind, I am forcibly reminded of the final scenes in the movie *Brazil*. The protagonist is being subjected to unbearable torture. We see him being miraculously rescued. He and the woman he loves reach safe haven in the countryside. But as the rescue proceeds, the sense of reality attached to it diminishes. We are not really surprised when we find ourselves back in the torture chamber. The protagonist, who throughout the film is portrayed as a dreamer of the most vivid dreams, has escaped into a split-off, erotic dream state, but his tormented body remains behind.

IV. Ecce Homo

13.

When we turn from the text to the author, we find ourselves viewing a drama staged against the backdrop of Nietzsche's prior relationships with women and consisting of three acts: his experience of eternal return, his encounter with Lou Salomé, and the massive internalization of the feminine that resulted in the birth of his "son" Zarathustra.

Second only to his mother, the most important woman in Nietzsche's life was his sister, Elisabeth. Although he consistently treated her with big brotherly and characteristically masculine condescension, and while he manifestly placed a greater value on his male friendships, she was his most intimate childhood companion. During the 1870s, he often relied on her as fellow traveler, manager of his household, and attendant to him in his illness. He also periodically tired of her company and found it necessary to escape from her.

Elisabeth, for her part, idealized her brother. She was very possessive of him and especially of his good reputation. She defined the latter in largely conventional terms. Hence she was gratified and reflexively dignified by his early appointment to the professorate and his position as an esteemed member of the Wagner circle. She was disapproving when his devotion to Wagner was replaced by his friendship with the young philosopher and psychologist Paul Rée, who was Jewish; and she was appalled at his intensifying immoralism, which she attributed in part to Rée's influence. But before the appearance of Lou Salomé, the differences between brother and sister could be contained by familial loyalty, shared aristocratic pretensions, and a mutual concern for outward propriety.

Although, for all members of the family, proper conduct included a strict correctness in relationships between the sexes, Nietzsche took sexual propriety a significant step further. The sexual passions were to be overcome, and chastity was their self-overcoming. From his perspective, abstinence was self-affirming and self-expressive. But from another angle, chastity can be seen as a defense against castration and other sexual anxieties. Remember in this regard the brothel incident from Nietzsche's student days: confronted with women's sexuality, he was *médusé*—frozen in terror and disgust. This is not to say that he completely repudiated sexual activity. After the onset of his insanity, he told a doctor that he had "infected himself twice in 1866" (Hayman 1980, p. 10). The presumption is that the disease was venereal, hence that he had sexual intercourse at least twice. If in these instances sex was a disease, in others it was prescribed as a cure: Nietzsche apparently reported having had sex several times in Italy, "on doctor's orders" (in Salomé 1988, p. xli). This might be the basis for Lou Salomé's claim that Rée warned her that Nietzsche "was not as innocent as he seemed: Nietzsche had sworn him to secrecy when they were together several years earlier in Sorrento and it was obvious to Rée that his friend had entertained visits from a village girl" (p. liii). Rée was Nietzsche's rival for Salomé, hence his testimony must be taken with a grain of salt. But even if we credit it, along with such other evidence as exists concerning Nietzsche's sexual experience, we would have to conclude that he was largely, if not entirely, "innocent."[18]

Thus while Zarathustra may proudly proclaim that he never ran after women, Nietzsche can be viewed as running away from them. And speaking both for himself and through his double, he scarcely bothers to conceal the reasons for his flight. The "free spirit" of *Human, All Too Human* "will breathe a sign of relief when he has finally resolved to shake off that motherly watching and warding with which women govern him." In *The Gay Science*, he finds them easy to hate "on account of all the repulsive natural functions" to which they are subject, and he views it as a matter of "decency and shame" to keep their pudenda veiled. And Zarathustra, who praises sexual abstinence for those who are chaste "through and through," prefaces his teaching on chastity this way: "I love the forest. It is bad to live in cities: there too many are in heat. Is it not better to fall into the hands of a murderer than into the dreams of a woman in heat? And behold these men: their eyes say it—they know of nothing better on earth than to lie with a woman. Mud is at the bottom of their souls; and woe if their mud also has spirit!" (*TSZ*, p. 166). Men's sexual desire muddies the soul, women's sexual desire is murderous or worse. Thus sexuality goes the way of the mother-world. It is abjected.

14.

In the early versions of psychoanalytic theory, spiritual or cultural creativity is seen as resulting from the sublimation of the sexual drives. If we extend the concept of sexuality to the erotic as a life-drive (as does Freud in his late metapsychology), then we would say that the life of the mind comes at the expense of the life of the body. Although I do not share this conceptual perspective, it provides a convenient metaphor for Nietzsche's creativity. One could say that his life drives were so mentalized that almost no life-giving eros was left for his body. Hence, on the one hand, his psychophysiological abjection and, on the other, his access to spiritual sublimity.

Metaphors aside, I have argued that the idea of eternal return arose out of the conjuncture of the abject and the sublime and that this experience was the matrix of *Thus Spoke Zarathustra*. What needs to be emphasized here is that the initial experience of eternal return had a profound effect on Nietzsche's view of himself and his mission. He believed that he had unlocked the basic secret of the spiritual and moral, perhaps also the physical, universe, and he was eager for students and disciples. His mood is reflected in Zarathustra's opening speech. He too was like "a bee that has gathered too much honey" and "need[s] hands outstretched to receive it." And so Nietzsche prepared to "go under"—to forsake his solitude and once more attempt to live among men.

Let me put the point more theoretically. By the late 1870s, Nietzsche's tolerance for intimate interaction with other people had been reduced to a minimum. The social other was almost always persecutory or suffocating; he preserved himself by withdrawal and isolation. For example, Rée came to visit him in Genoa in early 1882. After one week, he wrote to Elisabeth: "With Dr. Rée's visit so far, as was to be expected, all has *not* gone well. The first day, best of spirits; the second endurable only with the help of restoratives; exhaustion the third, fainting in the afternoon; the attack came that night; the fourth in bed; the fifth up again, only to lie down again in the afternoon; the sixth and till now, perpetual headaches and weakness" (in Binion 1968, p. 48). In this instance, Nietzsche acclimated himself to company and was in good health until the day Rée left, when he again fell ill. But the basic point seems clear: both closeness to and separation from other people were painful and debilitating. Hence his isolation—his persistent occupancy of the schizoid extreme of the paranoid-schizoid position.

The experience of eternal return did not change this basic personality configuration. But it did, albeit intermittently, give Nietzsche access to hitherto abjected life forces. These forces themselves constituted a pressure and a demand. Indeed, perhaps Zarathustra's opening speech understates Nietzsche's sense of pent-up potency and we should turn instead to the opening of part 2: "My impatient love overflows in rivers, downward, toward sunrise and sunset. From silent mountains and thunderstorms of suffering my soul rushes into the valleys" (*TSZ*, p. 196). So when Paul Rée wrote to him about a fascinating and intelligent young Russian girl, he wrote back: "Greet this young Russian from me if you think it does any good. I am greedy for her kind of souls. In the near future I am going to rape one" (in Peters 1962,

p. 86). It is souls, not bodies, that Nietzsche desires to ravish, and the letter was written in a high-spirited and prankish mood, but one can still read in it the disaster that lay ahead. Salomé—fiercely intelligent, strong willed, and determined to make her own way in the world—was not about to be overcome by Nietzsche's will to power, be it spiritual or carnal.

Nietzsche was introduced to Salomé in April 1882, and was immediately captivated.[19] He wrote to Peter Gast (Heinrich Köselitz): "She is twenty years old; she is shrewd as an eagle and brave as a lion, and yet still a very girlish child, who perhaps will not live long. . . . She is most amazingly well prepared for *my* way of thinking and my ideas" (in Middleton 1969, p. 186). Partially, as we see here, he viewed her as his perfect student. At a deeper level, he thought she might be his heir and—at the same time—his spiritual bride. In June, he wrote to her, "I am now seeking people who could be my heirs; I carry something around with me absolutely not to be read in my books—and am seeking the finest, most fertile soil for it" (Binion 1968, p. 67). He would implant his ideas in her. Most of all, he thought she was his feminine counterpart. Ida Overbeck, the wife of his loyal friend Franz, insightfully commented that, in Lou, he thought he had found his *"alter ego"* (p. 55). Nietzsche himself wrote to Franz Overbeck, "Our mentalities and tastes are most deeply akin—and yet there are so many contrasts too that we are for each other the most instructive of subjects." Lou agreed: "How alike we think and feel . . . and how we do take the thoughts and words out of each other's mouth" (p. 82). In September, he wrote to her, "Your idea of reducing philosophical systems to the personal records of their originators is truly an idea arising from a 'brother-sister brain'" (Salomé 1988, p. 3). And the sense of kinship and union had even deeper resonances. He wrote to Gast concerning Lou's poem "An Den Schmerz" (To pain), "It is among the things which quite overpower me; I have never been able to read it without tears coming to my eyes; it sounds like a voice for which I have been waiting and waiting since childhood" (Middleton 1969, p. 186).

Again using a concept as a metaphor, we imagine a nursing interaction of infant and mother that has routinely failed to yield pleasure to either party. The two participants are locked into a vicious circle of recurrent pain, the continuation of which is assured by their anticipation of mutual failure. But one day, quite inexplicably, the baby awakens in a mood of pure sunshine, while his mother is in a benignly forgetful state of mind. The burden of the past slips away; mother and child enjoy a blissful, unburdened moment of mutual gratification.

In using this metaphor, I hope to convey something of the wonder and vulnerability that characterized Nietzsche's relationship with Salomé. He had experienced years of suffering, then the great noon of eternal recurrence with its gift-giving demands—and now there was Lou, his perfect erotic/intellectual/spiritual other. He was convinced that his life had changed directions and that his exile from human relations had come to an end. For her part, Lou was assuredly in search of spiritual inspiration. Yet, despite their very real affinity, the two spiritual lovers were destined to part. He was looking for a disciple and (at least) spiritual bride; she was determined to retain her independence. She did not want to lose her personality in his, although she had a susceptibility to sublimated erotic union. And he was unable to resist attempting to imprint himself on her, although he had a sincere desire that she become her own woman. In the end, she would go her own way, and he would have to return to his mountain and his solitude.

Thus the structure of *Thus Spoke Zarathustra* is reflected in the life of its author: from solitude to erotically tinged interaction and back into solitude. Nietzsche finds his "feminine" side externally embodied in Salomé and takes it back into himself when she is no longer available. At the same time, Nietzsche's vision of women darkened. This was not simply, or even primarily, the result of his disappointed hopes in Salomé; he was capable of affirming the tragedy of a great loss. It was rather how the relationship ended, and not the mere ending of it, that embittered him.

The story has four central characters, each of whom could tell it from his or her own perspective. There is first Paul Rée. From the beginning, Salomé had been involved with Rée as well as with Nietzsche. Indeed, her bond with Rée was more reliable and less oppressive—he was more interested in serving her than in imposing his philosophical will on her. But it seems he could not resist competing for her love and loyalty by sullying the reputation of his friend (Binion 1968, pp. 71–80). Presumably he portrayed Nietzsche as wanting to use her as both secretary and sexual object. His remarks on Nietzsche's sexual experiences in Italy probably were made in this context, and one can imagine that he was trying to undermine Nietzsche's claim to purely spiritual interest in Salomé.

Next there is Salomé. Her emotional connection to Nietzsche was profound, and her interest in his philosophy, sincere. But quite apart from her determination to retain her independence, she does seem to have kept from him her evolving relationship with Rée, and she reportedly bragged about her influence on him to the Wagnerites, when she attended the Bayreuth festival in the summer of 1882 (ibid., p. 74). From Nietzsche's perspective, each of these actions was a humiliating betrayal.

The third character in the piece is Elisabeth, who, I think it is fair to say, played the most destructive role. Her motives were no doubt complex. An improper and immodest woman was stealing her beloved brother, bringing out all his least admirable traits and beliefs, and holding him up to social ridicule. Initially, she tried to be sympathetic to Salomé, but two incidents decisively undermined this attempt. First, at Nietzsche's request, she had accompanied Salomé to Bayreuth and witnessed the latter's presumed toying with her brother's reputation. Second, just after the festival, she was assigned the task of accompanying Salomé to Tautenberg, where Nietzsche had secured a summer retreat for them. The two women met in Jena. Under the guise of giving Lou big-sisterly advice, Elisabeth reproached her for her behavior at Bayreuth. She also condemned as immoral the plan that Rée, Salomé, and Nietzsche then had of living and studying together in Paris or elsewhere. Salomé did not take kindly to these admonishments. She replied: "Don't get the idea that I am interested in your brother, or in love with him. I could spend a whole night with him in one room without getting excited. It was your brother who first soiled our study plan with the lowest intentions" (in Peters 1962, p. 117). A screaming match followed, and peace was never truly restored.

Elisabeth reported both the Bayreuth and Tautenberg incidents to her brother, but in the short run Nietzsche's bond to Salomé withstood these assaults. He broke with Elisabeth rather than with his friends. And when his mother—responding to reports from Elisabeth—reproached him for his philosophical immoralism by saying that he was a disgrace to the grave of his father, he broke off relations with her as well (Middleton 1969, p. 206).

The fourth player is Nietzsche himself. There is some evidence that he belittled Rée to Salomé, thus mirroring Rée's belittling of him. But for the most part, he conducted himself honorably, although foolishly. He met Salomé after years of encapsulation in a schizoid shell—after years of withdrawal from ordinary human contact, much less something as explosive as a sublimated erotic union with a young woman. The paranoid potential in such a situation was enormous. Moreover, he was in a state of pronounced narcissistic vulnerability. He was the teacher of eternal return, the almost-overman who had risen above morality and all other human, all-too-human experiences. He was descending from his great heights to give humankind its most precious and dangerous gift. Hence nothing could be more devastating than to feel that he had been made to play the fool. And this is just what he felt, when he perceived or realized that Rée and Salomé were a couple, if a chaste one, and that he was the odd man out. Here we have an enactment of the oedipal primal scene, in which the son experiences not only the pain of exclusion but also the humiliation of being the one his mother does not desire. In body language, the father's large penis satisfies the mother's desire as the son's small penis cannot. His oedipal ambitions are laughable. And this laughter, echoing internally, is persecutory. Thus in losing Lou to Rée, Nietzsche resembled nothing so much as the nauseating small man who recurs eternally in *Thus Spoke Zarathustra*. And in this condition, he was vulnerable to emotions he prided himself on having overcome. Spurred on by his sister, with whom he was more or less reconciled, he found himself wanting to counterattack. He craved vengeance. He thought of challenging Rée to a duel, and he wrote bitterly of Salomé that she was "a dried-up, dirty, ill-smelling monkey with false breasts" (Hollingdale 1965, p. 187). So much for the voice he had longed for since childhood!

In one of the despairing moods that accompanied the death throes of the Salomé affair, Nietzsche wrote to Overbeck (December 1882): "This last *morsel of life* was the hardest I have yet to chew, and it is still possible that I shall *choke* on it. I have suffered from the humiliating and tormenting memories of this summer as from a bout of madness. . . . Unless I discover the alchemical trick of turning this—muck into gold, I am lost" (in Middleton 1969, p. 199). He added, emphatically and ironically, "Here I have the most splendid chance to prove that for me 'all experiences are useful, all days holy and all people divine!!!'" (ibid.). And here we have the biographical subtext of the "Tomb Song," which echoes Nietzsche's bitterness and pain:

> "All days shall be holy to me"—thus said the wisdom of my youth once; verily, it was the saying of a gay wisdom. But then you, my enemies, stole my nights from me and sold them into sleepless agony; alas, where has my gay wisdom fled now? . . .
>
> All nausea I once vowed to renounce: then you changed those near and nearest to me into putrid boils. Alas, where did my noblest vow flee then?
>
> I once walked as a blind man along blessed paths; then you threw filth in the path of the blind man, and now his old footpath nauseates him.
>
> And when I did what was hardest for me and celebrated the triumph over my overcomings, then you made those who loved me scream that I was hurting them most. (*TSZ*, pp. 223–24)

Yet to a remarkable extent, Nietzsche was able to turn the muck into gold and to affirm this most painful of experiences. The euphoric moods in which Zarathustra was born are precisely the overcoming of his lacerating pain and depression. Salomé is there symbolically from the beginning: the young woman, shrewd as an eagle, becomes Zarathustra's eagle, appropriately mated to the snake of sexual temptation. The narrative's turning point, at least from this perspective, is constituted by the three songs in which Zarathustra gives voice to his loneliness, sexual desire, and sense of betrayal. One might also read the allegorical moment in "On the Vision and the Riddle" from this angle. As before, the snake on which the shepherd chokes symbolizes an abjective relationship to an object. But now it may be seen as

Nietzsche's desire for union and communion with Salomé, transformed and deformed by his hurt and rage. Biting off the head of the snake is then both a violent breaking off of contact with the woman who betrayed him and an act of autocastration.

To put it perhaps too crudely, with Salomé, Nietzsche bit off more than he could chew; he will not bite again. Zarathustra's plunge into isolation mirrors his creator's surrender of all possibility of intimate interaction. Nietzsche, who hoped to give birth to Zarathustra through Salomé, is forced to give birth to him through himself; Zarathustra, who longs for the other who would give as well as receive in "The Dancing Song," is compelled to play both parts in his ultimate, solitary, erotic union with life—with his own life.

Although *Thus Spoke Zarathustra* may be read as Nietzsche's sublimation of the Salomé affair, a residue was left behind in this process of (al)chemical transmutation. The whole section on "woman as such" in *Beyond Good and Evil* is a sarcastic and condescending rewrite of an essay and aphorisms on women written by Salomé and revised under Nietzsche's supervision in 1882 (Binion 1968, p. 129). We could see this as a belated and misbegotten attempt to generate a text from their "brother-sister brain," but it is more plausibly viewed as the product of Nietzsche's inability to turn all his own emotional muck into philosophical gold: "So much for the 'emancipated woman' who dared to reject me. I'll put her back in her place!"

15.

In *Thus Spoke Zarathustra*, the moment in which one experiences the disorientation of the eternal return of the same is represented as a gateway between past and present (p. 270). The argument put forward in Chapter 4 was that Nietzsche was trapped in the transitional space created by his abjective identification with his mother and his melancholic identification with his father. Or, in his own autobiographical terms, he is dead as his father—his hopes for normative heterosexual masculinity have died—while he is alive as his mother—but under protest. He wishes to go beyond being her but finds himself recurrently returned to his identification with her. This position is simultaneously fixated and fluid. Although he cannot transcend it, it does provide him with a kind of doubled sexual perspective and identity. For just this reason, he is psychologically more interesting than philosophers who, securely identified with the patriarchal order, simply presuppose it. Yet we must remember that the Nietzschean doppelgänger (*EH*, p. 225) lives within masculine phantasy. It would take a separate inquiry to bring the experiences of women into conjunction with this doubled but still masculine imago.

By way of concluding this biographical engagement with Nietzsche, let's briefly retrace the history of gender in his philosophical career. *The Birth of Tragedy* was written when he was in good health, when his academic prospects seemed bright, and when he seemed to have solved the problem of the lost father. He had accepted Schopenhauer as his philosophical guide and Wagner as his musical one. And in the triangular relationship with Wagner and his wife Cosima, he was occupying the space of the oedipal configuration. From this secured position, he precociously and portentously delineated a veritably psychoanalytic model of gender development. The maternal/feminine Dionysian is countered by the individuated/masculine Apollonian. Oedipus signifies the problematic relationship between them. His attempt to penetrate the Dionysian violates the natural order of things and is self-destructive.

Although the psychosexual meanings are here so plain that they hardly require translation, Nietzsche was not yet a psychologist when he wrote *The Birth of Tragedy*. He did not become one until the Schopenhauerian and Wagnerian solution to his version of the oedipal problem failed—that is, when he found himself compelled to reject the authority of both father figures and launch himself along a perilous road of self-definition in defiance of them. The *Untimely Meditations*, which include essays on both Schopenhauer and Wagner, mark this transition. *Human, All Too Human*, written against the background of his deepening psychophysiological crisis, stakes a claim to normative heterosexual identity. Although the free spirit views intimate involvement with women as dangerous and limiting, Nietzsche's approach is quite conventionally masculine in both style and substance. We might see him as simulating postoedipal masculinity, writing as if he were a man among men.

When he passed the age at which his father died, Nietzsche more genuinely entered into the oedipal sphere. *The Gay Science* is far more erotic than the works preceding it. Masculine and feminine, although filled with conventional meaning, are treated more delicately and playfully than hitherto. And the consanguine drama of sexual violence begins to emerge. Yet, if Nietzsche was struggling his way into the oedipal arena when he was working on *The Gay Science*, the Salomé affair pushed him out of it. Viewed one way, he lost out to a male rival (Paul Rée). Viewed another, he was rejected by Lou herself. Either way, he was driven out of the world of male-female interaction. In this context, we have the massive internalization of the feminine in *Thus Spoke Zarathustra*—which, it might be added, follows Nietzsche's established pattern of melancholic identification with a lost love object. And as in the case of all such identifications, there is a substantial residue of hostility. This is managed through splitting. Everything good about women, the feminine, and the maternal is taken into the male self, who thereby becomes self-procreative and self-sufficient. Everything bad about women, the feminine, and the maternal is externalized and essentialized. We end up with the bitter caricature of sexual relationships in *Thus Spoke Zarathustra* and of emancipated women in *Beyond Good and Evil.*

As we know, the story does not have a happy ending. During the autumn of 1888, Nietzsche believed he had finally outlasted his illness. In fact, he was moving ever closer to catastrophic breakdown. He was struggling frantically for self-control and self-preservation, but madness—the Dionysian in its most destructive manifestation—was overpowering him (see Hayman 1980, chap. 13). This is the struggle that is registered in and as *Ecce Homo.* And here we also have Nietzsche's last words about the sexual wars. He claims a profound knowledge of women as part of his "Dionysian dowry." Perhaps, he speculates, he is "the first psychologist of the eternally feminine." All women love him except "*abortive* females, the 'emancipated' who lack the stuff for children" (*EH*, p. 266). But love is inherently deceptive and dangerous. At bottom it is the "deadly hatred of the sexes" (p. 267). So he avoids even, or especially, those who love him: "I am not willing to be torn to pieces: the perfect woman tears to pieces when she loves.—I know these charming maenads" (p. 266).

The reference here is unambiguously to *The Bacchae,* as well as to Lou Salomé and all other emancipated women. Gone is the longing of the first "Dancing Song" and the triumphant sexual fusion of the second. In its place we have the Euripidean original. Pentheus, under the spell of Dionysus and driven by his own sexual curiosity, dresses as a woman to spy on the maenads. Betrayed by Dionysus, he is torn apart by the women, who—also bewitched—mistake him for a lion. The leader of the maenads is his mother, Agave. The climactic moment comes when she awakens from the spell and recognizes that the head she had torn from the blond beast's body was that of her son.

This is the catastrophic conclusion to Nietzsche's engagement with the feminine. The penalty for piercing the veil that conceals the pudendum, perhaps also for the appropriation and internalization of the feminine / maternal, is not merely castration but rather death—if not physically, then psychologically. Intercourse with women leads to psychic dismemberment and disintegration of the self. One could see this as a rounding of a circle— bringing the vision of *The Birth of Tragedy* back home. But, ironically and sadly, it is Nietzsche who is brought home. After his madness, it is first his mother who patiently and lovingly cares for him and finally, when she dies, his sister who exploits what's left of him.

16.

Nietzsche often viewed himself as a posthumous man and so it is only appropriate that he should have a posthumous lover. The "marine lover of Friedrich Nietzsche" (Irigaray 1991) is not his other or double.[20] She is a woman, existing outside of him, who willingly blurs the boundaries between them. In both regards, she differs from him, but this difference calls into question that other difference through which he became himself. *That* difference is doubly the disavowal of femininity: of the feminine in the masculine and of women self-constituted outside the male imaginary. *This* difference proceeds from the other direction. But it is not an inverse Cartesianism, the replacement of "I(he) am, therefore she is" with "I(she) am, therefore he is." Rather, the marine lover comes back to him and brings him back to himself in the process. She confronts Nietzsche with his inability to touch anything outside of himself, or even to recognize that the self he constitutes within himself requires the existence of an other he cannot reduce to himself.

"The eternal recurrence," she asks, "what is that but the will to recapitulate all projects within yourself?" (p. 69). A reactive will at that: a woman refuses to be "the guardian of your hearth, so that your work can be accomplished. She [Frau Lou?] refuses. Stresses her freedom in the face of your will" (p. 72). What then?

> You try to find your balance again, fail. Except in the eternal recurrence that creates an autological movement that cannot be reopened. By giving yourself up wholly to a center in which the other has no role except as counterweight or balance arm between you and yourself, you cannot get out of the circle. . . .
>
> The limit traced in this way is achieved by and against her. It is a closure that reacts to the effects of her "no." And to what you fail to decathect of her. Without being able to interpret her. Lost as you are in a labyrinth. For the first time you measure yourself up against a will of equal strength, yet different from your own, and you are lost. (P. 73)

Irigaray sees clearly that eternal return, for all its appearance of affirmation, is a "no" to a "no"—not an overcoming but rather a denial and a disavowal, an unwillingness or inability to accept the act through which the woman expresses her independent existence. If it is liberating, this is because it detaches its creator from a problem he cannot solve, so that the problem temporarily disappears. But so long as he cannot tolerate her appearing, it will reappear.

Viewed this way, eternal return is a horizon drawn around the male imaginary. Irigaray, more than any other writer, deserves credit for specifying *this* imaginary as male and for beginning the task of locating and articulating a female imaginary. Perhaps she has some trouble escaping the binary determination of sexuality so characteristic of masculine phantasy. Yet compare her "woman" with Nietzsche's "now you see it, now you don't" evocation of Baubô: "Woman 'touches herself' all the time, and moreover no one can forbid her to do so, for her genitals are formed of two lips in continuous contact. Thus, within herself, she is already two—but not divisible into one(s)—that caress each other" (Irigaray 1985, p. 24). At a minimum, this caress is not bestowed by men.

Irigaray is not, it should be stressed, proposing the substitution of one autoeroticism for another. To the contrary: the marine lover is attempting to liberate Nietzsche (and not only Nietzsche) from his self-encapsulation:

And, forever covered over or possessed by your projections, she will give them back to you as things neither she nor you want, and in which you will not recognize your will. Beyond the horizon you have opened up, she will offer you that in which she still lives and that your day has not even imagined. And yet, the multiple layers of veil and disguise are hiding such depth. Are calling on you to drop the mask and stop the show so that you may marry and make merry (faire la noce) at last—that is not your fortune! (Irigaray 1991, p. 73)

"That is not your fortune": the marine lover seemingly knows her love is and must be unrequited. Yet I'm not sure that Irigaray understands that Nietzsche was a man in a bubble—that he could not survive without or outside the male imaginary. Standing alone at the edge of an emotional abyss, he filled the void with images of a castrated/castrative Medusa and the bawdy, fecund Baubô. But these were, at least, his images, the products of his will. And as he comments in *On the Genealogy of Morals*, "man would rather will *nothingness* than *not* will" (p. 163).

This brings us to a last thought about gender and phantasy. Whether masculine or feminine, whether constructed by one sex or both, gendered phantasies function as defenses against psychic and psychophysiological pain. They are the product of our merely animal/sensuous vulnerability, our sexuality, and our distinctively human capacity for self-deception. Thus Janet Adelman says, in refusing to split herself off from the passions of Shakespeare's Lear, "For I too inhabit the terror of finitude and the desire for merger with the infinitely kind nursery that can undo the pain of separation; I too long for her return" (1992, p. 126).

6

After Nietzsche

Emancipate yourselves from mental slavery,
None but ourselves can free our minds.
　　　　　—Bob Marley, "Redemption Song"

1.

It is time to effect a transition from Nietzsche's world to our own. The first task is to make good on the promise of thinking through the relationship between dialectical reason, perspectivism, and the will to power. Next we round the hermeneutic circle and ask, "Under what conditions did men devise these value judgments good and evil, *and what value do they themselves possess?*" We will answer the question from Nietzsche's perspective, although we will find that so doing leaves us painfully short on both love and compassion. Finally, we return to our own hard times, where we will use a critical theory mediated by Nietzschean and Foucauldian concepts to investigate the contemporary configuration of hegemony and resistance. Here the rules devised to guide our clinical practice will be adapted to the exigencies of political judgment.

I. The Power of the Negative

2.

"A commentator on Nietzsche," Gilles Deleuze warns, "must, above all, avoid any kind of pretext for dialectising his thought" (1962, p. 10). Yet in Chapter 2, I not only reconceptualized the will to power from my own perspective but also articulated it as a dialectical manifold of forces and counterforces. Then in Chapter 3, I compounded the damage by setting perspectivism within a dialectical frame—displacing the frame but not replacing it. And in Chapter 4, I added the final insult of interpreting Nietzsche's own emotional and philosophical development dialectically. Deleuze and Nietzsche must be turning, if not quite eternally, in their graves.

Deleuze claims that "anti-Hegelianism runs through Nietzsche's work as its cutting edge." This would not have been Nietzsche's view of the matter. The enemies he needed and honored most were Kant and Schopenhauer among the moderns, and Socrates, Plato, and Christ among the ancients. But if given the chance, Nietzsche might agree that "pluralism [Deleuze's term for the interplay of will to power and perspectivism] sometimes appears to be dialectical—but it is its most ferocious enemy, its only profound enemy" (p. 8):

> It is sufficient to say that dialectic is a labour and empiricism [pluralism] an enjoyment. And who says there is more thought in labour than in enjoyment? Difference is the object of a practical affirmation inseparable from essence and constitutive of existence. Nietzsche's "yes" is opposed to the dialectical "no"; affirmation to dialectical negation; difference to dialectical contradiction; joy, enjoyment, to dialectical labour; lightness, dance, to dialectical responsibilities. The empirical feeling of difference, in short, hierarchy, is the essential motor of the concept, deeper and more effective than all thought about contradiction. (P. 9)

For Deleuze, the opposition between Nietzsche and Hegel is absolute—no free man would undertake Hegel's "strenuous effort of the Notion" (Hegel 1977, p. 34). Moreover, the stakes in the game are not merely epistemic. Deleuze invokes the famous battle for recognition in *The Phenomenology of Spirit:*

> If the master-slave relationship can easily take on the dialectical form, to the point where it has become an archetype or schoolboy exercise for every young Hegelian, it is because the portrait of the master that Hegel offers us is, from the start, a portrait which represents the slave, at least as he is in his dreams, as at best a successful slave. Underneath the Hegelian image of the master we always find the slave. (Deleuze 1962, p. 10)

Nietzsche, by contrast, criticizes from above, actively and not reactively.

If we identify Hegelian problematics of recognition with the foundational values of critical theory, then Deleuze's Nietzschean challenge to the one is ipso facto a challenge to the other. I will attempt to counter this attack in the following sections. But for the moment, let's consider only the epistemological issue. Nietzsche's perspectivism encounters characteristically Kantian problems when it reaches the boundary of language and logic. In Chapter 3, where I was intent on broadening the horizons of clinical practice, I resisted the temptation of bringing Hegelian dialectics to bear on this matter. But the temptation remains. On the one hand, Hegel's liquefaction of both language and logic dissolves those parts of Nietzsche's perspective that presuppose concepts as essences and thinking as binary. On the other, the will to power, the "whither" of Nietzsche's perspectivism, overcomes the rigidities peculiar to dialectical reason. This suggests, contra Deleuze and despite the evident opposition between the will to power and dialectical reason, the possibility of epistemological reconciliation.

3.

Hegel sees fluidity where Nietzsche sees fixity because he adopts the perspective of transitive verbs and replaces the traditional philosophical copula with—if you will—copulation. Or if this odd erotics of language seems too willful, we may say that the "is" (as in, A is A, $A = A$) is replaced by a symbol of transformation (arbitrarily, $A \rightarrow A$). This has the effect of making language and logic into mirrors of life processes. It also involves the moment of internal negation that is the object of Deleuze's criticism.

The discussion of predication in the preface to *The Phenomenology of Spirit* may be taken as exemplary. The object of Hegel's criticism is argumentative or ratiocinative thinking, in which the subject is externally related to the predicate. The ratiocinative thinker either accepts or rejects the postulated identity of subject and predicate; either way the judgment remains external to the terms themselves. Subject and predicate remain fixed and impenetrable, looking for all the world like the linguistic essences of which Nietzsche, too, is critical. But simple propositions can also be conceived speculatively:

> Speculative thinking behaves in a different way. Since the Notion [in the initial position of subject] is the object's own self, which presents itself as the *coming-to-be of the object*, it is not a passive Subject inertly supporting the Accidents; it is, on the contrary, the self-moving Notion which takes its determinations back into itself. In this movement the passive Subject itself perishes; it enters into the differences and the content, and constitutes the determinateness, i.e. the differentiated content and its movement, instead of remaining inertly over against it. The solid ground which argumentation

has in the passive Subject is therefore shaken, and only this movement itself becomes the object. (Hegel 1977, p. 37)

Reading Hegel writing creates an immediate sympathy for Deleuze, who rejects dialectical labor for pluralist enjoyment. But consider this roughly speculative interpretation of the proposition, the will to power = overcoming resistance:

1. The will to power = the will to power. Although this statement of identity can be interpreted speculatively, Hegel would treat it as an almost meaningless tautology, yet another night in which all cows are black. We therefore assume its nullity and must predicate something of the term to give it meaning—hence will to power = overcoming resistance.

2. The statement will to power = overcoming resistance is plainly self-contradictory. The will to power is not overcoming resistance; it is the will to power, and conversely. By the rules of ratiocinative argument, each term remains fixed in its meaning and cannot penetrate the other. If we are not to lapse back into a now doubled nullity, we must rethink how the terms are related—hence will to power → overcoming resistance. The will to power, initially in the position of subject, passes over into the predicate and becomes what it initially was not—that is, overcoming resistance. Changing the relationship of the terms is to change the terms themselves.

3. This movement is inherently reflexive. Overcoming resistance has become subject just as much as the will to power has become predicate. It is no longer predicated of the subject but has become the subject itself. Hence overcoming resistance → will to power.

4. When we reflect on this dialectical interpretation of predication, we see that there is difference within the proposition—the twofold process of negation that constitutes it. But this is a difference which is no difference, that is, a difference that establishes selfsameness or identity. The proposition as a whole is nothing other than this movement of simultaneous negation and affirmation. Its difference from other propositions is established by the contained difference that constitutes it.

Hegel is not content with formally speculative propositions of this kind. In *The Phenomenology of Spirit* the shift from thinking about things to immersion in life processes comes when consciousness finds it both necessary and possible "to think pure change, or *think antithesis within the antithe-*

sis itself, or *contradiction.*" Antithesis within antithesis, difference within difference—self-negating and just as much self-affirming—is the thought of the infinite, infinity itself, which "may be called the simple essence of life, the soul of the world, the universal blood, whose omnipresence is neither disturbed nor interrupted by any difference, but rather is itself every difference, as also their supersession; it pulsates within itself but does not move, inwardly vibrates, yet it is at rest" (p. 100).

Leaving to one side any problems we may find with Hegel's articulation of dialectical reason, the striking thing in this brief philosophical dalliance is how close Hegel and Nietzsche come to each other. On the one hand, they are both philosophers of becoming—but Hegel can conceptualize processes of transformation that Nietzsche can only metaphorize. Not that Hegel abjures the use of metaphors; indeed, at times he almost seems to be evoking Nietzsche's restless play of will and wave. He can speak conceptually, however, where Nietzsche is forced to remain silent. Hence we might say that Nietzsche requires Hegel to complete his own project. On the other hand, because dialectical negation seems fatally attracted to the will to power, Hegel cannot really escape the trap Nietzsche sets for him. What "really" happens when the subject becomes what it is not (the predicate) and the predicate becomes what it is not (the subject)? Don't we have here a mutual, internal overcoming of resistance? The subject says, "you are not the predicate, I am," while the predicate says, "you are not the subject, I am." Thus we have a bilateral declaration of civil war, followed by thrusts and counterthrusts, a syntactical duel in which each party penetrates and conquers the territory of the other—albeit with the paradoxical feature of not losing its own. Or, if concepts are preferred to metaphors: *Immanent negation (the negation of negation) is precisely the overcoming of internal resistance.* For both Hegel and Nietzsche, self-overcoming is the name of the ontological / epistemological game. So while Deleuze has good reasons for ruling out the dialectising of Nietzsche's thought, Hegelians have equally good ones for resisting the willful Nietzscheanizing of theirs.

Thus Nietzsche and Hegel are the most intimate of enemies, fighting the same battle with very much the same weapons. They might even be allies on occasion, as when confronted by the common enemy of merely ratiocinative or argumentative thinking. But the language of social interaction falls short of expressing the relationship between the two perspectives. Better to say that Nietzsche and Hegel are the inside and outside of each other—not merely mirror images, external and specular, but rather (here some poetic license is required) yang-in-yin and yin-in-yang. Experienced one way, Hegelian dialectics take form within the incessant self-overcoming of the will to power (yang-in-yin). Negation and negation of negation explode out of their position as middle term and mediation, with the consequence that any position within the dialectical manifold is simply a perspective, a placement of power contending for priority with every other placement of power. Apollo, caught off guard, loses himself in Dionysian ecstasy. Yet experienced the other way around, potentiality and actuality—the extremes of the dialectical manifold—come before and after the moment of overcoming resistance (yin-in-yang). Life is not an undifferentiated oneness of temporal and spatial elements, all equally and indistinctly beginning, middle, or end. Whatever its built-in entropic tendencies, it takes form, emerges in the form of distinct identities that remain selfsame in the midst of their self-overcomings. Knowing this about life, dialectical reason places the will to power in perspective, confines it to the role of mediation, forces its shoulder to the wheel of development, and thereby reimposes sobriety and order on "the Bacchanalian revel in which no member is not drunk" (p. 27). Trapped by the need to make sense out of the things of this world, Dionysus is forced to dance to Apollo's tune.[1]

This cosmic dance can continue, infinitely and recursively (yin-in-yang and yang-in-yin). We turn one way and are immersed in "the simple essence of life, the soul of the world, the universal blood, whose omnipresence is neither disturbed nor interrupted by any difference, but rather is itself every difference, as also their supersession; it pulsates within itself but does not move, inwardly vibrates, yet it is at rest." We turn another and find ourselves inside "a monster of energy, without beginning, without end; a firm, iron magnitude of force that does not grow bigger or smaller, that does not expend itself but only transforms itself . . . a sea of forces flowing and rushing together, eternally changing, eternally flooding back . . . [a] *Dionysian* world of the eternally self-creating, the eternally self-destroying, [a] mysterious world of twofold voluptuous delight" (*WP*, p. 550). Neither partner has the epistemic power to bring this dance to an end.

We might take a (no doubt metaphysical) step beyond. Yin and yang, darkness and light, distinct and interpenetrating, waxing and waning infinitely, are forms of *t'ai chi t'u* (the Primal Beginning) in the *I Ching* (Baynes 1967, p. 298) or of the Tao in *The Way of Life* (*Tao Tê Ching*) (Blakney 1955). They intimate a power and a perspective in which the distinction between inside and outside is not. All mystics turn themselves in this direction— from different directions, along different paths, and with correspondingly different definitions of their goals. So too Hegel and Nietzsche, each of whom attempts the transcendence of time and space, the one by the thought of infinity itself and the other by the thought of eternal return. Held back by competitive desire, however, they fall short of the goal. One insists that light must limit darkness and the other that darkness explodes into light. Yang and yin are out of harmony, imbalanced, and so the Way is missed and the experience of *t'ai chi t'u* is precluded.[2]

Tennyson would have Ulysses "follow knowledge like a shooting star, beyond the utmost bound of human thought" (Andrews and Percival 1928, p. 21). As critical theorists and psychoanalysts, we are not free to sail so far into the mystic. We are charged with attending to our mundane, everyday, and this-worldly affairs. More soberly, then. Because the will to power takes the limitations of language and logic as resistances to be overcome, it can disrupt any dialectical unfolding, annihilate and go beyond any horizon that is imposed on it. Yet in so doing it reaffirms its dialectical nature. We might instance the ultimate Nietzschean overcoming: Saying "yes" to eternal return is to overcome the human, all-too-human need to say "no" to it. This yes-saying is precisely the negation of a negation and, for just this reason, a most profound affirmation. Hegel proves irresistible because he can make sense of Nietzsche's most inspired moment.

Confronted by these opposing Nietzschean and Hegelian claims, it is tempting to take sides with one or the other. This is precisely the yinist and yangist trap we must avoid. The will to power becomes monotonous, nearly meaningless, when it is monistically maintained—the same singsong refrain sung over and over again. Dialectical reason, so easily dogmatized, desiccates the very things that it desires, sucks the life out of them—formalizes them. Everything becomes an epistemological waltz, a predictable and boring three-step. When the two perspectives are used in tandem, however— and this use is possible just because the will to power and dialectical negation are so inside/outside each other—dialectical reason becomes a flexible way of thinking about processes of transformation, while the will to power is reflexively restrained. And once joined together, their operations can be suspended together. This is the demand which the clinical practice of psychoanalysis imposes on us and which, more generally, opens up the space where the unknown can take form.

4.

In thinking about the relationship between the will to power and the determinacy of pleasure and pain, a definite resolution was required. The two psychological orientations are truly opposed, the actual mirror images that the will to power and dialectical reason only appear to be. But the will to power was not adequate to the exigencies of psychological understanding. Hence its required reformulation as overcoming pain to gain pleasure, including the pleasure of overcoming pain. Epistemologically, however, no such resolution or reformulation is needed. The will to power, pristine and simple, slips into and through dialectical reason, reconstituting it as a dialectical perspectivism. If the determinacy of pleasure and pain, in its very determinacy, directs us toward our human, all-too-human core, dialectical perspectivism creates a nondogmatic way of experiencing it.

II. Beneath Good and Evil

5.

In the preceding discussion, I separated epistemological and moral issues. Although one may question the legitimacy of such a bracketing procedure, it facilitates the work of conceptual clarification. That having been done, there is no reason to postpone an engagement with Nietzsche concerning the genesis and nature of moral valuations.

In his preface to *On the Genealogy of Morals*, Nietzsche notes that *Human, All Too Human* contained the first, provisional statement of his views concerning the origin of moral prejudices (*GM*, p. 16); in *Ecce Homo* he says that his "campaign against morality" began in *Daybreak* (*EH*, p. 290). This rightly suggests that we could follow our familiar developmental path by tracing the evolution of his thinking about morals into and out of *Thus Spoke Zarathustra*. Our interests will be better served, however, if this time we focus on *Genealogy*. This is Nietzsche's most provocative treatment of morality and the one in which the will to power is applied most insistently and even ruthlessly. The result is an extraordinary analysis of moralized self-torture—an unsuccessful analysis, however, if Nietzsche's aim was to cure a disease.

We might orient ourselves toward *Genealogy* by considering this statement of perspectivist method from the 1886 preface to *Human, All Too Human*:

It may finally happen that, under the sudden illumination of a still stressful, still changeable health, the free, ever freer spirit begins to unveil the riddle of the great liberation which had until then waited dark, questionable, almost untouchable in his memory. If he has for long hardly dared to ask himself: 'why so apart? so alone? renouncing everything I once reverenced? renouncing reverence itself? why this hardness, this suspiciousness, this hatred for your own virtues?'—now he dares to ask it aloud and hears in reply something like an answer. 'You shall become master over yourself, master also over your virtues. Formerly *they* were your masters; but they must be only your instruments beside other instruments. You shall get control of your For and Against and learn how to display first one and then the other in accordance with your higher goal. You shall learn to grasp the sense of perspective in every value judgment—the displacement, distortion and merely apparent teleology of horizons and whatever else pertains to perspectivism. . . . You shall learn to grasp the *necessary* injustice in every For and Against, injustice as inseparable from life, life itself as *conditioned* by the sense of perspective and its injustice.' (*HH*, p. 9)

Yet there is an "order of rank": injustice is greatest where life is weakest, whereas "power and right and spaciousness of perspective grow into the heights together" (ibid.).

This statement of method resembles a Rosetta stone. Turned one way, it points toward eternal return, the "great liberation"; turned the other, it initiates the genealogy of morals, the investigation of the order of rank among peoples and values. Its premise is years of self-renunciation. The self of the free spirit is identified with certain virtues, including the virtue of truth. At first serving them, accepting their authority, over time it calls them into question, exerts its will to power against them, overcomes and rises above them. They become perspectives, instruments of knowledge deployed by a self that knows no moral master. The last thread of morality is snapped by the affirmation of eternal return. Now, seen from that great height and in the light of that great noon, the injustices, distortions, and falsifications attached to all judgments, to every Pro and Con, become apparent. We might be tempted to say that a goodly part of the falsification results from Nietzsche's entrapment in the either/or of ratiocinative logic, his failure to see the doubled negativity internal to every judgment and value. But putting such epistemic concerns aside momentarily, the point is that Nietzsche's genealogical investigations are conducted from the perspective of eternal return.

Genealogy is divided into three essays overlaid on but not isomorphic with a threefold evolutionary conception of morals. The first essay, a general depiction of the slave revolt in morality, establishes the "what" of the inquiry. The second yields a conception of the dynamus, the "how," of the process of moral development—the internalization of cruelty that creates bad conscience. The third gives us the "why," an examination of the will to nothingness that runs like an invisible thread through all moral valuations. Within this expository frame, Nietzsche depicts an initial position of untrammeled, freely expressed animal will, the inversion and internalization of the will—its self-alienation and drive toward nihilism—and then the (prospective) negation of the negation, that is, the transcendence of moral

alienation resulting from the affirmation of eternal return. The third substantive step is taken beneath the surface of the text, however, by implication
and not by explication. Thus we have one story embedded within another
and are challenged to find our way from genealogical surface to emancipatory depth. If we do this successfully, we join Nietzsche in the dialectical
joining of manifest and latent content. Along with him, we bring *Thus Spoke
Zarathustra* into *On the Genealogy of Morals* and could then, if we wished,
read *On the Genealogy of Morals* back into *Thus Spoke Zarathustra*.[3]

Nietzsche begins his polemic by positing a "before good and evil"—the
existence of "good" and "bad" as premoral valuations. Initially "good" is the
self-designation and self-affirmation of aristocrats and nobles, while "bad"
means "base" or "lowly"—the commoner as seen from above. These judgments are active, are indeed little more than enactments. They involve no
reflection, no criticism or self-criticism. They begin their evolution when
"the highest caste is at the same time the *priestly* caste" (*GM*, p. 31), with the
consequence that the judgments of purity or impurity can both be applied to
those who are good. From the standpoint of animal health and vigor, this
priestly intervention is a poisoning disguised as medicinal treatment, a poisoning so thorough that "mankind itself is still ill with the effects of this
priestly naïveté in medicine" (p. 32). Yet this development is not to be
regretted:

> With the priests *everything* becomes more dangerous, not only cures and
> remedies, but also arrogance, revenge, acuteness, profligacy, love, lust to
> rule, virtue, disease—but it is only fair to add that it was on the soil of this
> *essentially dangerous* form of human existence, the priestly form, that man
> first became *an interesting animal*, that only here did the human soul acquire
> *depth* and become *evil*—and these are the two basic respects in which man
> has hitherto been superior to other beasts. (Pp. 32–33)

If we take this as an ontogenetic tale, then we are talking about bowel and
bladder training, the first imposition of moral, really protomoral, discipline
on infantile life. In this context, one is proud to be clean and ashamed to be
dirty. This is quite universally the first step in the domestication of the
"beast of prey" (p. 40) in each of us. It does not always create cages, of
course, but it does result in a modicum of self-restraint or basic repression
(as Marcuse would say). And as Nietzsche, Marcuse, and we ourselves would
have it, these interventions by priests and parents are humanizing. We can
no more regret them than we can regret being ourselves.

Things take a nastier turn when the site of value-formation shifts to the
lower classes. Members of these classes, looking up at the nobles, react to

them and their valuations resentfully. The existence of something superior to them is, so to speak, an intolerable, narcissistic affront. It evokes rage and that most destructive of desires, envy. The lowly wish to sully, stain, besmirch, and ruin the nobles, so that they will no longer be reproached by an embodied ideal they cannot attain. This, at least, is a plausible psychoanalytic interpretation of Nietzsche's conception of ressentiment.

If one wishes to see ressentiment unadorned, one might attend a performance of Shakespeare's *Othello*. There Iago, the veritable embodiment of envy, poisons Othello, infects and inflames him—transforms him from a magnanimous, loving warrior-ruler into an enraged, jealous, and murderous beast.[4] Cloak Iago in priestly robes and align him with the lowly and one has the "slave revolt in morality" (p. 34). The priestly classes—preeminently the Jewish Pharisees and their Christian successors—revalue the unfettered strength, the good, of the nobility as evil. They value noble virtue negatively because they are negatively valued by it. This is the expression of their will to power. But their transvaluation of values would be truly impotent if the nobles were able to resist it. Hence a problem is posed: where is the noble's Achilles' heel, his point of vulnerability to priestly poisoning? The example of *Othello* would suggest that envy attaches itself to the worm of self-doubt in even the most self-affirming nobleman. "Am I worthy of respect? Of her love? Do I have reason to be ashamed? Am I less than I appear or aspire to be?" These are the questions that actual warriors ask themselves or that haunt them even when unasked. They reflect the first-order domestication of the blond beast. But Nietzsche would view the posing of such questions as begging a prior question. His noble warrior has no second thoughts of this kind, indeed no intrasubjectivity of any kind. He is a "bird of prey" who finds nothing "more tasty than a tender lamb" (pp. 44–45), and he has no choice in this matter: a bird of prey or a wolf on the fold cannot elect to be a lamb or a sheep any more than a lamb or a sheep can elect to be a bird of prey or a wolf on the fold. There is no accountability, certainly no moral accountability, in this predatory relationship. Through a trick of language, however, accountability can be introduced: "A quantum of force is equivalent to a quantum of drive, will, effect—more, it is nothing other than precisely this very driving, willing, effecting, and only owing to the seduction of language (and of the fundamental errors of reason petrified in it) which conceives and misconceives all effects as conditioned by something that causes effects, by a 'subject,' can it appear otherwise" (p. 45). Even blond beasts, those healthy embodiments of the will to power, are users of logic and language and therefore liable to self-falsification. This is their Achilles' heel: "No wonder if the submerged, darkly glowering emotions of vengefulness and hatred exploit this belief to their own ends and in fact maintain no belief more ardently than the belief that the strong man is free to be weak and the bird of prey to be a lamb [even, no doubt, the lamb of God]—for thus they gain the right to make the bird of prey accountable for being a bird of prey" (ibid.).

This genealogical construction is not without its difficulties, including the fact that, as every parent of a preverbal child knows, self-accountability does not depend on language. But many of these difficulties can be resolved within the epistemic limits of constrained perspectivism. Moreover, Nietzsche's analysis of ressentiment is psychoanalytically plausible, and there are both historical and ontogenetic equivalents to the slave revolt in morality. Whatever its psychological and existential status, however, the situation he depicts is paranoid-schizoid, replete with the narcissistic trends that are characteristic of that psychic position. Members of the lower classes are filled with envy and resentment, as if they were infants who could not tolerate the distance between their pitiful neediness and their mother's bountiful sufficiency. The members of the upper classes are solitary beasts who disavow their own frailties, maybe even project them downward—who are in any case contemptuous of their inferiors and at best mutually admiring of each other. Love plays no constitutive role in these social relations, not even the pleasure-seeking precursors of love that make occupancy of the paranoid-schizoid position humanly tolerable. We have, to put it another way, a depiction of a psychic or social situation in which the only effective force is the will to power. Resistances are joyfully overcome by some, resentfully overcome by others, and these are the only possibilities—or almost the only possibilities. When the opposed positions are figured as extremes of one personality—Nietzsche's, for instance—we also have the elements for a dialectic of self-overcoming: an initial position of strength; the negation of that position through weakness, hatred, and envy (through the infusion of abjective affect); and the challenge of negating the negation by affirming even the abjective mediation. What we do not have is a basis for the kinds of moral relationships that originate in the depressive position, where compassion and concern become available for the healing of emotional wounds.

6.

The second essay in *Genealogy* depicts the process through which the noble warrior, a heedless ravisher of others, becomes a man of bad conscience, a guilty ravisher of the self. The first step is to take the potential for accountability in language and transform it into an actuality. Because one cannot be held accountable for commitments one cannot remember making, this requires the creation of memory or, stated negatively, overcoming the natural proclivity for forgetfulness. (Recall the happy and unhistorical cattle of "On the Uses and Disadvantages of History for Life.") And how do things come to be remembered? "'If something is to stay in the memory it must be burned in: only that which never ceases to *hurt* stays in memory'" (*GM*, p. 61). Nodal points of pain serve to remind us of our duties. Systematically generated, they are the product of punishment.

Punishment is initially a two-party affair with no relationship to utilitarian values and only a perverse relationship to hedonic ones. Tellingly, Nietzsche sees it as akin to parent-child relations in which parents "punish their children, from anger at some harm or injury, vented on the one who caused it" (p. 63). A child intrudes on a parental domain and is angrily rebuked. This crude discharge of anger takes on a more sophisticated form when it is embedded in contractual (creditor—debtor) relations. A debtor promises repayment and accepts responsibility for providing an equivalent if he fails to repay. But in the event of failure, material equivalents are not at issue:

> An equivalence is provided by the creditor's receiving, in place of a literal compensation for an injury (thus in place of money, land, possessions of any kind), a recompense in the form of a kind of *pleasure*—the pleasure of being allowed to vent his power freely upon one who is powerless, the voluptuous pleasure *"de faire le mal pour le plaisir de le faire,"* the enjoyment of violation.... The compensation, then, consists in a warrant for and title to cruelty. (Pp. 64–65)

The dynamic element in the genealogy of morals is here revealed. The untamed noble warriors were naturally cruel. They discharged their instincts and inflicted pain without a second thought. Punishment in the instance of creditor-debtor relationships formalizes this expression of the will to power and brings it into sharper focus. We are witness to cruelty for its own sake, gaining pleasure from inflicting pain. This is a perversion of the will to power in *our* sense of the word, where pleasure is a function of overcoming, not inflicting, pain. But think of the adolescent Nietzsche holding burning matches in his outstretched hand. From one perspective, as the one on whom pain is inflicted, he is proving his indifference to suffering. The pleasure is a derivative or by-product of not giving in to self-protective impulse. From another, as the one inflicting the pain, the pleasure is in the action, and the enjoyment comes from inflicting pain on himself. The two sides of the action are joined in the Nietzschean concept of self-mastery or self-overcoming, and no judgment of perversity attaches to it. Here, then, is a clear measure of the distance between Nietzsche's conception of the will to power and our own.

Be that as it may, for Nietzsche the internalization of cruelty is the decisive moment in moral development. The noble warrior, equipped with both language and memory and therefore accountable for his actions, is confined in society and deprived of the natural outlet for his cruelty. Blond beast or wolf that he is, he is reduced to preying on himself, and in this *"internalization* of man" (p. 64) we have the origin of bad conscience:

> The man who, from lack of external enemies and resistances and forcibly confined to the oppressive narrowness and punctiliousness of custom, impatiently lacerated, persecuted, gnawed at, assaulted, and maltreated himself; this animal that rubbed itself raw against the bars of its cage as one tried to "tame" it; this deprived creature, racked with homesickness for the wild, who had to turn himself into an adventure, a torture chamber, an uncertain and dangerous wilderness—this fool, this yearning and desperate prisoner became the inventor of the "bad conscience." (*GM*, p. 85)

In Chapter 4 we applied this characterization of moral development to Nietzsche's life history; here Nietzsche applies it to social history. We are again reminded that "every great philosophy" is "the personal confession of its author" (*BGE*, p. 13).

This self-punishing creature is protomoral but not yet fully moral. Only when God becomes the creditor and man the debtor do we arrive at guilt in the proper sense and at full-blown morality: "This man of bad conscience . . . [seizes] upon the presupposition of religion so as to drive his self-torture to its most gruesome pitch of severity and rigor. Guilt before *God:* this thought becomes an instrument of torture to him. He apprehends in 'God' the ultimate antithesis of his own ineluctable animal instincts; he reinterprets these animal instincts themselves as a form of guilt before God" (*GM*, p. 92). Thus we have the internalization of the slave revolt in morals. The ressentiment of the lowly transforms good into evil, bad into good. The notion of subjective causality built into language is the noble's Achilles' heel. But ressentiment cannot take advantage of this opening until it tips the arrow of internalized cruelty. Then the blond beast, wounded and poisoned, becomes a guilty Christian, and Iago's revenge is complete.

The second stage in Nietzsche's genealogy of moral development is subject to the same psychoanalytic interpretation as the first. Leaving aside the fact that memory is no less natural than forgetfulness and that it is not necessarily a source of emotional disturbance, the major point is that guilt is not simply cruelty turned inward. Although it is self-punishing and can certainly be tormenting, the self-persecution Nietzsche depicts is guilt as it takes form within the paranoid-schizoid position, indeed in a quite extreme version of that situation—one where, for instance, parents punish their children out of anger. It is not the more developed form of guilt, emergent within the depressive position, that results from intentionally or even unintentionally injuring someone loved—guilt that, redemptively, leads to attempts at repair and reconciliation. Because Nietzsche closes off this pathway to moral development, he remains trapped within a world of solitary self-torture. We might acknowledge moments when we are driven to resemble him. But in the end, a pathos of difference as well as distance separates us from him. At least, so I would like to believe.

7.

The noble warrior who became a guilty Christian through the internalization and moralization of cruelty is one of the many servants of ascetic ideals. Understanding him, placing him in proper perspective, requires a general understanding of asceticism. Thus we have the third essay, "What Is the Meaning of Ascetic Ideals?" Here, again, the end is in the beginning, and this in a double sense. First, the essay is staged as an exegesis of the now familiar aphorism from *Thus Spoke Zarathustra:* "Unconcerned, mocking, violent—thus wisdom wants *us:* she is a woman and loves only a warrior" (*GM*, p. 96). Taken strictly in context, the philosopher, identified with an unconcerned, mocking, and violent warrior, is linked to the nobleman of the first essay. He treats wisdom as a woman and, it will be guessed, seeks to overcome her resistances. This Zarathustrian figuration of the philosopher also points beyond the text itself to the overman and eternal return. Second, Nietzsche begins by answering his own question about the meaning of ascetic ideals: "*That* the ascetic ideal has meant so many things to man, however, is an expression of the basic fact of the human will, its *horror vacui: it needs a goal*—and it will rather will *nothingness* than *not* will" (p. 96). Because we are familiar with Nietzsche's critique of metaphysics from the perspective of the will to power, we might anticipate the meaning of this concise formulation. But Nietzsche does not assume such familiarity and therefore treats his explanatory conclusion as an investigative beginning.

Nietzsche's typology of asceticism begins with artists and philosophers—predictably enough, Wagner and Schopenhauer, with Nietzsche himself positioned between the two. But as he himself remarks, only when we come to the ascetic priest does the "self-contradiction" of the ascetic life come fully into view: "Here rules a *ressentiment* without equal, that of an insatiable instinct and power-will that wants to become master not over something in life but over life itself, over its most profound, powerful, and basic conditions; here an attempt is made to employ force to block up the wells of force" (pp. 117–18). Our exploration of perspectivism has familiarized us with this kind of metaphysical asceticism, in which will to power is life-denying rather than life-affirming. But Nietzsche goes on to offer a more subtle interpretation of this nihilistic tendency, one that subsumes the analyses of the first two essays. Again there are two classes of individuals. On the one side are the "rare cases of great power and soul and body, man's *lucky hits*." These are the healthy noblemen of this or any age. But for the most part and on the other side, man is a "sick animal" (p. 121). The great mass of humanity is a diseased herd, overflowing with ressentiment, all too pitiable and nauseating to behold—a threat to the lucky few who, viewing them, may fall victim to pity and become infected with their poison. In this context, the ascetic priest appears as both herdsman and mediator. Partly, he is an enemy of the healthy and noble, at war with the "beasts of prey" whom he fights with cunning rather than with force, seeking to infect them with "misery, discord, and self-contradiction" (p. 126). Here we have a return of the original moral poisoning of the blond beast. But the ascetic priest's primary aim is to retain his power over the herd, which he does by laying hold of its ressentiment and redirecting it against itself (pp. 126–27). The herd is sick and suffering, in pain from its incapacity and degeneracy, eaten up with envy of the healthy, blaming those who are stronger for its own weakness. The priest shifts the blame onto the sufferers themselves, sickens them further with their own disease, maintains his power over them the way a heroin dealer maintains his power over a junkie. In the process, he quarantines his charges and indirectly protects the lucky few from infection, but he also and more fundamentally gives the members of the herd what they need to survive, namely, a meaning for their suffering. For although man is "in the main a sickly animal," his "problem was *not* suffering itself, but that there was no answer to the crying question, *'why* do I suffer?'" (p. 162). The ascetic ideal answers this question and makes it possible to go on living. Thus we see that *"the ascetic ideal springs from the protective instinct of a degenerating life* which tries by all means to sustain itself and fight for its existence" (p. 120).

"Degenerating life" refers to a built-in, physiological weakness or decadence, at once irremediable and intolerable. It is the ultimate source of ressentiment, which at root is an inability to bear being oneself. All manner of suffering and numbing are preferable to experiencing this incapacity directly, and thus we have a more developed interpretation of guilt or bad conscience:

Man, suffering from himself in some way or other but in any case physio-logically like an animal shut up in a cage, uncertain why or wherefore, thirsting for reasons—reasons relieve—thirsting, too, for remedies and narcotics, at last takes counsel with one who knows hidden things, too—and behold! he receives a hint, he receives from his sorcerer, the ascetic priest, the *first* hint as to the "cause" of his suffering: he must seek it in *him-self*, in some *guilt*, in a piece of the past, he must understand his suffering as punishment. (P. 140)

The invalid has been transformed into a sinner and his (or her) sufferings have become morally meaningful.

Nietzsche does not collapse all of asceticism into its especially malignant, priestly form, but he does collapse all existing valuations into asceticism, including those of modern science (*Wissenschaft*, science in the broad—cultural as well as natural—sense). In the latter instance, "truth" replaces God as master but is served with the same unconditional faith and belief. Its value is not questioned, and just so, it functions as an ascetic ideal. It no less than God is an escape route, an evasion, a nullity placed defensively against the superabundance of life. It preserves life precisely by denying it. It bespeaks a refusal to live or a kind of living death. Yet when life cannot be affirmed in its Dionysian fullness—when, indeed, it is all but intolerable—this profoundly negative expression of the will to power is preferable to giv-ing up the ghost. And so Nietzsche ends as he began: "man would rather will *nothingness* than *not* will" (p. 163).

Although Nietzsche arrives at this conclusion along a road we had not previously traveled, it is the very one we anticipated. Asceticism is restrained nihilism, the will to power deployed as a defense against the Dionysian excess of life. And I would grant that Nietzsche is depicting a real phenom-enon. Think of his ascetic restraint in the face of his abject suffering and his quite heroic struggle to make this suffering meaningful. Yet there is a char-acteristic distortion in his analysis, one that reflects precisely his experience: he was not able to remedy his own suffering and correspondingly tends to treat suffering as irremediable. It is built-in physiologically, and nothing is to be done about it. Like the disarmed critical theorists evoked in Chapter 1, Nietzsche's ascetic, unable to change his world, can only interpret it dif-ferently. Thus suffering is split off from meaning, with the former treated as a constant and the latter as a variable. This is a defensive retreat from activ-ity to passivity, one that makes sense in a situation like Nietzsche's in which no practical remedy for intense suffering is available. When suffering does not have to be treated as an existential given, however, when it is potentially remediable, there is proportionally less reason to split experience and the meaning of experience. Then we are not forced to identify ourselves with the will to power, gaining pleasure only from imposing meaning on and thus overcoming pain. Rather, we restore the will to power to its position within the determinacy of pleasure and pain, using it as a means to hedonic and utilitarian ends instead of treating it as an end in itself. Then, too, passivity gives way to activity, and we orient ourselves toward changing the world.

Thus *On the Genealogy of Morals* offers us a one-sided and truncated depiction of moral development. An uncivilized creature is placed into a situation of instinctual restraint. At first proud and relatively autonomous, it becomes increasingly guilt-ridden and ascetic. Even if it passes beyond sacred to secular conceptions of morality, it turns away from life instead of living it fully. It seems to be devoid of social relationships and unable to transform the inverted world within which it is trapped. No wonder it screams out, "Too long, the earth has been a madhouse!" (p. 93). But the life-world of this tormented and self-tormenting creature is diseased and out of balance, or diseased because it is out of balance. The rhythm of life, the metabolic cycle within which pleasure and pain play their determining roles, has been fatefully if not fatally disrupted. The predominance of pain over pleasure forces a twofold misidentification of the self with the will to power and of the will to power with cruelty. Constructed from this perspective and on this basis, morality is persecutory and self-punishing. But this is only one form of morality—morality in the paranoid-schizoid position, morality as an attempt to impose order on a disordered world. The problem is not, to put it another way, that the blond beast has been moralized but rather that morality has been bestialized. No doubt, this bestialized morality is human, all-too-human, but this is because arrested and perverted moral development is human, all-too-human.

8.

The preceding analysis suggests that one should aim to take the beast out of morality rather than morality out of the beast. This is not the path that Nietzsche elects to follow. Although he neither advocates reversion to purely predatory relationships nor seeks to undo the work of civilization, he aims to go beyond morality rather than to redeem it. And this brings us to the dialectic of liberation that underlies and frames the manifest dialectic of moral development in *Genealogy*. It, too, begins with the values of the premoral warrior nobility and proceeds in like fashion to the internalization of the slave revolt in morals. But at this level, asceticism does not bring the story to an end. It simply completes the process of alienation and poses the question, "Where is the match of this closed system of will, goal, and interpretation? Why has it not found its match?—Where is the other '*one* goal'?" (p. 146). Although the answer is not given in the text, Nietzsche points us in its direction. In the first essay he evokes a warrior of the mind who can endure a "subterranean life of struggle" and emerge "again and again into the light," experiencing "again and again one's golden hour of victory." Although here the allusion is plainly to his experience of eternal return, he backs away from stating or claiming it. Instead he imagines "divine goddesses in the realm beyond good and evil" who might grant him the sight of a "redeeming lucky hit," a man "wholly achieved" and "still capable of arousing fear" (p. 44).

A few pages later Nietzsche resumes the advance. His aim, he says, "is inscribed at the head of my last book *Beyond Good and Evil.*—At least this does not mean 'Beyond Good and Bad'" (p. 55). It might seem that he is identifying his warrior of the mind with the blond beast. The mental warrior is not the blond beast as he existed in the first instance, however, but rather someone who has passed through morality and emerged on its other side. Early in the second essay, Nietzsche offers us a portrait of a "*sovereign individual*" who is "liberated again from morality," who is "autonomous and supramoral," and who "has his own independent, protracted will and the *right to make promises*" (p. 59). The "power over oneself and over fate" has in this case "penetrated to the profoundest depths and become instinct, the dominating instinct," and this dominating instinct is his conscience (p. 60). Needless to say, this is not bad conscience but rather self-overcoming elevated to a postmoral principle of autonomous individuality. Think back to the passage from *Human, All Too Human* cited earlier, in which Nietzsche asks, "Why this hatred for your own virtues?" He answers, "You shall become master over yourself, master also over your virtues." In this way, one's own will becomes sovereign, and values become instruments (perspectives) through which the will is expressed. Each value or virtue becomes a placement of one's will to power. But to achieve this end, one must pass beyond both priests and philosophers, the servants of God and the servants of the truth, and one must abjure the search for a meaning (a higher purpose) for one's suffering. The "great liberation" comes when one is able to affirm life just as it is, without addition or subtraction—and this is the perspective from which all other valuations (beyond perhaps the most primitive ones) may be viewed as ascetic. Unsurprisingly, therefore, Nietzsche ends the second essay by evoking Zarathustra, that most sovereign of individuals:

This man of the future, who will redeem us not only from the hitherto reigning ideal but also from that which is bound to grow out of it, the great nausea, the will to nothingness, nihilism; this bell-stroke of noon and of the great decision that liberates the will again and restores its goal to the earth and his hopes to man; this Antichrist and antinihilist; this victor over God and nothingness—he must come one day. (P. 96)

Nietzsche, not yet on the verge of madness, again backs away from identifying himself with Zarathustra and the overman. But only the experience of eternal return gives him the right to promise that this peculiar redeemer "must come one day." And only the affirmation of eternal return is the negation of our moralized self-negation and hence the "match" for asceticism.

Once we recognize eternal return as the light Nietzsche shines into the moral darkness, an additional interpretation of *Genealogy* becomes available. The history of morals, it now seems clear, has been constructed as a dialectical progression from natural health through abjection to sublimity. Morality is identified with the experience of abject misery, and we are encouraged to abject it. We must see ourselves in the image of the shepherd of "On the Vision and the Riddle." Morality is a nauseating, poisonous black snake stuck in our throats and filling us with disgust. We must bite off its head and spit it out if we are to lift the crown of thorns from off our own heads. Then, and only then, will we be sovereign individuals.

We are not persuaded. We see at once that Nietzsche offers us an idealized reproduction of his own life history, challenging us to identify ourselves with it. But however much we may respect the struggle that gave rise to his depiction of moral darkness and postmoral light, we must keep our distance from it. For one thing, Nietzsche's antithesis of health and decadence splits a far more complex manifold of interpenetrating tendencies. It is, oddly or not so oddly, rather too dialectical, too simply antithetical, and, in its resolution, too totalizing and absolute—whatever the ironic and parodic brackets he might wish to place around it. Even more important, his cure is better seen as part of the disease. Assume that I am able to affirm all aspects of my solitary existence, as the Nietzschean challenge demands—that I am capable of willing their infinite repetition, no matter how painful or nauseating. But what about the life experiences of other people, including those whose lives intersect with my own? What if (to take an obvious case) someone I love is suffering intolerable pain? Am I to will its eternal return? Am I truly to view my empathic connection to other human beings as a part of a human, all-too-human condition that I must overcome to fully realize myself as an autonomous individual?

At this juncture, a reader of *Thus Spoke Zarathustra* might protest that we have fallen victim to pity, that greatest of all moral temptations and

Zarathustra's "final sin"—the last step of his self-overcoming (*TSZ*, p. 354). Perhaps. But we might want to draw a distinction between pity and compassion. Pity is characteristically inflected with condescension. We "take pity on" people, judge their suffering from outside and above and, by so doing, make ourselves into objects of their resentment. Viewed this way, acts of pity involve a failure of mutual recognition. They enact a relationship of lordship and bondage—noblesse oblige, as the saying goes. By contrast, compassion—and, even more, commiseration—involves a sharing of feeling. This experience was toxic for Nietzsche. Intimacy made him ill. Consequently compassion, which is the only reliable affective basis for a morality of mutual recognition, is removed from the picture at the outset.[5] Again, therefore, although we may respect his struggle and even share the profoundly disturbing feelings it involves, we must insist on our differences with and distance from him.

9.

To clarify further where we stand in relationship to Nietzsche and the world of psychic experience beneath good and evil, let's briefly return to the psychoanalytic consulting room. We remember that Nietzsche offered us meaningful interpretations of both Maya and Anna. Maya's erotic transference to me gave meaning to her suffering, her experience of internal persecution fit the model of bad conscience, and her mother treated her emergent selfhood as a resistance to be overcome. Anna was also the victim of internal persecution, and, struggling with the legacy of maternal neglect rather than maternal intrusion, at times she very nearly plunged into a psychophysiological abyss quite like the pre- or postmetaphysical world in Nietzsche's philosophy. But neither the cause nor the cure for these conditions fits the Nietzschean model. In the former regard, the experience of internal persecution and endangered selfhood reflects the necessity of creating personal meaning in pathologizing circumstances. If the two women's development seems to conform to Nietzsche's genealogy of morals, this is because moral development was perverted in the one case as in the other. In the latter regard, the aim of clinical interaction was not the affirmation of this painful life experience, along the lines of the affirmation of eternal return. Rather, the psychoanalytic encounter was oriented toward an acceptance of losses and a healing of wounds through mutual compassion and recognition. Only from this perspective might both parties to the interaction say, "Too long, the earth has been a madhouse!"

From this vantage point, we might consider once more Foucault's analysis of psychoanalysis in volume 1 of *The History of Sexuality*. As we saw in Chapter 1, his interpretive optic is a sociologized rearticulation of the will to power. This monocular instrument brings important aspects of psychoanalysis to light, but in characteristically Nietzschean fashion, it also blinds its user to the qualities of mutuality and concern that distinguish psychoanalysis from power / knowledge relationships. Moreover, Foucault's conception of human subjectivity is virtually as monadic as Nietzsche's. Jane Flax observes, when discussing Foucault's late ideas concerning subjectivity, that his "constant remaking of the self presupposes a socially isolated and individualistic view of the self. It precludes the possibility of enduring attachments and responsibilities to another in which the other can rely on one's stability and 'continuity of being'" (1990, p. 217).[6] Thus his perspective is doubly one-sided. Methodologically monistic and psychologically monadic, it precludes recognizing the very qualities that psychoanalysis both presupposes and engenders.

It might be protested that we have displaced the object of Foucault's analysis, that is, psychoanalysis as practiced by Freud and his French followers. There is some legitimacy to this protest: if the analyst occupies the paranoid-schizoid position with its characteristic narcissistic features, then clinical inquiry will approximate to Foucault's power / knowledge depiction of it. Although we are entitled to view this as a perversion of the psychoanalytic process, it is not just a paranoid phantasy. Moreover, if psychoanalysis had been left in the hands of its male practitioners, we might not have recognized this as a perversity. Given men's typical path to gender identity, they (at least in Western cultures) are far more likely than women to take isolated individuality as normal and normative. When they become psychoanalysts, they are also more likely than women to use interpretation intrusively, in phallic fashion, and to interpret interpretation as an overcoming of resistance. The consequence is that the will to know rather than compassion becomes the basic determinant of clinical interaction. Women psychoanalysts, by contrast, have been better attuned to the relational and caregiving nature of analytic work. Thus Flax comments in the course of her respectful appraisal of Freud:

Had he been able to respect the therapeutic value and power of the analytic relationship, he could have thought about analysis as a means of charting and recovering not only the repressed but the healing power of "caretaking" itself, for a central insight of analysis is that our relationships with others can make us ill, and hence such illness can be overcome by entering into relationships that offer the possibility of experiences that are different from past, pathogenic ones. (P. 86)

Approaching clinical practice from this deeply relational perspective has its risks. But the risks must be taken if the emancipatory potentialities of psychoanalysis are to be realized.

III. Hegemony and Resistance

10.

We close the consulting room door behind us and stand again on political ground. This does not mean that we leave Nietzschean and psychoanalytic insights behind. But now these notions must be linked to the objectivities of political life. Nietzsche is notably deficient in establishing such linkages. His untimeliness consisted in part of a stubborn refusal to think from within modern economic and political structures. Although this may have enabled him to be a "free spirit" and a "good European" who was not tied down by, especially, nationalist loyalties, it also resulted in the substitution of atavistic aristocratic fantasies for empirically based political analysis.[7] Thus in *Beyond Good and Evil*, after imagining a future Europe of sickened will and parliamentary domestication, he goes on to articulate his conception of "great politics":

> I do not say this because I want it to happen: the opposite is rather to my heart—I mean such an increase in the menace of Russia that Europe would have to resolve to become menacing, too, namely, to acquire one will by means of a new caste that would rule Europe, a long terrible will of its own that would be able to cast its goals millennia hence—so the long-drawn-out comedy of its many splinter states as well as its dynastic and democratic splinter wills would come to an end. The time for petty politics is over: the very next century will bring the fight for dominion of the earth—the compulsion to [great] large-scale politics. (*BGE*, p. 131)

Here the will to power, identified with national or even supranational entities, reverts to its simplest, martial meaning, and we have a new race of blond beasts ruling over Europe. It is easy to see how the Nazis could grab hold of this vision and bend it to their own uses. Or, to take another example, one might even imagine Hitler seeing himself in *Ecce Homo*:

> When truth enters into a fight with the lies of millennia, we shall have upheavals, a convulsion of earthquakes, a moving of mountains and valleys, the like of which has never been dreamed of. The concept of politics will

have merged entirely with a war of spirits; all power structures of the old society will have been exploded—all of them are based on lies: there will be wars the like of which have never been seen on earth. It is only beginning with me that the earth knows *great politics*. (*EH*, p. 327)

It might be protested that great wars and great politics are to be interpreted figuratively rather than literally, that Nietzsche is envisioning spiritual rather than material combat. But a perspectivist philosophy grounded in the will to power provides no defense against such a literal appropriation, and— however *that* interpretive issue might be resolved—I do not see a place for Nietzsche's politics of the will in critical social theory.

There is, however, a place for the will to power, and a vital one at that. Recall the anthropological model presented in Chapter 1, in which human individuality is conceptualized as this dialectical manifold: sensuousness → work / desire → consciousness. The will to power modifies and clarifies the first of these dimensions. There is still a drive toward pleasure—the life-drive—and a drive away from pain—the death-drive. But the third basic drive, which was identified rather vaguely as aggression, can now be conceptualized as the will to power, in our reformulated sense of overcoming pain to gain pleasure, including the pleasure of overcoming pain. Thus redefined and relocated, the will to power stands at the doorway of individuation, indeed in the very place where selfhood first takes form. For in situations that approach being purely pleasurable and ones that approach being purely painful, the life- and death-drives operate quite automatically or even instinctually. No development is called for. But when pleasures, especially vital pleasures, must be extracted from integuments of pain, problems must be solved. The will to power is the locus for solving them, hence also the point at which we begin to be self-determining. Moreover, this is the developmental nexus at which the reality principle begins to be differentiated from the pleasure and Nirvana principles. But reality in this sense—that is, reality experienced as a problem and as a resistance to be overcome—is a stimulus to nonliteral mentation. Thus the reality principle is just as much the principle of imagination, and in this double aspect, it both originates in and regulates the activity of the will to power.[8]

The meaning of the life-drive, death-drive, and will to power is progressively reconstituted as further development occurs. One developmental possibility is that their relationship to each other will be inverted or perverted: when pain is overwhelming, the pleasure of overcoming it may become a first principle and an end in itself. But whether or not development includes this characteristically Nietzschean deformation, the modalities of human sensuousness will be formed and re-formed through the inscription of work, desire, and consciousness. Although it then becomes quite impossible to experience them "as such," they do not fall into the position of inaccessible things-in-themselves. Rather, they make their presence felt in all aspects of our living, and for just this reason, the dialectical manifold of human sensuousness constitutes an interpretive perspective.

In the version of critical theory framing the present inquiry, work, desire, and consciousness also constitute interpretive vantage points. Or, to keep things from unduly proliferating, we might unite sensuousness, work, and consciousness under the aegis of interests and utilities and sensuousness, desire, and consciousness under the aegis of the passions and hedonic satisfactions. We then have the basis for the characteristic valuations of critical theory, with respect to which power in the ordinary sense plays its instrumental part. Given their conceptual derivation and historical specificity, these values can never be absolutized or maintained with apodictic certainty. But this does not mean that we are condemned to a Nietzschean or Foucauldian collapse of values (including truth and knowledge) into power. To be sure, political knowledge is never innocent—never purely detached, purely disinterested, purely objective. This does not mean, however, that it is only guilty—only partisan, only interested, only subjective. Rather, the needs, interests, and desires of individuals and collectivities of individuals constitute quite definite if situationally contingent standards of judgment. We may not be able to escape the element of contestation in this orientation toward ethical life and therefore must necessarily think about how to establish rules of political fair play. But so long as we are content with being human, all-too-human, we do not need metaphysical certainties to preserve us from postmetaphysical nihilism and moral suicide.

11.

With these very general features of critical theory in mind, we might view capitalist development from the perspective of resistance and resistance overcome. Here, again, is the basic Nietzschean formulation:

> The will to power can manifest itself only against resistances; therefore it seeks that which resists it—this is the primeval tendency of the protoplasm when it extends its pseudopodia and feels about. Appropriation and assimilation are above all a desire to overwhelm, a forming, shaping and reshaping, until at length that which has been overwhelmed has entirely gone over into the power domain of the aggressor and increased the same. (*WP*, p. 346)

The establishment of capitalist hegemony requires overcoming anticapitalist resistances. And, bowing in Foucault's direction, we might claim that power here has a juridico-discursive form: the emergent bourgeoisie seeks to gain control of political institutions that are then utilized in its own interests. As Foucault would certainly insist, this bourgeois deployment of juridico-discursive power was productive as well as repressive and far more complex than either structural or top-down models would suggest. But for all its strategic and tactical complexity, it is interpretable in terms of the legitimating codes of liberal political theory and from the perspective of Marxist ideology critique.

In the present context, we cannot attempt either a demonstration of the preceding historiographical claim or a strategic analysis of capitalist development. We can, however, briefly adumbrate the resistances confronting the emergent capitalist system. There was first the resistance offered by the preexisting mode of production in Europe and then resistance to the spread of capitalism from its geographic point of origin. Here lies the genesis of the system—the economic and political processes through which it emerged from feudalism, the bloody progress of colonialism and imperialism through which it expanded its scope, and the step-by-step creation of a world market. Starting with the primitive accumulation of capital, the process culminates in the defeat of peoples and cultures existing outside the capitalist ambit.

Third, capitalism encounters internal resistance. The capitalist ruling class, the bourgeoisie, confronts labor, the modern working class, its necessary counterpart in the operation of the system. One can debate just when, in the more rapidly developing capitalist nations, the class struggle between labor and capital became a structural feature of political life. But it was plainly visible by the early 1800s, and Marx, not only a young Hegelian but also the young Hegel of his time, grasped its theoretical and practical significance. He articulated its parameters and possibilities so well that his name came to signify the working-class movement against capitalist domination.

This brings us back to our point of departure in Chapter 1—the hard times confronted by contemporary critical theory. Although working-class interests and aspirations continue to have political effects and working-class organizations can still disrupt the ordinary functioning of the system, the working classes of the world no longer pose a credible threat to the viability of the system itself. Even the various specters of communism—the ideological apparitions of the cold war—have been dispelled. Depending on one's political interests, one can celebrate this state of affairs or lament it, but it seems hard to deny the end of the class struggle as we knew it.

"Not so fast," it might be objected, "you have been blinded by the short-run success of post–cold war capitalism. You seem to be presupposing more or less steady economic growth, maybe even the conquest or at least sub-stantial smoothing out of the business cycle. Naïvely, you are taking the apologists of capitalism at their word. But severe economic crises cannot be ruled out, and in the event of sustained economic decline, one might witness a renewal of effective leftist politics."

Possibly so. And one might add that the ruling classes themselves have been making haste to strip away the state welfare provisions that have given workers something to lose. They have been relentlessly turning back the clock and perhaps re-creating the conditions for working-class struggle. Indeed, it might even be claimed that we are oddly, or perhaps perversely, in a situation resembling that in which Marxism originated—a situation in which political democracy and social inequality advance concomitantly. But these conditions powerfully animate the irrationalist political tendency that Umberto Eco characterizes as "ur-fascism." And this is the fourth form of resistance to capitalism, one that—like working-class struggle—its normal operations incite.

According to Eco, ur-fascism is a loosely organized set of contradictory elements that can be combined in varying ways. These include cult of tradi-tion, maintained in a syncretistic fashion; rejection of modernism; action for action's sake; rejection of critical reason; fear of difference; appeal to frus-trated middle classes; obsession with a plot; envy of powerful enemies, whom one is nonetheless destined to defeat; pacifism as betrayal of the cause, life as incessant warfare; contempt for the weak combined with a pop-ulist elitism; education of everyone to be a hero; and sexual machismo that is easily displaced onto weapons (Eco 1995, pp. 14–15). Classically ur-fascis-tic movements grow in the soil of lower-middle-class discontent. Whatever their precise social location, however, they are fed by the fear of things get-ting worse and by ressentiment against those who are perceived as the cause of their distress. The less this fear and ressentiment can be warded off by economic prosperity and the less it can be contained by progressive social movements, the more it strengthens the ur-fascistic potentialities of capital-ist economies.

So to return to the objection, my brief, stylized sketch of capitalism as a world system is not intended to imply the inevitability of unrestrained capi-talist hegemony. A revival of effective leftist politics cannot be ruled out. But the socioeconomic conditions that would seem to favor interest-based, working-class action also feed ur-fascistic fevers.

Ur-fascistic movements are particularly primitive forms of group-emotional activity, or modalities of collective action in which interest-based rationality is overcome by irrationalizing psychological forces. The wide-spread anti-immigrant hysteria of the late 1990s and the reemergence of

long-latent ethnic hostilities in Eastern Europe and elsewhere are characteristic instances. I am not arguing that we are about to be swept away by
great ur-fascistic waves but only that the structural conditions of contemporary capitalism accentuate irrationalist political tendencies. These tendencies are irrational in the specific sense that they do not serve the interests of
those adhering to them. No gains in socioeconomic well-being result from
them. They function instead as conduits for the displacement of the locus of
conflict. Anger and frustration are directed away from those in power onto
racial and other scapegoats. In this way, ur-fascism, which in one sense is a
resistance to capitalist hegemony, is simultaneously a means for stabilizing
it. Or, to be more precise, ur-fascism stabilizes capitalist systems so long as
it can be structurally contained. If it becomes the dominant political trend,
it may very well explode them.

In their relatively domesticated forms, ur-fascism and related political
tendencies are cases of *mass motives serving ruling-class interests.* Ordinary
people are massed into an emotional group on the basis of identification
with their oppressors. Class oppositions disappear in an intensely charged
sense of national identity. Hostile impulses are then directed, indeed projected, outward. A paranoid situation is created in which the foreign or racial
Other is endowed with all the malignant and destructive impulses that have
been split off from the purified nation. And because this intergroup formation massively reduces complexity and correspondingly reduces anxiety, it is
extremely resistant to rational discourse. Indeed, reasoned argument is
interpreted as a threat to group identity and tends to be viewed as treaso-
nous.

If we shift the angle of psychoanalytic vision just a bit, it is easy to see that
with ur-fascism politics is in the paranoid-schizoid position. That is, the vir-
ulent scapegoating of outsiders and immigrants proceeds from and rational-
izes collective paranoid-schizoid defenses. The deployment or mobilization
of these defenses is determined objectively and subjectively: objectively by
the uncertainty concerning well-being that is the common lot of (especially)
middle classes in the current, predatory phase of late capitalist development,
subjectively by the anxiety that accompanies this insecurity. The malignancy
of the paranoid-schizoid group process is proportional to the anxiety it
expresses and defends against. The more intense the anxiety, the more the
group process approximates to psychosis, and the less amenable it becomes
to rational discourse.

Thus we—critical theorists—find ourselves not only in hard times but
also between a rock and a hard place. On the one side, we face a victorious
capitalism identified with interest-based rationality and claiming a monop-
oly on moral and ethical valuations. It constitutes an overwhelmingly formi-

dable resistance to the emancipatory project of critical theory. On the other side, we see diffuse ur-fascistic tendencies and movements, suffused with rage and ressentiment, aligned with and justified by appeals to national and ethnic sentiments—and carrying with them the recurrent threat of bestialized politics and a relapse into barbarism. Hence we might ask, how are we to keep our political heads about us when the space for emancipatory politics is so maddeningly constricted? And when, as I now would like to argue, we can feel the metabolic ground shifting disturbingly under our feet.

12.

In the preceding analysis of capitalist hegemony, I utilized the double optic of interests and desires. Although these two perspectives were inflected with Marxist and psychoanalytic meaning, they are quite conventional modalities of political interpretation. We find them deployed in Plato's *Republic* and Aristotle's *Politics*, as well as in the classical texts of liberal political theory. They also fit together easily with a juridico-discursive conception of power—not surprisingly, given that Foucault characterizes emergent capitalist systems in these terms. Our brief orchestration of political themes suggests that power retains a juridico-discursive form in late as well as emergent capitalist systems, likewise that interests and desires maintain their interpretive efficacy. But it is also true that social power in the contemporary world extends beyond or below collective interests, desires, and political institutions, that it penetrates into our life-worlds to an extraordinary degree and in unprecedented fashion. Hence the interpretive appropriateness of Foucault's notions of biopower and biopolitics—power that aims at control over life processes rather than the right of restricting freedom and putting to death.

I think it is fair to say that biopower is not a historical novelty, indeed that in all societies life processes are regulated and disciplined. Hence the task of the historian of power relationships would be to trace out the variable ways in which juridico-discursive power and biopower interact in different societies, along with the cultural variation in their content and form. Within this analytic framework, one would then attempt to specify the distinctive features of the capitalist, especially the late capitalist, deployment of power. And in this regard, anthropological schemata might be of some use. What if— exercising the right to reorient concepts for pragmatic purposes—we were to identity juridico-discursive power with control over individual and collective interests and desires and biopower with control over the field of sensuous or metabolic interaction? This would fit tolerably well with Foucault's specification of the "*anatomo-politics of the human body*" and "*a bio-politics of the population*" as the principal modalities of biopower (Foucault 1990, p. 139). It would also permit us to put forward the proposition that *capitalist development has disrupted the field of sensuous interaction to a historically unprecedented degree.* This is not an unmitigated disaster. The extraordinary efficacy of modern medicine, for example, is an instance of such metabolic disruption. But there are manifold ways in which the yin and yang of human / natural existence have been thrown quite desperately out of balance by the technological and cultural impact of the capitalist mode of production.[9]

I am not contending that metabolic disruption is uniquely a feature of capitalist systems but rather that capitalist economies do have a unique capacity for overcoming "natural"—human natural and ecological—resistances. We might avail ourselves of a classical analogy in this regard, namely, Aristotle's analysis of natural and perverse acquisition in the *Politics*. The aim of natural acquisition is use, specifically securing the amount and kind of property that "suffices for a good life" (Barker 1958, p. 21). Sufficiency provides the limit of acquisition. In the perverse instance, by contrast, the concern is only with getting a fund of money through the exchange of commodities. This form of acquisition "may be held to turn on the power of currency; for currency is the starting-point, as it is also the goal, of exchange." It follows that "the wealth produced by . . . [the perverse] form of the art of acquisition is unlimited" (p. 25). Thus the ends-means relationship of natural acquisition is inverted (money becomes an end in itself instead of a means to the end of need-satisfaction), and the limit of use and sufficiency is violated.

Aristotle's analysis of acquisitive perversity is cast in terms of interests. He himself links it to human passions, especially to "men's anxiety about livelihood" (p. 26); we could say, in tried and true Marxist fashion, that Aristotle's perverse mode of acquisition becomes the norm in capitalist systems. Legitimate in its own eyes, it is perverse when viewed from the perspective of human flourishing. More to the present point, we can restate Aristotle's argument in terms of human sensuousness. Then the perversity consists of inverting the relationship between the life-drive and death-drive and the will to power. The former, like the criteria of utility and the good life in the *Politics*, provide organism-specific standards of health and well-being, bases for judging what is too much and what is too little. The will to power, when it displaces the life- and death-drives within the determinacy of pleasure and pain, knows no such limitations. It presses on restlessly and endlessly, unmindful of the damage done in the course of its advance.

I should emphasize that this line of argument is not reductive. The aim is not to replace interests and desires as standards for assessing human flourishing but rather to augment them with the perspective of human sen-suousness. Nor am I contending that the life-drive, death-drive, and will to power require no guidance and cultivation, that we instinctively know what is too much and too little. Creatures of imagination that we are, we must learn from experience how to establish and maintain metabolic balance. But I am claiming that the characteristically Nietzschean inversion of the will to power and the determinacy of pleasure and pain is perverse, precisely a pre-scription for human suffering rather than human flourishing. Thus to return to the former point from this direction: the perversion of acquisition and the perversion of the determinacy of pleasure and pain are not unique to capitalist systems, but capitalist systems both join and empower them. The will to power drives the acquisitive impulse, the acquisitive impulse dri-ves the will to power, and—mobilized through the self-expanding tech-nologies of capitalist production—they conjointly penetrate life-worlds and disrupt their organic balance.

Fatefully, this overpowering and overturning of natural limits is sup-ported by our sexual arrangements, specifically by our deeply rooted ten-dency to identify the natural with the feminine-maternal. As Dorothy Din-nerstein argues, the mother of a neonatal infant is its

> main contact with the natural surround, the center of everything the infant
> wants and feels drawn to, fears losing and feels threatened by. She is the
> center also of the non-self, an unbounded, still unarticulated region within
> which the child labors to define itself and to discover the outlines of durable
> objects, creatures, themes. She is this global, inchoate, all-embracing
> presence before she is a person, a discrete finite human being with a sub-
> jectivity of her own. (1976, p. 93)

This relationship of mother and child has a twofold implication. On the one hand, a gendered split is established, in which women figure as the natural and men as the human. The woman, not-quite-human and with her subjec-tivity denied, is obliged to satisfy the needs of the man. She is to be used, and he is entitled to use her. On the other hand, the natural world is figured as maternal, with the same consequence: "She"—mother nature—is to be used, and he—mankind—is entitled to use "her":

> Inextricable from the notion that nature is our semi-sentient early mother
> is the notion that she is inherently inexhaustible, that if she does not pro-
> vide everything we would like to have it is because she does not want to,
> that her treasure is infinite and can if necessary be taken by force. This view
> of Mother Earth is in turn identical with the view of woman as Earth

Mother, a bottomless source of richness, a being not human enough to have needs as primary, as self-evident, as the importance of our own needs, but voluntary and conscious enough so that if she does not give us what we expect she is withholding it on purpose and we are justified in getting it from her any way we can. *The murderous infantilism of our relation to nature follows inexorably from the murderous infantilism of our sexual arrangements.* (Pp. 109–10; emphasis added)

Very much in line with the present analysis, Dinnerstein does not see this doubled perversity as uniquely a feature of our own society but rather as built into any society in which mothers and other women are the sole nurturers of infants. But she notes that "men's exploitation of Mother Nature has so far been kept in check largely by their conception of the practical risk they themselves ran in antagonizing, depleting, spoiling her" and that this check on male rapacity has been significantly weakened. The fear of antagonizing Mother Nature has decreased as technological potency has increased. Consequently, we now have the illusion that "the son has set his foot on the mother's chest, he has harnessed her firmly to his uses, he has opened her body once and for all and may now help himself at will to its riches" (p. 104). Beneath the juridico-discursive Law of the (oedipal) Father, we have the envious, greedy, and destructive will to (bio)power of the infant son. Women's embodied will and the boundaries of the biosphere are equally resistances to be overcome.

Thus the capitalist mode of social production involves the development and mobilization of technological instrumentalities that transform and disrupt human life-worlds to an unprecedented degree. The ameliorative potential of this enhanced human capability is undercut not only by the purely economic features of the system—the laws of the market and the imperatives of the profit motive—but also by the ways in which capitalist production has overcome the natural resistances to the exercise of masculine will to power. With mechanized shovels and motivated by ressentiment at imagined maternal domination, we dig our own metabolic graves.

13.

When we see our situation through the optic of juridico-discursive power, we orient ourselves toward matters of justice and rights. When we view it through the optic of biopower, our concerns are with the health of the body politic, quite literally with the psychophysiological integument of human flourishing. In both regards, the picture is disquieting, anxiety-provoking, and frustrating. It is so easy to imagine the utilization of technological means for richly humanizing ends and so hard to imagine, given the existing power relationships, how these ends are to be achieved. Consequently, one might foresee a time when the adherents of critical theory, despondent and afraid, turn away from the political world and devote themselves to tending their private gardens. These might not be Nietzschean gardens, sealed off from meaningful human intercourse. They might be rich in love and rewarding work. But from a political perspective, the attempt to live such a strictly private existence would be nihilistic, an abandonment of the task of finding value in and establishing values for public life. Thus we come to the question broached earlier: how are we to keep our political heads about us when the stakes in the game are high and the chances of winning are low?

Let me grant, first, that one might reject this line of inquiry altogether. Maybe human values can be realized within rather than through the transformation of capitalism. Maybe the either/or of capitalist hegemony and ur-fascism distorts the prospects for progressive political development. Maybe our lives are not so far out of metabolic balance after all. Maybe so. It would take a far more detailed and empirically based analysis than has been possible here to counter such claims, and even then the matter would be open to dispute. Perhaps it will be granted, however, that the preceding depiction of capitalist hegemony is discursively meaningful, that it is worth thinking and talking about. On this assumption, I will proceed to consider its epistemological, psychological, and pragmatic implications.

Once upon a time and in certain quarters, it was believed that epistemological orientations were inherently political—that, for example, dialectical reason was by its very nature radical and critical, whereas empiricism was necessarily affirmative of existing situations. This belief is hard to sustain on logical grounds and even more on empirical ones: reactionary dialecticians are just as common as radical ones, and healthy common sense can easily turn critical when circumstances warrant it. Still, I believe that the union of dialectical reason and constrained perspectivism does help us to stay oriented to the political things of this world. Unlike classical dialectics, perspectivism precludes (or ought to preclude) the a priori valorization of any one position within a dialectical manifold and the dogmatic assumption that, in the course of dialectical development, reason and reality will be definitively joined. Unlike Nietzsche's perspectivism, dialectical reason precludes the reduction of knowledge to power and the nihilistic tendency, built into an ontology of the will to power, toward negation without end— the overcoming of resistance for its own sake. Or, to put it another way, perspectivism has a built-in proclivity for fission and entropy, while dialectical reason is all too fusional and neg-entropic. Because everyday and political life pull in both directions, our epistemological orientation should help us to follow and think through these oscillations. And because even stable political situations involve incessant small changes and adjustments while unstable ones involve large-scale transformations, we require concepts that focus our attention on change and movement to keep us attuned to the dynamic aspect of social processes. Hence the utility of thinking in terms of the will to power when it is joined to the concept of immanent negation.

Here is a pertinent example of applied dialectical perspectivism. Foucault offers us a distinction between juridico-discursive power and biopower. Only partially following his lead, we treated these as interpretive perspectives rather than as conceptual rivals. But in the course of our discussion, the meaning of the concepts started to change. When we align biopower with the field of sensuous or psychophysiological interaction, we are placing it at the beginning of a process of development. Whether ontogenetically or phylogenetically (historically), the first order of business is the establishment of some kind of metabolic balance—limited by the built-in features of the human species but variable with circumstance and custom. In psychoanalytic terms, biopower is played out in the preoedipal realm and under the shadow of the determinacy of pleasure and pain. It tends to take form as the paranoid-schizoid position, the first and last defense against abjective disintegration.

The second step in this developmental process is the crystallization of juridico-discursive power in familial and other institutions that function under the aegis of patriarchal law. This involves a profound negation of the feminine-maternal and of women. Stated more concretely, it sets men and women as well as male and female identities in binary opposition to each other—although the antagonism in this oppositional relationship may be covered over by mutual acquiescence to these power / gender relationships. And, as Dinnerstein emphasizes, both sexes may settle for this arrangement rather than risk regression into the terrors of the mother-world.

A third step occurs if and when the two forms of power are fused, in such a way that discipline, regulation, and normalization replace or supplement the play of juridico-discursive power. One might even state this possible development in classical dialectical terms: biopower in Foucault's sense is precisely the sublation of the distinction between biopower in our sense and juridico-discursive power. It combines, in a totalizing fashion, the metabolic permeability of the one with the social control and legitimacy of the other, while preserving the two forms of power as moments in its overall operation.

Each of these three stages in the postulated dialectical manifold is an interpretive perspective that must be experienced as such and not in the light of future development. But if development does occur, then each stage is reinterpreted from the perspective of development itself. Meanwhile, we who are attempting to think perspectivally and dialectically about these power relationships have an interest in going beyond them. Our values—establishment of metabolic balance and reduction of unnecessary pain, satisfaction of needs and creative work, gratification of desire and fulfilling relationships, compassion and mutual recognition—are more negated than realized within such patterns and structures of social interaction. To be sure, our world has not really been one-dimensionalized in this fashion. It is a complex of emancipatory and normalizing, humanizing and dehumanizing, tendencies and forces. For just this reason, it demands of us something akin to the mental discipline required for the practice of psychoanalysis, namely, the ability to tolerate the anxiety that necessarily accompanies uncertainty and complexity. Faced with highly problematic political circumstances, it is tempting to batten down the intellectual hatches—to retreat to simplifying assumptions and dogmatic positions, narrow our interpretive horizons, and substitute metaphysical beliefs for political reasoning. Dialectical perspectivism encourages us to move in the opposite direction.

This line of reasoning does not eventuate in prescriptions for either the realization of the aims of critical theory or the maintenance of political sanity. Rather, the present analysis suggests that political sanity is difficult to preserve and that it requires quite considerable self-discipline and self-overcoming. The example of clinical psychoanalysis provides some guidance in this regard but of a rather peculiar sort: when it comes to broadening the horizons of personal and political judgment, there are very few rules to guide.

As to the matter of political aims, we have no choice but to live with the disjunction between the potential for realizing the project of human emancipation and the recognition that this potential is not going to be realized any time soon. In the foreseeable future, we are not going to be able to go beyond capitalism. We cannot hope for the emergence of a society in which the free development of each individual is a condition for the free development of all. Capitalism is a system of structurally determined inequality; its normal and necessary operations preclude genuine social democracy. This is the sobering premise of contemporary emancipatory politics. Yet from its inception, capitalism has combined emancipatory and oppressive tendencies. We must resist the temptation of one-dimensionalizing it one way or the other. Putting the point pragmatically, we can hope and work for the realization of progressive policy aims so long as these do not (unduly?) inhibit the process of capital accumulation or threaten the power relationships that maintain them. This defines a substantial field for political action, one in which outcomes are contingent and not determinable in advance. It is an abnegation of political responsibility not to take advantage of these potentialities, even if social injustices and metabolic imbalances cannot be altogether eliminated.

To carry the argument a bit further, the realization of progressive political aims depends on collective action, ultimately at national or even international levels. Local action, vital as it may be, just is not enough. We—critical theorists—must be prepared for a war on two fronts: against the hegemonic power of capitalist ruling classes, on the one side, and against sometimes diffuse, sometimes organizationally embodied, ur-fascistic tendencies, on the other. The fissiparous tendency in leftist politics, sometimes celebrated in postmodern discourse, puts us at a terrible strategic and tactical disadvantage. The dangers of a dissent-stiffling leftist hegemony, although not a mere phantasy, are far less pressing than the risks of self-fragmentation and political incoherence. In this regard, the more things change, the more they stay the same: resistance politics must be both dialectically self-unifying and perspectivally self-differentiating.

Finally, we might remind ourselves of the concluding words of Max Weber's "Politics as a Vocation," which, with their Nietzschean resonances, fit both our times and the inquiry that is now coming to an end:

> Politics is a strong and slow boring of hard boards. It takes both passion and perspective. Certainly all historical experience confirms the truth—that man would not have attained the possible unless time and again he had reached out for the impossible. But to do that a man must be a leader, and not only a leader but a hero as well, in a very sober sense of the word. And even those who are neither leaders nor heroes must arm themselves with that steadfastness of heart which can brave even the crumbling of all hopes. . . . Only he has the calling for politics who is sure that he shall not crumble when the world from his point of view is too stupid or too base for what he wants to offer. Only he who in the face of all of this can say 'In spite of it all!' has the calling for politics. (1958, p. 128)

We are not overmen, and most of us are not heroes. But in ways great and small, we are participants in the politics of our time, with a responsibility toward our future as well as our present well-being. It may be that, when we draw back the curtain of political civility, we see an ongoing war of attrition in which neither quick victories nor lasting peace is to be anticipated. Yet it would be a mistake to equate these battles with a politics of the will to power. As I have attempted to demonstrate, such a politics leads only into darkness. If, by contrast, we are to emerge from the darkness of our own times, moral valuations grounded in love and compassion must light our way.

14.

In the end, then, we do not stand on Nietzschean ground, and we do not aim at becoming the sovereign individuals he depicts in *On the Genealogy of Morals*. But we do accept the goal of a certain self-overcoming—of emancipating ourselves from mental and other forms of slavery. And in this regard, we cannot but be grateful to Nietzsche, whose interior explorations lead us into our own personal depths, where, if we survive, we may discover or create the capacity to overcome those resistances that keep us from being more fully ourselves.

Notes

Chapter 1

1. The difference between a psychology based on the will to power and one oriented toward hedonic and utilitarian ends has not received the attention it deserves. But see the excellent essay by Ivan Soll (in Schacht 1994), in which the will to power is seen as successfully challenging hedonic and utilitarian explanations of cruelty and asceticism.

2. There are many and fairly obvious affinities between Nietzsche and Freud, as well as some evidence of a more Nietzschean contribution to the origins of psychoanalysis than Freud was wont to admit (see Lehrer 1995). Moreover, C. G. Jung had a serious interest in Nietzsche. But it cannot be said that Nietzsche is commonly read as someone whose thinking has implications for psychoanalytic practice. Daniel Chapelle (1993), who attempts to align eternal return with the repetition compulsion, the uncanny, and transference, is pretty much alone in seeing the clinical implications of Nietzschean notions.

For other but less sustained studies in this general area, see Ginsberg 1973, Monette 1989, and Stauth and Turner 1988, chap. 4.

3. On this issue, see Megill 1996.

4. An early example is Francis Fukuyama (1992), although his argument has an interesting Nietzschean twist. Since that time the literature on this newest of world orders has grown rapidly. If one were to use an economic metaphor, I'd say that supply now far outstrips demand.

5. See Chapter 3 of my *Psychoanalytic-Marxism: Groundwork* (1993) for a critical analysis of Marcuse, Reich, and Erich Fromm.

6. Foucault's relationship to Nietzsche is anything but straightforward. See especially the interview conducted by Gérard Raulet (in Kritzman 1988, pp. 17–46) and the one with Gilles Barbadette and André Scala (in Kritzman 1988, pp. 242–54). For Foucault's reading of Nietzsche, see his "Nietzsche, Genealogy, History" (1971).

Mahon (1992) provides a reading of Foucault as a Nietzschean genealogist, while Forrester (1990) does a nice job of tracing out Foucault's ambivalent relationship to Freud and psychoanalysis.

An earlier version of my analysis of Foucault and critical theory was published in the *South Atlantic Quarterly* 97, no. 2 (Spring 1998).

7. "Maurice Florence" is arguably Foucault himself (Gutting 1994, p. viii).

8. I must admit to taking a step too far when I translate Foucault back into Nietzsche in so direct a fashion. Nietzsche was quite comfortable with macrolevel concepts, including those of social class, whereas Foucault is much more skeptical concerning the descriptive accuracy, theoretical utility, and political value of such totalizations. One might also say that the will to power in Nietzsche sometimes merges with what, in Foucault's terms, is its juridico-discursive expression. Nonetheless, the Nietzschean resonances of Foucault's analysis of the deployment of sexuality are fairly unmistakable.

9. What follows is an extremely simplified and condensed representation of the propositions I put forward in, especially, chapter 6 of *Psychoanalytic-Marxism: Groundwork*. I have also modified the presentation so as to respond to some of the issues raised by Foucault.

10. The English middle school of psychoanalysis evolved as a meeting ground for the rival factions headed by Anna Freud and Melanie Klein and has proved to be a congenial location for American feminist psychoanalysts. Winnicott is the most influential of the middle school analysts.

My own approach to individuation and gender development follows the lead of Klein, Winnicott, and the post-Kleinian psychoanalyst W. R. Bion, on the one hand, and Jessica Benjamin (1980, 1988, 1995), Nancy Chodorow (1978, 1989, 1994), Dorothy Dinnerstein (1976), and Jane Flax (1990, 1993), on the other.

11. Foucault is somewhat equivocal in this regard.

12. See Jay 1993 for a delicate treatment of the problem of vision and the visible in Foucault.

Chapter 2

1. Wayne Klein (1997, p. 181 ff.) demonstrates rather convincingly that the arrangement of materials in *The Will to Power* is sometimes misleading. He does not succeed in demonstrating that the materials themselves are fundamentally misleading or interpretively useless.

For a careful review of Nietzsche's deployment of the will to power in his published and unpublished work, see Williams 1996.

2. Kaufmann traces the biographical emergence of the will to power in chapter 6 of *Nietzsche: Philosopher, Psychologist, Antichrist* (1956). The concept itself is clearly articulated by Danto (1965, chap. 8), Schacht (1983, chap. 4), and Stambaugh (1987, chap. 4).

3. George Stack (1994) offers a quite different explanation of Nietzsche's experimentalist bracketing. He contends that Nietzsche was self-consciously mythologizing when he characterized natural processes in what we would think of as psychological terms. In the present instance, he believes Nietzsche is being "cunningly misleading," that he dons an experimentalist guise to disguise his mytho-poetic intentions (p. 271).

I do not find this interpretation entirely implausible. It accounts for Nietzsche's parenthetical comment that he is pushing the reduction to "the point of nonsense" and it fits with Nietzsche's perspectival claims that we cannot help seeing things in our own terms—hence that we necessarily anthropomorphize the cosmos in our attempts to understand it.

We will return to this issue in the following chapters. But for now, two points are relevant. First, Nietzsche's deployment of the will to power in the cosmological field is helpful in clarifying the meaning of the concept. Second, whatever *his* intent in so doing, from our perspective he is creating at least the functional equivalent of a creation myth.

4. On the concept of the will in Schopenhauer and Nietzsche, see also Gillespie 1995, chap. 6.

5. Once, in his mother's absence, the little boy had made himself "gone" by first looking in a mirror and then crouching beneath its lower edge (p. 15). I mention this only because we sometimes forget that the issues of alienation and self-mastery that are central to Lacan's conceptualization of the mirror stage occur within an intersubjective field.

6. Here Freud was saying more than he knew. As Dorothy Dinnerstein (1976) recognized, the son's desire to punish his apparently all-powerful mother for her various sins is a principal determinant of normative masculine identity. See Section 13 below.

7. I hasten to add that it is not my intention to drag notions of psychic energy back into psychoanalytic discourse. But energic notions are convenient metaphors in the present context.

8. Readers of *The Phenomenology of Spirit* will recognize my indebtedness to Hegel's analysis of force in the third chapter of that work.

9. I am basing myself here on the much more detailed arguments I put forward in chapter 6 of *Psychoanalytic-Marxism: Groundwork* (1993).

10. Michael Lewis (1993) makes a related but more specific argument. Anger occurs, he contends, "when a goal is interfered with and when organisms wish to overcome the obstacle to that goal. Anger, at least as a primary emotion, is designed to provide the motivation, including internal affective states and behaviors, to overcome the obstacle" (p. 165).

11. We will see in Chapter 3 that Nietzsche takes up this problem from his own perspective.

12. The dream reflects Freud's guilt over the injury done to "Irma" by his friend Fliess's incompetent surgery. It could also be interpreted as a wishful assertion of patriarchal power and authority in relation to women, whose role it is to open their orifices for inspection and penetration without resistance.

I cannot resist mentioning that, when I last taught *The Interpretation of Dreams* in a political theory seminar, the women in the class immediately felt and were repelled by the way Freud, stylistically and substantively, turned women into specimens to be displayed before a masculine audience. The men, for the most part, simply responded to the content of Freud's argument.

Chapter 3

1. But one might also argue in Nietzschean fashion that the contradiction is purely verbal—that is, an artifact of the universalizing metaphysics of language.

On the paradoxes of perspectivism, see Section 5 below and Nehamas 1985, introduction.

2. It is quite possible to interpret Nietzsche's philosophy as a type of metaphysics, despite his own disclaimers. For a recent example, see Richardson 1996.

3. It would take me too far afield to review the now quite abundant literature on Nietzsche's perspectivism, but one of the interpretive issues is built into my staging of the investigation. Nietzsche does not distinguish between what I term "constrained perspectivism" and a perspectivist worldview or between perspectivist inquiry and inquiries about perspectivism. As categories, the former have to be interpretively extracted or abstracted from the latter. This does no violence to Nietzsche's philosophizing, however, because he both puts forward truth-claims about things and skeptical claims about the truth. Hence a tension exists within his thinking around which my interpretive categories are deployed.

One can also categorize the interpretive literature in these terms. One set of writers privileges Nietzsche's epistemological skepticism, indeed subsumes all his philosophizing within it. Nietzsche is seen as denying any possible realist truth-claims and as rejecting any version whatsoever of the correspondence theory of the truth. Bernd Magnus (1978) is an early and persuasive representative of this position, and the postmodern Nietzscheans are also its adherents. But the difficulty with this reading of Nietzsche is that it does not account for the extremely large number of instances, from the beginning of his work until its end, in which he makes perfectly straightforward empirical and other claims. These claims can be put into perspectivist brackets, but they cannot be plausibly disavowed.

By contrast, there are those who both insist on our distinction and privilege constrained perspectivism over the perspectivist worldview. Here, however, we have the opposite difficulty: proponents of this position are forced to disavow the epistemological skepticism that characterizes Nietzsche's work from beginning to end.

The most interesting writer in the second camp is Maudemarie Clark (1990). Clark sees the mature Nietzsche (the Nietzsche of his last six published books) as a sophisticated neo-Kantian who has outgrown his earlier (and untenable) belief that human knowing falsifies reality. To me, this seems like an obvious attempt to save Nietzsche from himself. Clark rejects as epistemologically immature everything published and unpublished through *Beyond Good and Evil*. The key perspectivist passage in *On the Genealogy of Morals* (p. 119) is given a strained interpretation (Clark 1990, p. 128 ff). A similar passage in the 1886 preface to *Human, All Too Human*, which is even less favorable to her interpretation, is ignored. Section 354 of *The Gay Science*, which is contemporary with *On the Genealogy of Morals* and in which Nietzsche again claims that our knowing falsifies reality, is treated as a survival of his outgrown epistemological position (p. 149). And, as one would anticipate, the abundance of material in *The Will to Power*, in which Nietzsche continues to experiment with the limits of human knowledge, is ruled out of order. Yet the unpublished material is of a piece with section 354 of *The Gay Science* and with Nietzsche's epistemological speculations more generally. Finally, there is nothing in the works that Clark is willing to include to suggest that Nietzsche rejected the larger problematic. The most that can be said is that epistemological issues are not the focus of these texts.

The upshot is that Clark, like so many others, has created a Nietzsche in her own image. And so, of course, have I. Yet I believe my interpretation can be defended on the basis of Clark's own constrained perspectivist position—that is, on evidential grounds. Rather than choosing one side or the other of Nietzsche's epistemological orientation, I seek to establish a relationship between them. I grant that Nietzsche is a neo-Kantian in his analysis of historical, cultural, and psychological phenomena, but I also argue that he does not stay within neo-Kantian limits. Although he does not really reject the Kantian problematic, his critique of logic and language, along with his linking of perspectivism to the will to power, calls into question precisely the boundaries and limits that neo-Kantians such as Clark wish to maintain.

There is at least one other approach to this matter, which is to reject the imposition of our usual epistemological categories and concerns on Nietzsche. Instead of saddling him with our Kantian or even post-Kantian distinction between epistemology and ontology, one credits him with an ontology (the will to power) that directly and indissolubly has epistemological implications (perspectivism). One then has a set of internal conceptual relations from within which to interpret any given empirical instance or situation. This is the path followed, with quite considerable persuasiveness and skill, by Ruediger Grimm (1977), and I arrive at a somewhat similar interpretation of perspectivism and the will to power, albeit via a different route. But Grimm views this Nietzschean theory of knowledge as epistemologically adequate, while I see it as an instance of monisms that are either meaningless but true or meaningful but false. By differentiating between constrained perspectivism and perspectivism as a worldview, I hope to preserve the tensions that make Nietzsche so epistemologically interesting and challenging.

For other discussions of perspectivism, see Schacht 1983, pp. 108–17; Schrift 1990, pt. 3; Strong 1988, chap. 10; Warnock 1978; and Wilcox 1974, chap. 6.

4. Nietzsche also identifies the defensive function of causal explanations: they reduce fear by transforming the strange into the familiar—something new into a mere example (TI, p. 497).

5. Some writers (for example, Magnus 1978; Clark 1990) use this progression as a kind of inverted divided line. Just as one follows the divided line upward until one escapes the realm of becoming and participates as fully as is humanly possible in the realm of being, so one follows these steps downward until one is as fully immersed in the world of becoming as is humanly possible.

6. This passage can be read as a sly allusion to eternal recurrence, or at least to the problems of temporality (such as willing backward, willing the past) that the concept of eternal return purports to solve.

7. For another approach to psychoanalysis and perspectivism, see Lehrer 1995, chap. 13.

8. As is well known, Jacques Lacan was the first psychoanalyst to make systematic use of these Hegelian notions. For my own development of them, see Wolfenstein 1993.

Chapter 4

1. Graham Parkes, who offers a stunning interpretation of Nietzsche as psychologist in his *Composing the Soul: Reaches of Nietzsche's Psychology* (1994), comments: "That his psychological acumen . . . should have gone uncelebrated for so long stems from a failure to discern the figure of the man behind the works, the person in the thoughts, the soul and life in the corpus" (p. 1).

2. On Nietzsche and abjection, see also Graybeal 1990 and Oliver 1995.

3. In what follows I lean heavily on Pletsch 1991 and Hayman 1980. For a compassionate and quite lovely biographical sketch of Nietzsche that emphasizes his last days, see Chamberlain 1998. And for an antibiographical approach to Nietzsche's biography, see Allison 1993.

It should also be noted that all interpreters of Nietzsche's early life must make use of Elisabeth Förster-Nietzsche's reminiscences of her brother (1912). This is at the very least awkward, given Förster-Nietzsche's interest in the "normalization" of Nietzsche's legacy. The awkwardness is slightly reduced in the present case, however, because—if one reads past her own piety and ostentatious reverence for her brother—her impressions fit with images of Nietzsche derived from a variety of other sources.

4. This is the archetypal instance of passive-aggressive behavior or, at a deeper level, of schizoid retreat from persecutory interaction.

5. Nietzsche's demand that his mother carry him to bed—that she do as he wills—is (with a few important exceptions) the prototype of his interpersonal relationships generally. He maintained relationships primarily with people who admired him and who, when so requested, carried out his will.

6. One is reminded here of Lacan's interpretation of the *fort! da!* game: "We can now grasp in this the fact that in this moment the subject is not simply mastering his privation by assuming it, but that here he is raising his desire to a second power" (1977, p. 103).

7. My interpretation of Nietzsche's relationship with his father is more or less conventionally psychoanalytic. For an alternative approach to Nietzsche and Oedipus, see Strong 1985a.

8. Nietzsche's health did not markedly improve in the immediately following years. Hence we should read his claim that his thirty-sixth year was the nadir of his vitality as an interpretation, and an essentially psychoanalytic one at that. He, at least retrospectively, understood his illness as a paternal legacy.

9. Note that his mother's taking piano lessons along with her son is also evidence of intrusive maternal desire (as well as, perhaps, a simple desire for creative self-expression).

10. See also Pletsch 1991, chap. 5.

11. In one letter, Nietzsche addresses Wagner as *Pater seraphice* (in Middleton 1969, p. 66).

12. The extraordinary individual anticipates the overman of *Thus Spoke Zarathustra*, while those occupying a suprahistorical vantage point anticipate the last men and exhausted spirits who induce Zarathustra's nausea.

13. Hayman (1980) is especially good in both tracing the course of Nietzsche's illness and recognizing the complexity of its meaning. See especially chapters 7 and 8.

14. As noted in Chapter 2, some interpreters of eternal return rely on and take seriously the thought-experiments in the notebooks, at least some of which treat the concept as an empirical or cosmological proposition. Others tend to dismiss the notebooks and these thought-experiments. Characteristically, they interpret eternal return in psychological or existential/ethical terms.

My own position falls between these extremes. Like those who view eternal return in ethical and psychological terms, I find Nietzsche's cosmological arguments unconvincing. But that is a matter of how *we* view them and does not bear on the question of how *he* viewed them. He quite obviously took them seriously, and thus we might ask why.

My answer to this question is easy to anticipate. Nietzsche was haunted by the idea of eternal return from early on, as can be seen from its intrusion into his thinking about history in "On the Uses and Disadvantages of History for Life." He not only accepted but also was overwhelmed by it in the inspired moments I will presently analyze. In a deep, prerational or more-than-rational way, he believed it to be true. Indeed, if he did not believe it to be true, it would have been quite weightless. A mere hypothesis or thought-experiment does not have the psychological consequences he attributed to it. Moreover, my guess is that at least a semblance of "scientific" argument was part of the experience itself.

In short, while we might like to identify ourselves with the perspectivist Nietzsche who proclaims that we cannot look around our own corner, he himself turned it. He was then left with the task of reconciling what we would call a metaphysical experience with his antimetaphysical perspectivism. Scientific proof of the doctrine would have been helpful in this regard. That is, eternal return would carry more weight if it could be demonstrated to be as "true" as the laws of Newtonian physics.

A different approach to finding a middle ground is taken by Ivan Soll. Although he rejects all the cosmological arguments for eternal return, Soll contends that Nietzsche may have believed that even the possibility or plausibility of the idea brings with it all the consequences of its being proven to be true (1973, p. 325). In other words, if the idea cannot be disproved, one must live as if it were true. I think Nietzsche may have fallen back to this position, when his belief in eternal return was not sustained by his elevated moods. But this only adds to the importance of the cosmological arguments, without which the claim to plausibility is considerably reduced.

Magnus, despite his self-characterization as a splitter rather than a lumper, provides a notably thorough and thoughtful review of the arguments concerning eternal return in the notebooks.

For sustained and serious treatments of eternal return, see Clark 1990, Danto 1965, Haar 1996, Higgins 1987, Klossowki 1997, Lampert 1986, Löwith 1997, Magnus 1978, Nehamas 1985, Sadler 1995, Smith 1996, Stack 1994, Stambaugh 1972, 1987, Wood 1988, and Zuboff 1973.

15. Although Karl Jaspers rejects psychologizing interpretations of eternal return, he does raise the question of "whether or not Nietzsche's abnormal states included the well-known *déjà vu*: the conviction that everything present, down to the smallest detail, has been experienced in exactly the same way once before" (Jaspers 1965, p. 357).

16. The recognition that Nietzsche is, in this strong sense, anti-Hegelian and antidialectical, is the central insight in Gilles Deleuze's *Nietzsche and Philosophy* (1962). But I find little evidence to support Deleuze's claim that "Nietzsche had a profound knowledge of the Hegelian movement" (p. 162). (I discuss Deleuze's interpretation of Nietzsche and Hegel further in Chapter 6.)

17. The view that eternal return renders choices of action meaningless seemingly captures two aspects of the notion but bypasses its central implication. First, because present and future are already past, everything has already been determined. Second, because all that was

and is will come again, one cannot act in such a way as to eliminate that which is repulsive, and so forth.

One could respond that these issues arise only from perspectives that Nietzsche rejects—to wit, that he does not think in terms of determinism versus free will, in the first instance, or teleological conceptions of history and time, in the second. But he does take both issues seriously. Indeed, they constitute major obstacles to Zarathustra's affirmation of eternal return. And this is precisely the point. Eternal return poses the problem of affirming life just as it is. If, therefore, the interpreter claims that it renders the making of choices meaningless, this only proves that she or he has not affirmed eternal return.

18. In Chapter 2 I noted the emergence of the will to power in the section on "will and wave" from book 4 of *The Gay Science*. This section, along with "The Greatest Weight," was written between Nietzsche's initial experience of eternal return and the inspired composition of *Thus Spoke Zarathustra*. Thus the concepts of will to power and eternal return were born together—born, I am now suggesting, out of Nietzsche's own experience, that is, precisely as the conceptualization of this experience. So when we find him saying in *Beyond Good and Evil* that "a living thing seeks above all to *discharge* its strength—life itself is *will to power*," we are reading biography in the form of philosophy. Which is not to deny that it is philosophy.

19. This must be kept in mind when we come, in Chapter 6, to the analysis of the bad conscience and Christianity in *On the Genealogy of Morals*. There Nietzsche both condemns any such moral values as a kind of madness and affirms their role in making man into an "interesting" animal.

20. Although the challenge turns out to be merely rhetorical, the specification of Zarathustra's auditors is nonetheless important. They are experimental thinkers and free spirits, not rationalists or dogmatists—Nietzsche's preferred if largely imagined audience, which we are hereby invited to join.

21. Laurence Lampert, who is a distinguished interpreter of *Thus Spoke Zarathustra*, contends that we are not intended to take the argument itself seriously: "this chapter seems to go out of its way to mock syllogistic or formal argument" (1986, p. 166). I find nothing in the text to support this contention, and the extratextual evidence is that Nietzsche experimented with precisely this line of reasoning (*WP*, pp. 548–49). But I do believe Lampert is correct in characterizing the interaction as a kind of dialectical combat, in which Zarathustra defeats the dwarf with the latter's own weapons.

For my part, I cannot help being reminded once again of Plato's divided line, although I would not claim that Nietzsche had it in mind. In *The Republic* Plato puts forward three arguments in favor of the proposition that wisdom is a form of the Good. The first is based on an analogy to natural processes (The Analogy of the Sun), the second (The Divided Line itself) is mathematical, and the third is a philosophical allegory (The Allegory of the Cave). These are presented in ascending order and in such a way that the last one simultaneously unifies and transcends the first two. So too in the present instance. Zarathustra articulates eternal return in more or less rationalist—I'm tempted to say mathematical—terms. The argument is meant seriously but is recognized as having a limited value. Of greater value is the experience of eternal return, and this is presented in the form of an allegory or parable.

22. One could conceptualize the this-worldly return of the same in terms of Freud's repetition compulsion. Along these lines, see Chapelle 1993, chaps. 8–9.

23. There is a specific biographical referent for the problem of the transcendence of vengeance, as it is here being presented, and that is the bitter and embittering aftermath of Nietzsche's relationship with Paul Rée and Lou Salomé. See Chapter 5.

24. Stack (1994), either independently or following Hollingdale (1969), claims that, on the occasion of the fateful and presumably fateful fall, Nietzsche "found his father lying unconscious on the ground in front of his house and saw a dog nearby and heard its piercing cry" (p. 230). I find no evidence for this claim. Förster-Nietzsche reports the fall and states that her father stumbled over the family dog (1912, p. 16). But there is no mention of her brother,

and given the aggrandizing nature of her narrative, one assumes she would have included him if the family history or mythology supported so doing. Still, it seems likely that Nietzsche blends his father's subsequent symptoms and his own recurrent nausea in the image of the shepherd and the snake.

25. Graybeal (1990) provides a stunning interpretation of the shepherd and the snake, focused on the relationship between abjection, the maternal body, and speech.

Chapter 5

My thanks to Ruth Abbey for her helpful comments on an earlier version of this chapter.

1. There is now a rather substantial literature on Nietzsche and the feminine. See Burgard 1994; Derrida 1979; Diprose 1995; Graybeal 1990; Irigaray 1991; Oliver 1995; and Patton 1993. The interpretive approach taken in these works is, however, neither biographical nor developmental. A notable exception is Allen 1979.

The organization of the chapter has a loose resemblance to dream interpretation. The first level takes place in the cultural daylight, the second level is the dreamscape of *Thus Spoke Zarathustra*, and the third level is the dreamer, hence also the latent content of the dream.

Kathleen Higgins also uses the analogy to dreams and dream interpretation in her reading of *Thus Spoke Zarathustra* (1988, pp. 140 ff), while Hans-Georg Gadamer provides thoughtful interpretation of its narrative line (1988).

2. See Section III of Chapter 6 for certain biopolitical implications of this developmental moment.

3. There are variants of this phantasy in which the father plays an earlier role, but for our purposes, these need not be adumbrated.

4. See also Ansell-Pearson 1992 and Koelb 1994.

5. Daniel Breazeale, who edited and translated "On Truth and Lies in a Nonmoral Sense," contends that Nietzsche "never modified . . . the theory of truth which he advanced in his unpublished writings of the early 1870's" (1990, p. xlvi). This places him in direct opposition to Maudemarie Clark (1990), who, as we recall, claims that Nietzsche eventually outgrew the position that human knowledge is a falsification of things as they are in themselves.

I would argue that neither party to this debate is quite clear about what changes and what remains the same in Nietzsche's epistemology. Along with Breazeale and in opposition to Clark, I do see a continuity in Nietzsche's theory of knowledge: from first to last, he views logic and language as falsifications and defensive stabilizations of the unutterable flux of becoming. But in his early work, his epistemology is fundamentally aesthetic, whereas in his later work it is psychological. Thus he privileges metaphor over concept in the first instance and derives both metaphor and concept from the will to power in the second.

The consequence of this change is not, as Clark would have it, the disappearance of the problem of knowledge of reality (however one might label it) but rather of an apparent solution to that problem. For so long as Nietzsche's epistemology is fundamentally aesthetic, the question of "the real" can be appropriately begged. The appearance of skepticism covers over aesthetic self-satisfaction. All is metaphor, so it goes. Although one might protest that, with this aestheticization of the world, we are again in the realm of monisms that are meaningful but false or meaningless but true, any such argument is ruled out in advance by the reduction of concepts to metaphors. But once the will to power is extracted from the signifying chains of concepts and metaphors, once it is seen as underlying both linguistic modalities, then aesthetic defenses against philosophical questions must be surrendered. And then one may rightfully be required to explain just *what it is* that one is talking about.

I might add that the deconstructionist or, more broadly, literary appropriation of Nietzsche does less violence to his earlier than to his later work. So long as he is privileging metaphor, interpretive approaches that do the same are in harmony with his intent. But once both the problem of knowledge and the process of artistic creation are seen from the perspective of the will to knowledge, aesthetic interpretations lose much of their resonance with the original texts. Thus with Nietzsche's later work, we do better following Foucault than Derrida.

See Schrift 1990, chaps. 3–4, for an exceptionally lucid treatment of (in his words) "Nietzsche in France." And see Kofman 1972 for the classic treatment of Nietzsche and metaphor.

6. The enduring tripartite depiction of Nietzsche's philosophical evolution (from metaphysical to positivist to postpositivist) originates in Salomé's quite extraordinary portrayal in her *Nietzsche*.

7. The continuation of the aphorism comes closer to Nietzsche's personal feeling about marriage: "Men who are too intellectual have great need of marriage, though they resist it as they would a foul-tasting medicine" (*HH*, p. 151).

8. Nietzsche includes comments on fathers as well as mothers: "If one does not have a good father one should furnish oneself with one. . . . Fathers have much to do to make amends for having sons. . . . In the maturity of his life and understanding a man is overcome by the feeling his father was wrong to beget him" (p. 150). Again, the empirical applicability of these comments is problematic. If we take them autobiographically, however, they shed an interesting light on Nietzsche's ambivalent attempt to ennoble his father and provide himself with Polish ancestry in *Ecce Homo*.

9. Nietzsche later subsumed *Assorted Maxims and Opinions* and *The Wanderer and His Shadow* into *Human, All Too Human*, and he viewed *The Gay Science* as the culmination of this series of investigations. (I also acknowledge that I am giving short shrift to *Daybreak*, which marks a considerable advance in the "Nietzscheanizing" of Nietzsche's thinking.)

10. Nietzsche was influenced by the positivism of his friend Paul Rée during this period and even punningly characterized *Human, All Too Human* as a work of "Réealism" (Peters 1962, p. 86).

11. There are, of course, forerunners and anticipations of the later aesthetic. See especially section 552 of *Daybreak*, on spiritual pregnancy as ideal selfishness.

12. In *Daybreak* we find this passage: "When man gave all things a sex he thought, not that he was playing, but that he had gained a profound insight: — it was only very late that he confessed to himself what an enormous error this was, and perhaps even now he has not confessed it completely" (Nietzsche 1881 [hereafter *D*], p. 9). To which one might respond, what's sauce for the goose is sauce for the gander.

13. "*Women and their action at a distance*" is famously or notoriously put into play by Derrida in *Spurs: Nietzsche's Styles* (1979). See also Diprose 1993 and Vasseleu 1993.

14. Shortly after *The Birth of Tragedy* was published and his reputation as a philologist had been called into question, Nietzsche wrote to Wagner: "But there is one point which troubles me greatly at present: our winter semester has begun, and I have no students at all! Our philologists have not appeared! This is actually a *pudendum* and should be fearfully concealed from the world" (Middleton 1969, p. 110).

Here it is plain that pudendum = lack, literally the lack of students. But students are what the professor ought to have, which implies the symbolic equation, student = phallus. The lack of students, in other words, is a narcissistic wound which symbolizes castration and which equates to female genitals.

15. Joachim Köhler (1989) reads *Thus Spoke Zarathustra* as constructed around Nietzsche's conflicts about his homoerotic tendencies. I would not deny that these tendencies exist and that, more obviously, Nietzsche's youthful longing for a philosophical brotherhood constitutes one of *Thus Spoke Zarathustra's* biographical subtexts. But the objects of Zarathustra's desires are represented as feminine, which I do not believe is an instance of Nietzschean masking.

16. As is well known, there are warriors whose violent side is displayed only in warfare and whose intimate relationships are characterized by tenderness. But one supposes that, if

Nietzsche had wanted us to imagine a tender warrior, he would have pointed us in that direction.

17. He is accompanied by friends, but their dramatic use is to frame his aloneness rather than to provide him with company.

18. As we saw in the last chapter, Nietzsche did have some "platonic" friendships with women. He adored Cosima Wagner, and he maintained his close friendship with Malwida von Meysenbug for quite some time. He even proposed to Mathilde Trampedach in 1876, but calling the effort halfhearted would be to overstate its seriousness.

19. The story of Nietzsche and Salomé has been often told. The most detailed treatment is by Rudolph Binion (1968), but his prejudices are clear from his subtitular depiction of Lou as "Nietzsche's wayward disciple." For more evenhanded descriptions, see Podach 1931; Peters 1962; Livingstone 1984; and Martin 1991.

20. For an excellent reading, see Oppel 1993, as well as Krell 1994. For a more general interpretation of Irigaray, see Whitford 1989.

Chapter 6

1. Ian Forbes, discussing politics and individuality, sees "Nietzsche as the Dionysus to Marx's Apollo" (1991, p. 163). Given Marx's relationship to Hegel, this is not an implausible interpretation.

2. After writing this section, I was amused to come on an enticing little essay by Peter Sloterdijk entitled "Eurotaoism" (1989, pp. 99–116).

3. David Allison (1990, pp. 56–57) argues that, after the failure of *Thus Spoke Zarathustra* to find comprehending readers, Nietzsche fell back on aposiopesis (becoming silent) with respect to eternal return. Henceforth he implied the idea without stating it, so that readers would be led toward rather than directly confronted by it.

See also Kathleen Higgins 1994, Sarah Kofman 1994, and Richard White 1994, all of whom put forward arguments that suggest the continued importance of eternal return in Nietzsche's thinking and writing.

4. For a stunning interpretation of the role of envy in *Othello*, see Adelman 1997.

5. This interpretation might seem to be at odds with section 338 of *The Gay Science*, in which Nietzsche rejects pity but affirms helping friends "whose distress you *understand* entirely because they share with you one suffering and one hope" (p. 271). But he goes on to abjure commiseration: "I want to teach them what is understood by so few today, least of all by these preachers of pity: *to share not suffering but joy*" (ibid.). This is not a particularly helpful teaching for either psychoanalysts or true friends.

Martha Nussbaum, while not differentiating between pity and compassion, recognizes that Nietzsche's criticism of pity assails "the roots of the deepest sort of human love" (1994, p. 140).

6. Flax's criticisms of Foucault come from a position of considerable sympathy. Indeed, in *The American Dream in Black and White* (1998) she utilizes his analysis of power in her own investigation of the Clarence Thomas confirmation hearings.

7. I am here distinguishing between politics and culture. Nietzsche has important things to say about the latter, especially with respect to postmetaphysical nihilism as a widely spread social phenomenon. But his own comments on such things as state power, class conflict, and social movements pale rather considerably when compared with the more robust traditions of both critical and liberal political theory.

For sustained interpretations of Nietzsche on culture and politics, see Strong's groundbreaking *Friedrich Nietzsche and the Politics of Transfigurations* (1975, rev. ed. 1988), as well as Ansell-Pearson 1994, Connolly 1988, Conway 1997, Detwiler 1990, Heilke 1998, Love 1986, and Warren 1988. Additionally, Leslie Paul Thiele's *Friedrich Nietzsche and the Politics of the*

Soul (1990) nicely captures the inwardness of Nietzsche's "politics" and hence the difficulty of constructing social theory on this foundation: "for all his evangelical endeavors, the higher man primarily addresses an inner audience. He is caught up with and in himself" (p. 212).

8. These principles of psychophysiological functioning are treated more thoroughly in chapter 6 of my *Psychoanalytic-Marxism: Groundwork* (1993).

9. See ibid., chap. 8, for a related version of this argument.

References

Adelman, Janet. 1992. *Suffocating Mothers: Fantasies of Maternal Origin in Shakespeare's Plays, "Hamlet" to "The Tempest."* New York: Routledge.

———. 1997. "Iago's Alter Ego: Race as Projection in *Othello.*" *Shakespeare Quarterly* 48, no. 2: 125–44.

Allen, Christine. 1979. "Nietzsche's Ambivalence about Women." In Clark and Lange 1979, pp. 117–33.

Allison, David B., ed. 1990. "A Diet of Worms: Aposiopetic Rhetoric in *Beyond Good and Evil.*" *Nietzsche-Studien* 19:41–58.

———. 1993. "Nietzsche's Identity." In Ansell-Pearson and Caygill 1993, pp. 15–42.

Andrews, C. E., and M. O. Percival, eds. 1928. *Victorian Poetry.* Columbus, Ohio: R. G. Adams.

Ansell-Pearson, Keith. 1992. "Who Is the *Übermensch?* Time, Truth, and Woman in Nietzsche." *Journal of the History of Ideas* 53, no. 2:309–31.

———. 1994. *An Introduction to Nietzsche as Political Thinker.* New York: Cambridge University Press.

Ansell-Pearson, Keith, and Howard Caygill, eds. 1993. *The Fate of the New Nietzsche.* Aldershot, England: Avebury.

Barker, Ernest, trans. 1958. *The Politics of Aristotle.* New York: Oxford University Press.

Baynes, Cary F., trans. 1967. *The I Ching.* Princeton: Princeton University Press.

Benjamin, Jessica. 1980. "The Bonds of Love: Rational Violence and Erotic Domination." *Feminist Studies* 6:144–74.

———. 1988. *The Bonds of Love: Psychoanalysis, Feminism, and the Problem of Domination.* New York: Pantheon.

———. 1995. *Like Subjects, Love Objects.* New Haven: Yale University Press.

Bernstein, Doris. 1990. "Female Genital Anxieties, Conflicts, and Typical Mastery Modes." *International Journal of Psycho-Analysis* 71:151–65.

Binion, Rudolph. 1968. *Frau Lou: Nietzsche's Wayward Disciple*. Princeton: Princeton University Press.

Bion, W. R. 1962. *Learning from Experience*. In Bion 1977.

——. 1967. *Second Thoughts*. New York: Jason Aronson.

——. 1970. *Attention and Interpretation*. In Bion 1977.

——. 1977. *Seven Servants*. New York: Jason Aronson.

Blakney, R. B., trans. 1955. *The Way of Life*. New York: Mentor.

Breazeale, Daniel, ed. and trans. 1990. *Philosophy and Truth: Selections from Nietzsche's Notebooks of the Early 1870's*. Atlantic Highlands, N.J.: Humanities Press.

Brennan, Teresa, ed. 1989. *Between Feminism and Psychoanalysis*. London: Routledge.

Burgard, Peter, ed. 1994. *Nietzsche and the Feminine*. Charlottesville: University Press of Virginia.

Burnet, John. 1930. *Early Greek Philosophy*. 4th ed. London: A. and C. Black.

Chamberlain, Lesley. 1998. *Nietzsche in Turin: An Intimate Biography*. New York: Picador USA.

Chapelle, Daniel. 1993. *Nietzsche and Psychoanalysis*. Albany: State University of New York Press.

Chodorow, Nancy. 1978. *The Reproduction of Mothering*. Berkeley: University of California Press.

——. 1989. *Feminism and Psychoanalytic Theory*. New Haven: Yale University Press.

——. 1994. *Femininities, Masculinities, Sexualities*. Lexington: University Press of Kentucky.

Clark, Lorenne, and Lynda Lange, eds. 1979. *The Sexism of Social and Political Theory*. Toronto: University of Toronto Press.

Clark, Maudemarie. 1990. *Nietzsche on Truth and Philosophy*. New York: Cambridge University Press.

Connolly, William E. 1988. *Political Theory and Modernity*. New York: B. Blackwell.

Conrad, Joseph. 1902. *Heart of Darkness*. In Zabel 1976, pp. 490–603.

Conway, Daniel W. 1997. *Nietzsche's Dangerous Game: Philosophy in the "Twilight of the Idols."* Cambridge: Cambridge University Press.

Danto, Arthur C. 1965. *Nietzsche as Philosopher*. New York: Macmillan.

Darby, Tom, Béla Egyed, and Ben Jones, eds. 1989. *Nietzsche and the Rhetoric of Nihilism*. Ottawa: Carleton University Press.

Deleuze, Gilles. 1962. *Nietzsche and Philosophy*. New York: Columbia University Press, 1983.

Derrida, Jacques. 1979. *Spurs: Nietzsche's Styles*. Chicago: University of Chicago Press.

Detwiler, Bruce. 1990. *Nietzsche and the Politics of Aristocratic Radicalism*. Chicago: University of Chicago Press.

Dinnerstein, Dorothy. 1976. *The Mermaid and the Minotaur*. New York: Harper and Row.

Diprose, Rosalyn. 1993. "Nietzsche and the Pathos of Distance." In Patton 1993, pp. 1–26.

——. 1995. "Nietzsche, Ethics, and Sexual Difference." In Sedgwick 1995, pp. 69–83.

Dorsey, Denise. 1996. "Castration Anxiety or Feminine Genital Anxiety." *Journal of the American Psychoanalytic Association* 44, suppl.:283–302.

Eco, Umberto. 1995. "Ur-Fascism." *New York Review of Books*, June 22.

Ellison, Ralph. 1989. *Invisible Man*. New York: Random House.

Epstein, Mark. 1995. *Thoughts without a Thinker*. New York: Basic.

Euripedes. *The Bacchae*. In Grene and Lattimore 1966, pp. 155–220.

Flax, Jane. 1990. *Thinking Fragments*. Berkeley: University of California Press.

——. 1993. *Disputed Subjects*. New York: Routledge.

——. 1998. *The American Dream in Black and White*. Ithaca: Cornell University Press.

Forbes, Ian. 1991. "Marx and Nietzsche: The Individual in History." In Ansell-Pearson 1994, pp. 143–64.

Forrester, John. 1990. *The Seductions of Psychoanalysis: Freud, Lacan, and Derrida*. New York: Cambridge University Press.

Förster-Nietzsche, Elisabeth. 1912. *The Young Nietzsche*. London: W. Heinemann.

Foucault, Michel. 1971. "Nietzsche, Genealogy, History." In Rabinow 1984, pp. 76–100.

——. 1990. *The History of Sexuality*. Vol. 1. New York: Vintage.

Freeman, Kathleen. 1978. *Ancilla to the Pre-Socratic Philosophers*. Cambridge: Harvard University Press.

Freud, Sigmund. 1895. "Project for a Scientific Psychology." In volume 1 of the *Standard Edition of the Complete Psychological Works of Sigmund Freud* [hereafter *SE*]. Edited and translated by James Strachey. 24 vols. London: Hogarth, 1953–74.

——. 1900. *The Interpretation of Dreams*. In *SE*, vols. 4–5.

——. 1912. "The Dynamics of Transference." In *SE*, vol. 12.

——. 1917. *Introductory Lectures on Psycho-Analysis*. In *SE*, vol. 16.

——. 1920. *Beyond the Pleasure Principle*. In *SE*, vol. 18.

——. 1921. *Group Psychology and the Analysis of the Ego*. In *SE*, vol. 18.

——. 1933. *New Introductory Lectures on Psycho-Analysis*. In *SE*, vol. 22.

Fukuyama, Francis. 1992. *The End of History and the Last Man*. New York: Free Press.

Gadamer, Hans-Georg. 1988. "The Drama of Zarathustra." In Gillespie and Strong 1988, pp. 220–31.

Gerth, Hans, and C. Wright Mills, eds. 1958. *From Max Weber*. New York: Oxford University Press.

Gillespie, Michael A. 1995. *Nihilism before Nietzsche*. Chicago: University of Chicago Press.

Gillespie, Michael A., and Tracy B. Strong, eds. 1988. *Nietzsche's New Seas: Explorations in Philosophy, Aesthetics, and Politics*. Chicago: University of Chicago Press.

Ginsberg, Mitchell. 1973. "Nietzschean Psychiatry." In Solomon 1983, pp. 293–315.

Glick, Robert, and Steven Roose, eds. 1993. *Rage, Power, and Aggression*. New Haven: Yale University Press.

Gordon, Colin, ed. 1980. *Power/Knowledge: Selected Interviews and Other Writings, 1972–1977, by Michel Foucault*. New York: Pantheon.

Graybeal, Jean. 1990. *Language and "the Feminine" in Nietzsche and Heidegger*. Bloomington: Indiana University Press.

Grene, David, and Richmond Lattimore, eds. 1966. *Euripedes V*. Chicago: University of Chicago Press.

Grimm, Ruediger H. 1977. *Nietzsche's Theory of Knowledge*. New York: Walter de Gruyter.

Gutting, Gary, ed. 1994. *The Cambridge Companion to Foucault*. New York: Cambridge University Press.

Haar, Michael. 1996. *Nietzsche and Metaphysics*. Albany: State University of New York Press.

Hayman, Ronald. 1980. *Nietzsche: A Critical Life*. London: Weidenfield and Nicolson.

Hegel, G. W. F. 1892. *The Logic of Hegel*. Edited by William Wallace. Oxford: Oxford University Press.

——. 1967. *The Philosophy of Right*. Translated by T. M. Knox. New York: Oxford University Press.

——. 1969. *Hegel's Science of Logic*. Translated by A. V. Miller. New York: Humanities Press.

——. 1977. *The Phenomenology of Spirit*. Translated by A. V. Miller. New York: Oxford University Press.

Heilke, Thomas. 1998. *Nietzsche's Tragic Regime*. DeKalb: Northern Illinois University Press.

Higgins, Kathleen. 1987. *Nietzsche's ZARATHUSTRA*. Philadelphia: Temple University Press.

——. 1988. "Reading *Zarathustra*." In Solomon and Higgins 1988, pp. 132–51.

——. 1994. "*On the Genealogy of Morals*—Nietzsche's *Gift*." In Schacht 1994, pp. 49–62.

Hollingdale, R. J. 1965. *Nietzsche: The Man and His Philosophy*. Baton Rouge: Louisiana State University Press.

——, trans. 1969. *Nietzsche: "Thus Spoke Zarathustra."* New York: Penguin.

Horney, Karen. 1933. "The Denial of the Vagina." In Horney 1967, pp. 147–61.

——. 1967. *Feminine Psychology*. New York: W. W. Norton.

Irigaray, Luce. 1985. *This Sex Which Is Not One*. Ithaca: Cornell University Press.

——. 1991. *Marine Lover of Friedrich Nietzsche*. New York: Columbia University Press.

Jaspers, Karl. 1965. *Nietzsche: An Introduction to the Understanding of His Philosophical Activity*. Tucson: University of Arizona Press.

Jay, Martin. 1993. *Downcast Eyes: The Denigration of Vision in Twentieth-Century French Thought*. Berkeley: University of California Press.

Kaufmann, Walter. 1956. *Nietzsche: Philosopher, Psychologist, Antichrist*. New York: World Publishing.

——, ed. 1954. *The Portable Nietzsche*. New York: Viking.

Kittay, Eva F. 1988. "Woman as Metaphor." In *Hypatia* 3, no. 2:63–86.

Klein, Melanie. 1952. "The Emotional Life of the Infant." In Klein 1975, pp. 61–93.

——. 1975. *Envy and Gratitude*. New York: Dell Publishing.

Klein, Wayne. 1997. *Nietzsche and the Promise of Philosophy*. Albany: State University of New York Press.

Klossowki, Pierre. 1997. *Nietzsche and the Vicious Circle*. Translated by Daniel W. Smith. Chicago: University of Chicago Press.

Koelb, Clayton. 1994. "Castration Envy: Nietzsche and the Figure of Woman." In Burgard 1994, pp. 71–81.

Kofman, Sarah. 1972. *Nietzsche et la métaphore*. Paris: Galilée.

——. 1988. "Baubô: Theological Perversion and Fetishism." In Gillespie and Strong 1988, pp. 175–202.

——. 1994. "Wagner's Ascetic Ideal according to Nietzsche." In Schacht 1994, pp. 193–213.

Köhler, Joachim. 1989. *Zarathustras Geheimnis: Friedrich Nietzsche und seine verschlüsselte Botschaft*. Cited in Megill 1996.

Krell, David. 1994. "To the Orange Grove at the Edge of the Sea: Remarks on Luce Irigaray's *Amante marine*." In Burgard 1994, pp. 185–209.

Krell, David, and David Wood, eds. 1988. *Exceedingly Nietzsche*. New York: Routledge.

Kristeva, Julia. 1979. "Women's Time." In Moi 1986, pp. 187–213.

——. 1982. *Powers of Horror: An Essay on Abjection*. New York: Columbia University Press.

——. 1989. *Black Sun: Depression and Melancholia*. New York: Columbia University Press.

Kritzman, Lawrence, ed. 1988. *Michel Foucault: Politics, Philosophy, Culture*. New York: Routledge.

Lacan, Jacques. 1977. *Écrits: A Selection*. Edited by Alan Sheridan. New York: W. W. Norton.

Lampert, Laurence. 1986. *Nietzsche's Teaching*. New Haven: Yale University Press.

Lehrer, Ronald. 1995. *Nietzsche's Presence in Freud's Life and Thought*. Albany: State University of New York Press.

Lewis, Michael. 1993. "The Development of Anger and Rage." In Glick and Roose 1993, pp. 148–68.

Livingstone, Angela. 1984. *Lou Andreas Salomé*. London: Gordon Fraser.

Love, Nancy S. 1986. *Marx, Nietzsche, and Modernity*. New York: Columbia University Press.

Löwith, Karl. 1997. *Nietzsche's Philosophy of the Eternal Return of the Same*. Berkeley: University of California Press.

Magnus, Bernd. 1978. *Nietzsche's Existential Imperative*. Bloomington: Indiana University Press.

Magnus, Bernd, and Kathleen Higgins, eds. 1996. *The Cambridge Companion to Nietzsche*. New York: Cambridge University Press.

Mahon, Michael. 1992. *Foucault's Nietzschean Genealogy*. Albany: State University of New York Press.

Marcuse, Herbert. 1966. *Eros and Civilization*. New York: Vintage.

——. 1991. *One-Dimensional Man*. Boston: Beacon.

Marley, Bob. 1980. "Redemption Song." Fifty-Six Hope Road Music, Ltd. and Odnil Music, Ltd.

Martin, Biddy. 1991. *Women and Modernity: The (Life)Styles of Lou Andreas-Salomé*. Ithaca: Cornell University Press.

Megill, Allan. 1996. "Historicizing Nietzsche? Paradoxes and Lessons of a Hard Case." *Journal of Modern History* 68:114–52.

Middleton, Christopher, ed. 1969. *Selected Letters of Friedrich Nietzsche*. Chicago: University of Chicago Press.

Miller, James. 1993. *The Passion of Michel Foucault*. New York: Simon and Schuster.

Moi, Toril, ed. 1986. *The Kristeva Reader*. New York: Columbia University Press.

Monette, Lise. 1989. "The Nietzschean Interpretation . . . of Freud as Thought on the Fragmentary, as Fragmented Thought." In Darby, Egyed, and Jones 1989, pp. 71–79.

Nehamas, Alexander. 1985. *Nietzsche: Life as Literature*. Cambridge: Harvard University Press.

Nietzsche, Friedrich. [1872] 1956. *The Birth of Tragedy*. Translated by Walter Kaufmann. New York: Doubleday. [*BT*]

——. [1873–76] 1983. *Untimely Meditations*. Translated by R. J. Hollingdale. New York: Cambridge University Press. [*UM*]

——. [1878–80; 1886] 1986. *Human, All Too Human*. Translated by R. J. Hollingdale. New York: Cambridge University Press. [*HH*]

——. [1881] 1983. *Daybreak*. Translated by R. J. Hollingdale. New York: Cambridge University Press. [*D*]

——. [1882] 1974. *The Gay Science*. Translated by Walter Kaufmann. New York: Vintage. [*GS*]

——. 1883–85. *Thus Spoke Zarathustra*. In Kaufmann 1954. [*TSZ*]

——. [1886] 1966. *Beyond Good and Evil*. Translated by Walter Kaufmann. New York: Vintage. [*BGE*]

——. [1887] 1967. *On the Genealogy of Morals.* Translated by Walter Kaufmann. New York: Vintage. [*GM*]

——. 1888a. *The Antichrist.* In Kaufmann 1954. [*A*]

——. [1888b] 1967. *Ecce Homo.* Translated by Walter Kaufmann. New York: Vintage. [*EH*]

——. 1888c. *Twilight of the Idols.* In Kaufman 1954. [*TI*]

——. [1901] 1968. *The Will to Power.* Translated by R. J. Hollingdale and Walter Kaufmann. New York: Vintage. [*WP*]

Nussbaum, Martha. 1994. "Pity and Mercy: Nietzsche's Stoicism." In Schacht 1994, pp. 139–67.

O'Hara, Daniel, ed. 1985. *Why Nietzsche Now?* Bloomington: Indiana University Press.

Oliver, Kelly. 1995. *Womanizing Nietzsche.* New York: Routledge.

Oppel, Frances. 1993. "'Speaking of Immemorial Waters': Irigaray with Nietzsche." In Patton 1993, pp. 88–109.

Parkes, Graham. 1994. *Composing the Soul: Reaches of Nietzsche's Psychology.* Chicago: University of Chicago Press.

Pasley, Malcolm, ed. 1978. *Nietzsche: Imagery and Thought.* Berkeley: University of California Press.

Patton, Paul, ed. 1993. *Nietzsche, Feminism, and Political Theory.* New York: Routledge.

Peters, H. F. 1962. *My Sister, My Spouse.* New York: W. W. Norton.

Plato. *Phaedo.* In Rouse 1956.

Pletsch, Carl. 1991. *Young Nietzsche: Becoming a Genius.* New York: Free Press.

Podach, Erich F. 1931. *The Madness of Nietzsche.* New York: Putnam.

Rabinow, Paul, ed. 1984. *The Foucault Reader.* New York: Penguin.

Reich, Wilhelm. 1929. "Dialectical Materialism and Psychoanalysis." In Baxandall 1972, pp. 1–74.

Richards, Arlene. 1996. "Primary Femininity and Female Genital Anxiety." *Journal of the American Psychoanalytic Association* 44, suppl.:261–81.

Richardson, John. 1996. *Nietzsche's System.* New York: Oxford University Press.

Rouse, W. H. D., ed. 1956. *Great Dialogues of Plato.* New York: New American Library.

Sadler, Ted. 1995. *Nietzsche: Truth and Redemption.* Atlantic Highlands, N.J.: Athlone Press.

Salomé, Lou. 1988. *Nietzsche.* Translated by Siegfried Mandel. Redding Ridge, Conn.: Black Swan Books.

Schacht, Richard. 1983. *Nietzsche.* London: Routledge and Kegan Paul.

——, ed. 1994. *Nietzsche, Genealogy, Morality.* Berkeley: University of California Press.

Schopenhauer, Arthur. 1969. *The World as Will and Representation.* Translated by E. F. J. Payne. New York: Dover.

Schrift, Alan. 1990. *Nietzsche and the Question of Interpretation.* New York: Routledge.

Sedgwick, Peter, ed. 1995. *Nietzsche: A Critical Reader.* Cambridge, Mass.: Blackwell.

Sloterdijk, Peter. 1989. "Eurotaoism." In Darby, Egyed, and Jones 1989, pp. 99–116.

Smith, Douglas. 1996. *Transvaluations: Nietzsche in France, 1872–1972.* New York: Oxford University Press.

Soll, Ivan. 1973. "Reflections on Recurrence: A Re-examination of Nietzsche's Doctrine, *die Ewige Wiederkehr des Gleichen.*" In Solomon 1983, pp. 322–42.

——. 1994. "Nietzsche on Cruelty, Asceticism, and the Failure of Hedonism." In Schacht 1994, pp. 168–92.

Solomon, Robert C., ed. 1983. *Nietzsche: A Collection of Critical Essays.* Garden City, N.Y.: Anchor Books.

Solomon, Robert C., and Kathleen M. Higgins, eds. 1988. *Reading Nietzsche*. New York: Oxford University Press.

Stack, George. 1994. *Nietzsche: Man, Knowledge, and Will to Power*. Durango, Colo.: Hollbrook Publications.

Stambaugh, Joan. 1972. *Nietzsche's Thought of Eternal Return*. New York: Taylor and Francis.

———. 1987. *The Problem of Time in Nietzsche*. Lewisburg: Bucknell University Press.

Stauth, Georg, and Bryan S. Turner. 1988. *Nietzsche's Dance: Resentment, Reciprocity, and Resistance in Social Life*. Oxford: Blackwell.

Strong, Tracy B. 1985. "Oedipus as Hero: Family and Family Metaphors in Nietzsche." In O'Hara 1985, pp. 311–35.

———. 1988. *Friedrich Nietzsche and the Politics of Transfiguration*. 2d ed. Berkeley: University of California Press.

Tennyson, Alfred Lord. 1842. "Ulysses." In Andrews and Percival 1928.

Thiele, Leslie P. 1990. *Friedrich Nietzsche and the Politics of the Soul*. Princeton: Princeton University Press.

Tucker, Robert, ed. 1978. *The Marx-Engels Reader*. New York: W. W. Norton.

Tyson, Phyllis. 1994. "Bedrock and Beyond: An Examination of the Clinical Utility of Contemporary Theories of Female Psychology." *Journal of the American Psychoanalytic Association* 42:447–67.

Vasseleu, Cathryn. 1993. "Not Drowning, Sailing." In Patton 1993, pp. 71–87.

Warnock, Mary. 1978. "Nietzsche's Conception of Truth." In Pasley 1978, pp. 33–63.

Warren, Mark. 1988. *Nietzsche and Political Thought*. Cambridge: MIT Press.

Weber, Max. 1958. "Politics as a Vocation." In Gerth and Mills 1958, pp. 77–128.

Whitford, Margaret. 1989. "Rereading Irigaray." In Brennan 1989, pp. 106–26.

Wilcox, John T. 1974. *Truth and Value in Nietzsche*. Ann Arbor: University of Michigan Press.

Williams, Linda L. 1996. "Will to Power in Nietzsche's Published Works and the *Nachlass*." In *Journal of the History of Ideas* 57, no. 3:447–63.

Winnicott, Clare, Ray Shepherd, and Madeleine Davis, eds. 1989. *Psycho-Analytic Explorations: D. W. Winnicott*. Cambridge: Harvard University Press.

Winnicott, D. W. 1963. "The Development of the Capacity for Concern." In Winnicott 1965, pp. 73–82.

———. 1965. *The Maturational Processes and the Facilitating Environment*. New York: International Universities Press.

———. 1969. "The Use of the Object and Relating through Identifications." In Winnicott 1971, pp. 86–94.

———. 1971. *Playing and Reality*. New York: Basic.

———. 1974. "Fear of Breakdown." In Winnicott, Shepherd, and Davis 1989, pp. 87–95.

Wolfenstein, E. Victor. 1985. "Three Principles of Mental Functioning in Psychoanalytic Theory and Practice." *International Journal of Psycho-Analysis* 66: 77–94.

———. 1993. *Psychoanalytic-Marxism: Groundwork*. New York: Guilford Press.

———. 1998. "Michel Foucault and Psychoanalytic-Marxism." *South Atlantic Quarterly* 97, no. 2, pp. 361–87.

Wood, David. 1988. "Nietzsche's Transvaluation of Time." In Krell and Wood 1988, pp. 31–62.

Zabel, Morton D., ed. 1976. *The Portable Conrad*. New York: Penguin.

Zuboff, Arnold. 1973. "Nietzsche and Eternal Recurrence." In Solomon 1983, pp. 343–57.

Index

abjective, the, 147, 190, 212; biopower and, 234; eternal return and, 146, 156, 158, 159; the feminine and, 126; Kristeva and, 116–18; the moral and, 220; nausea and, 170; Nietzsche and, 112, 138–39; sexual desire and, 189; Zarathustra and, 190

Adelman, Janet, 200

aesthetic, the, 79, 84, 112, 174, 246n. 5

alienation, 209–10, 218

analyst, the, 4, 31, 89–91, 93–100, 109; interpretation and, 36; will to power and, 2, 63–65, 68; women as, 222

analytic reduction, 36–38, 44, 52, 55

anger, 25, 213, 227, 241n. 10

Anna case, 105–08

anthropological, the, 13, 21, 23, 27, 28, 32, 229

Antichrist, The (Nietzsche), 39, 78, 97, 167

anxiety: the analyst and, 68; Anna case, 106; in clinical psychoanalysis, 64, 94; the infant and, 115; Maya case, 101, 102, 104; minimum defense and, 2, 64, 68, 94, 104, 106; pain and, 25; the political and, 2, 228, 230; tolerating the maximum, 2, 64, 68, 94, 104, 106; will to power and, 2, 104, 106

Apollonian, the, 40, 42, 182; *The Birth of Tragedy* and, 183, 196; falsification and, 84; the mother-world and, 169–70; redemption and, 47; will to power and, 206; Zarathustra and, 187

apparent, the, 70, 72–73, 79, 81, 84, 97

appropriation, 41, 46, 49

artistic, the, 166, 167, 176, 177

ascetic, the, 215–17, 219–20; nausea and, 170

assimilative, the, 41, 42, 46, 49

Bacchae, The (Euripides), 161, 183, 197

Baubô, 84, 87, 164, 165

becoming, 9, 70, 72–73, 84, 129–30, 168

being, 8, 9, 70, 71, 84, 168

Beyond Good and Evil (Nietzsche), 39, 180–81, 197; analytic reduction and, 44; conceptual analysis and, 45; experiment and, 46; the moral and, 219; on philosophers, 69; the political and, 223; Salomé and, 195; thought-experiment and, 52; truth in, 178; women in, 69, 95, 178, 181

Beyond the Pleasure Principle (Freud), 50, 51, 52, 55, 137, 148

Bion, Wilhelm Ruprecht, 64, 67, 98
biopower, 16, 18–19, 29, 229–30, 232, 234
Birth of Tragedy out of the Spirit of Music, The
(Nietzsche), 40, 84, 171, 196; Kofman
and, 183; Nietzsche's intercourse with
women and, 197; Schopenhauer and, 42,
47; self-unification and, 129; *Thus Spoke
Zarathustra* and, 168–69; Wagner and,
173
blond beast, the, 214, 218, 219
body, the, 8, 18–19, 31, 162–63, 164
boundary, 85–86, 92, 93
bourgeoisie, the, 6, 10, 16, 17, 226

capitalist, the, 225–33, 235; the anthropological and, 29; critical theory and,
5–7; Foucault and, 10; the sexual and,
12, 14, 18
castration (anxiety), 247n. 14; auto, 195;
Nietzsche and, 126, 162–64, 176–77,
188; Zarathustra and, 184, 187
child, the, 11, 181, 213
Christ, 97, 150, 202
Christian, the, 69, 72, 87, 245n. 19; the
ascetic and, 215; the blond beast and,
214; eternal return and, 145; the moral
and, 211
class (social stratum), 16–18, 226–28
collective, the, 17–18, 23, 28, 225, 229,
236
compassion, 201, 221, 222, 237
concept, 166–68, 191, 246n. 5
confession, 13, 17, 29, 76, 88, 214
conscience, 245n. 19; the ascetic and, 216;
instinct and, 219; Maya case, 102, 221;
the moral and, 209; noble warrior and,
212, 214; in *On the Genealogy of Morals*,
125
consciousness, 11, 22, 49, 204, 224–25
cosmological, the, 39, 85–86, 111
creation (creativity), 60, 105, 133, 134, 166,
177, 189–90
critical theory, 2–7, 9–12, 16–17, 29, 202;
Foucault and, 31, 32; the political and,
225, 226, 229, 233, 235
cruelty, 169, 213–15; Maya case, 102, 105;
the moral and, 209; self-overcoming and,
125; will to power and, 60, 218

death-drive, 7, 53–55, 59–60, 224, 230–31
decadent, the, 73, 179; the ascetic and, 216;
eternal return and, 147; the feminine and,
126; versus health, 133, 220; misery and,
174–75; Nietzsche and, 138; perspective
and, 76; as quiescence, 50–51; the will
and, 48; will to power and, 57, 60, 126

defense, 164; abjection and, 138; the analyst
and, 68; Anna case, 106; anxiety-driven,
144; in clinical psychoanalysis, 94; illusion as, 170; logic and, 92; minimum, 2,
64, 68, 94, 106; neonatal, 61; paranoid-
schizoid position and, 25; phantasy and,
163, 199; the political and, 2, 228; tolerating maximum anxiety and, 2, 64, 68, 94,
106; will to power and, 2, 106
Deleuze, Gilles, 201–2, 204
Demeter, 84, 164
democracy, 5, 227, 235
depressive position, the: the anthropological and, 21; in clinical psychoanalysis, 90;
guilt and, 215; the infant and, 115; Klein
and, 23–24; Maya case, 99–101, 103–4;
the moral and, 212; Nietzsche and, 194;
the political and, 30; will to power and,
59; Zarathustra and, 150
desire: in clinical psychoanalysis, 90; Foucault and, 14; Foucault on, 31; in *The Gay
Science*, 177; gender and, 26; in interaction of individuals, 22; parental, 117; the
phallus and, 27; the political and,
224–25; sexual, 189; transitional space
and, 118; the vagina and, 164; Zarathustra and, 181, 187
destructiveness, 59–60, 105
"determinacy of pleasure and pain," 22, 24,
38, 58, 61, 139, 231, 234
dialectical reason, 70, 89, 90; in clinical psychoanalysis, 109; Hegel and, 205; perspectivism and, 233–34; the political and,
233; will to power and, 201, 203, 207–8
dialectical, the, 210, 220; eternal return
and, 141; in interaction of individuals, 22;
manifold, 202, 206; Marcuse and, 7;
monism and, 37; Nietzsche and, 133; the
political and, 224, 234–35; power and,
234–35; resistance politics and, 236; will
to power and, 58, 204, 207
difference, 27–28, 163, 204–6, 227
Dinnerstein, Dorothy, 231–32, 234
Dionysian, the, 40, 42, 84, 182, 184; *The
Birth of Tragedy* and, 196; energy and, 206;
eternal return and, 142; as madness, 197;
the mother-world and, 169–70; Oedipus
and, 171; Schopenhauer and, 47, 48; will
to power and, 217; Zarathustra and, 187
disidentification, 115–16
displeasure, 49–50
dogmatic, the, 69, 74, 97
dream interpretation, 106–8, 123–24,
149–50, 246n. 1
drives, 7, 44, 81, 189, 224
dwarf, the, 153–55

Ecce Homo (Nietzsche): illness and, 133; madness in, 197; the moral and, 208; Nietzsche's mother and, 121; perspectivism and, 76; the political and, 223; time and, 119

Eco, Umberto, 227

ego, 63, 70, 93

emancipate, to, 2, 8, 19, 30, 31, 235, 237

energy: bodily, 19; the epistemic and, 206; labor force and, 16; origins of life and, 53; overcoming resistance and, 57–58; psychic, 27; resistance and, 56

envy, 60, 211, 212, 216

epistemic, the: in clinical psychoanalysis, 109; energy and, 206; interpretation and, 79; metaphor and, 166; will to power and, 85; will to truth and, 43

epistemological, the, 89, 241n. 3; analytical reduction and, 37; in clinical psychoanalysis, 93; critical theory and, 2, 9; falsification and, 83–84; language and, 81; logic and, 81; metaphor and, 166; the metaphysical and, 72; perspectivism and, 67–69, 75, 77, 203; the political and, 233–34; reduction and, 45; self-overcoming and, 205

Epstein, Mark, 65, 107

Eros and Civilization (Marcuse), 7, 9

erotic, the, 7, 8, 9, 174; eternal return and, 159; gender and, 26; individuation and, 122; Maya case, 221; Nietzsche on, 176; sublimation and, 189; transference, 99–102, 103; will to power and, 59

eternal return (recurrence), 60, 139–49, 151–59, 219, 244n. 14; aposiopesis and, 248n. 3; the ascetic and, 215, 220; being and, 8–9; conceptualization of, 87; critical theory and, 3; *On the Genealogy of Morals* and, 39, 199, 210; the historical and, 111–13, 132; making choices and, 245n. 17; the marine lover and, 198; the melancholic and, 123; the moral and, 209–10; Nietzsche's mother and, 121; the overman and, 39; pain and, 134; perspectivism and, 40; Plato and, 245n. 21; *Thus Spoke Zarathustra* and, 190; transitional space and, 118, 195; will to power and, 245n. 18; Winnicott and, 33; yin-yang and, 206; Zarathustra and, 43, 175

eternal womanly, the, 131–32

Europe, 179, 223, 226, 228; women and, 175

evangelical temptation, 97, 107

false, the, 37, 242n. 3; the metaphysical and, 78–79, 85; neonatal, 61; perspective and, 74; transitional space and, 118

falsification, 82–84, 92, 167, 209, 246n. 5

father, the, 147, 163–64; gender identity and, 26; God and, 145; Kristeva and, 122–23; the mother and, 114, 115; Nietzsche and, 113, 138, 170–71, 195, 196; Nietzsche on, 247n. 8; the penis and, 193; the son and, 135, 232

"father's time," 113–14, 133, 141

female, the, 164; the assimilative and, 42; juridico-discursive power and, 234; male phantasy and, 162–63; paranoid-schizoid position and, 62; time and, 114

feminine, the, 118; degeneration and, 72; Dionysian, 169; eternal return and, 87, 141, 152, 159; Europe and, 175, 179; gender identity and, 26–27; juridico-discursive power and, 234; marriage and, 173; masculine phantasy and, 165; the natural and, 231; Nietzsche and, 112, 132, 133, 136, 171, 192, 196–98; *Thus Spoke Zarathustra* and, 3; time, 114; Zarathustra and, 180, 183–84, 187–88

fetish, 19, 31, 82

force, 15, 48, 49, 50, 57–58, 80, 202

forgetting, 129–30, 167

fort! da! game, 51–52, 54–55, 93, 97

Foucault, Michel, 27; the anthropological and, 21; critical theory and, 5, 9–10; the political and, 226; power and, 28–32; sexuality and, 11–20; will to power and, 222

free spirit, the, 172, 174, 179, 209, 223

Freud, Sigmund, 7, 11, 56, 73, 137, 148; *fort! da!* game and, 51–52; Foucault and, 222; Marcuse and, 9; psychoanalysis and, 63; the schizoid and, 62; stimulation and, 52–55; will to power and, 58–59

future, the, 133, 141, 142, 154, 244n. 17

Gast, Peter, 143, 145, 191

Gay Science, The (Nietzsche), 43, 73, 87, 177, 179, 180, 181; Baubô in, 164, 165; eternal return and, 39, 139; God in, 84; the oedipal and, 196; pain in, 133; perspectivism and, 75; will to power and, 40; women in, 189

gender, 231; in clinical psychoanalysis, 222; eternal return and, 113; feminine, 118; individuation and, 25; the infant and, 115; Nietzsche and, 168, 175, 196; overcoming and, 180; paranoid-schizoid position and, 62; power and, 234; the sexual and, 162, 166, 177; *Thus Spoke Zarathustra* and, 3; time and, 133, 136; Zarathustra and, 152, 159

genitals, the, 163–65, 176; lack and, 247n. 14; Nietzsche on, 199; Zarathustra and, 184

Gersdorf, Carl von, 135, 139
God, 217; castration anxiety and, 164;
Christ and, 150; death of, 87; the father
and, 145; in *The Gay Science*, 84; Maya
case, 99; the melancholic and, 135; the
moral and, 212, 214; Nietzsche on, 220;
Zarathustra and, 186
Good, the, 70, 73, 85, 245n. 21
good and evil, 1, 43, 201, 210, 214
Greeks, the, 85, 86, 139
guilt, 30; the ascetic and, 215, 216–17;
Christ and, 97; the infant and, 25; Maya
case, 102; the moral and, 214–15,
216–17, 218; Nietzsche and, 147; *On the
Genealogy of Morals* and, 125; transitional
space and, 127

health: eternal return and, 147; the moral
and, 210, 220; Nietzsche and, 133–35,
138, 139; perspective and, 76; the political and, 230; the priest and, 216; reality
and, 78; will to power and, 57, 60
hedonic, the: critical theory and, 2; Marcuse
and, 8; Nietzsche and, 32, 55; the political and, 225; the psychophysiological and,
58; will to power and, 218
Hegel, Georg Wilhelm, 37, 88, 206, 226;
clinical psychoanalysis and, 89, 91; the
dialectical and, 202–5; Marcuse and, 9;
philosophy and, 4; thought-experiment
and, 52; will to power and, 58
hegemony, 226–29, 236
Heracleitus, 70, 86, 130
historical, the, 16, 17, 130–34; eternal
return and, 111–13; Foucault and, 10–14,
18–21, 27; the moral and, 214, 220;
Nietzsche and, 6, 244n. 14, 245n. 17; philosophy and, 166
History of Sexuality, The (Foucault), 5, 9–10,
13, 29, 32, 222
horizon, 74; in clinical psychoanalysis,
92–93; as disgust, 117; as eternal return,
199; eternal return and, 141; the false
and, 78; as metaphor, 167; Nietzsche and,
132; paranoid-schizoid position and, 139
Human, All-Too-Human (Nietzsche), 168,
171, 181, 196; Enlightenment and,
173–74; *The Gay Science* and, 177; the
moral and, 208, 219
human nature, 12, 21–22

identity, 25–27, 28, 204, 241n. 6; national,
228
illness, 137; Europe and, 175; Nietzsche
and, 133–35, 243n. 8; perspective and,
76; postmetaphysical nihilism and, 73;

suffering and, 125; transitional space and,
127; will to power and, 57
imagination, 22, 167, 224
individual, the, 183; in clinical psychoanalysis, 222; individuation and, 25–26; interaction of, 21, 28; the moral and, 219, 220;
the political and, 224, 225, 229, 235
individuation, 114–15; abjection and, 138;
gender and, 25–27; Kristeva and,
122–23; Nietzsche and, 3, 121; the political and, 224
infant, the, 61, 157, 231–32; individuation
and, 26; Klein and, 24–25; the moral and,
210; the mother and, 114–18, 177, 191;
yearning of, 183; Zarathustra and, 181
infinite, the, 133, 140, 141, 205
injustice, 85–86, 209
inorganic, the, 48, 53–54
instinct, 7–8, 22, 53, 219
interaction: clinical, 32; identity and,
27–28; of individuals, 21–23; mother-
child, 24; psychoanalytic, 89–90; sexual,
62; social, 20, 21, 29
interpret, to, 69, 70, 75–79, 93–96, 222
Irigaray, Luce, 198–99

judgment (discernment), 78, 82–83, 112,
203, 209
juridico-discursive, the, 14, 16, 28–29, 226,
232, 234
justice, 85–86

Kantian, the, 70, 72, 83, 203, 242n. 3
Klein, Melanie, 24–25, 104
knowledge, 166, 233, 242n. 3; critical theory and, 2; falsification and, 246n. 5; Foucault and, 29, 30, 32; versus life, 130; the
metaphysical and, 78–79; the moral and,
209; the ontological and, 69–71; perspective and, 81, 83–84, 131; political, 225;
the sexual and, 13
Kristeva, Julia, 113–14, 116–18, 122–23,
131, 157

lack, 47, 48, 73, 247n. 14
language, 241n. 1, 246n. 5; the body and,
162, 164; in interaction of individuals, 22;
the metaphysical and, 81–84; Nietzsche
and, 121; Nietzschian perspectivism and,
203; noble warrior and, 212, 214; nonverbal experience and, 91–92; perspectivism
and, 86, 87; as resistance, 207
law, 14–15, 27, 74, 86, 164, 171, 232
left Freudians: critical theory and, 2, 5;
Foucault and, 10, 11, 12, 20, 28; human
emancipation and, 19

liberation, 8, 9, 20, 218, 219
libido, 8, 12, 14, 27, 53
life, 217, 218; the ascetic and, 216; Baubô and, 164; eternal return and, 148; injustice and, 209; versus knowledge, 130; liberation and, 219; the metaphysical and, 73; versus thinking, 204; as will to power, 46; will to power and, 55, 58; Zarathustra and, 186
life-drive, 7, 54–55, 58–59, 189, 224, 230–31
limits, 85–86, 92, 93
logic, 246n. 5; the metaphysical and, 81–84; the moral and, 209; Nietzschian perspectivism and, 203; nonverbal experience and, 91–92; perspectivism and, 86, 87; as resistance, 207
love, 177, 212, 237; the free spirit and, 172; Nietzsche and, 197, 201; shame and, 176; women and, 172; Zarathustra and, 183

Magnus, Bernd, 38, 40
male, the, 187; the assimilative and, 42; individuation and, 122–23; juridico-discursive power and, 234; paranoid-schizoid position and, 62; pregnancy, 180; time and, 114
Marcuse, Herbert, 6–9, 10–11, 16, 17, 20
marine lover, the, 198–99
marriage, 17, 181, 182; Nietzsche on, 247n. 7
Marx, Karl, 9, 226
Marxism, 7, 8, 20, 227
masculine, the, 169, 232, 241n. 6; abjection and, 138; castration anxiety and, 162; in clinical psychoanalysis, 64; eternal return and, 141, 153; *fort! da!* game and, 62; gender identity and, 26–27; Nietzsche and, 112–13, 125–26, 132, 133, 171–72, 195–96; *Thus Spoke Zarathustra* and, 3; time, 114, 129
mastery, 51, 54, 61–62
maternal, the, 116–17; Dionysian, 196; eternal return and, 87, 145–46, 157; gender identity and, 26; juridico-discursive power and, 234; Maya case, 103, 221; the natural and, 231; Nietzsche and, 172, 243n. 9; paranoid-schizoid position and, 62; in *Thus Spoke Zarathustra*, 197; Zarathustra and, 177
Maya case, 99–105
meaning, 96, 168; death of God and, 87; experience and, 217–18; the infant and, 24; liberation and, 219; limits and, 86; logic and, 92; Maya case, 221; neonatal,

61; perspective and, 37, 83, 91; the priest and, 216; will to power and, 69, 167
Medusa, 87, 164, 199
melancholic, the, 112, 123–25, 127, 146, 147, 156, 158
memory: the infant and, 117; of intrauterine existence, 162; Maya case, 99–100; noble warrior and, 213–14; the suprahistorical and, 132; Zarathustra and, 150
men, 172, 173, 176–81, 189, 231, 247n. 7
metabolic, the, 218; the capitalist and, 29; capitalist production and, 232; the infant and, 24; interaction of individuals and, 28; Nietzsche and, 134; the political and, 229–32, 234–35; transitional space and, 118
metaphor, 166–67, 168, 191, 205, 246n. 5
metaphysical, the, 13, 72–74; in clinical psychoanalysis, 96–97; Foucault and, 27; God and, 87; language and, 81–84; logic and, 81–84; Maya case, 103; perspectivism and, 69, 77–79, 85, 244n. 14; Plato and, 84; the political and, 225
Meysenbug, Malwida von, 138, 139
monism, 37–38, 58, 61, 242n. 3
moral, the, 193, 208–12, 214–21, 245n. 19; the analyst and, 64; clinical psychoanalysis and, 221; eternal return and, 142; Foucault and, 14; Klein and, 25; Maya case, 102; the political and, 12, 225, 228
mother, the, 147; individuation and, 26; the infant and, 114–16, 118, 177; Klein and, 25; Kristeva and, 122–23; male phantasy and, 162–63; masculine identity and, 241n. 6; as nature, 231–32; Nietzsche and, 113, 138, 165, 171, 195; paranoid-schizoid position and, 62
"mother's species," 113–14, 133, 141
mother-world, the, 114, 117, 137, 169–70, 184, 189, 234

narcissistic, the, 62, 124, 138, 193, 211, 222, 247n. 14
nature, 84–85, 231–32; Baubô and, 165; male phantasy and, 163; the mother-world and, 169–70; Nietzsche and, 137, 175
nausea, 117, 138, 220, 246n. 24; the ascetic and, 170
negation, 116, 204–5, 207, 209, 212, 220
Nehamas, Alexander, 112, 139
neonatal, the, 61–62, 163, 231
Nietzsche, Elisabeth Therese (sister), 120, 123, 124, 125, 155, 188, 190; Salomé and, 193

Pentheus, 183, 197

persecutory, the, 99; Anna case, 108; the infant and, 24, 117; Maya case, 101–3, 221; the moral and, 218; Nietzsche and, 138, 190, 193; paranoid-schizoid position and, 30

perspective, 37, 167, 209, 236; interpretation and, 81

perspectivism, 131, 241n. 3; in clinical psychoanalysis, 36, 91, 94, 96, 109; clinical reports and, 99; constrained, 112; critical theory and, 2–4; as critique of metaphysics, 69, 72–81, 85–88, 244n. 14; the dialectical and, 201–3, 233–34; the epistemological and, 67–69; eternal return and, 40; language and, 83; the moral and, 212; the political and, 233–34; will to power and, 33, 208–9, 224; worldview and, 72–74, 80–81, 242n. 3

phallic, the, 27, 126, 163, 182, 184

phantasy, 162–63, 177, 195, 199

phenomenological, the, 4, 36, 89–90

Phenomenology of Spirit, The (Hegel), 52, 89, 202–3, 204

philosophy, 5–6, 76, 168; clinical psychoanalysis and, 105; the epistemic and, 69; eternal return and, 111; history of, 166; the moral and, 214; Nietzsche and, 4, 7; perspectivist, 224; psychoanalytic perspectivism and, 88

pity, 220–21

Plato, 20, 69–70, 84, 166, 202, 245n. 21; limits and, 86; the ontological and, 71

Platonic, the, 69, 72, 85

pleasure: in contractual relations, 213; critical theory and, 2; determinacy of, 22, 24, 38, 58, 60, 139, 231, 234; drives and, 54; *fort! da!* game and, 51–52; Foucault on, 31; Freud v. Nietzsche, 56; the infant and, 24; in interaction of individuals, 22; meaning and, 218; Nietzsche and, 148; of overcoming pain, 59–60, 93, 207; the political and, 224–25; power and, 49–50; will to power and, 38, 58–61, 93, 231

pleasure principle, 2, 7, 51–52, 54, 59

Pletsch, Carl, 124, 126

political, the, 2, 10–12, 17–18, 30, 223–29, 233–37

Politics (Aristotle), 229, 230

postmetaphysical, the, 96, 97, 103

power, 14–15, 206, 219; the dialectical and, 234–35; Foucault and, 11–16, 18–19, 29–32; gender and, 27, 28; interpretation and, 83; knowledge and, 233; pleasure and, 49–50; the political and, 225; psychological interpretation and, 34; in rela-

tionship of individuals, 23; resistance and, 48, 56

power/knowledge relationship, 9, 13, 32, 166, 233

Powers of Horror (Kristeva), 113

pregnancy, 183; male, 180; spiritual, 177

preoedipal, the, 163, 171, 184, 234

present, the, 154, 195, 244n. 17

priest, the, 64, 174, 210, 211, 216, 219

principle of constancy, 54–55, 60

production (economic), 8, 10, 28, 230; the anthropological and, 29; the sexual and, 12, 18; the technological and, 232

psychoanalytic, the: Anna case, 105–8, 221; clinical, 36, 63–65, 89–91, 207, 221–23; clinical reporting and, 98–99; confession and, 17; creativity and, 189; critical theory and, 2–4, 7; Foucault and, 14, 27, 28, 31–32; interpretation and, 95; Klein and, 24; Marcuse and, 9; Maya case, 99–105, 221; the metaphysical and, 73, 97; perspectivism and, 94, 96; power and, 29; redefinition of will to power and, 3–4, 9, 37, 58–59, 68, 93, 102–5, 158, 222; the self and, 93, 94; the sexual and, 11–12, 13; shepherd and the snake and, 158; time and, 114; Wolfenstein and, 88–91

psychological, the, 58, 72, 82, 112, 135, 207, 246n. 5

psychophysiological, the: in clinical psychoanalysis, 90; the infant and, 24; interaction, 234; in interaction of individuals, 22; life-drive and, 58; Nietzsche and, 137, 138; paranoid-schizoid position and, 61

quiescence, 9, 50–51

rage, 59, 101–2, 104–5, 115, 211, 229

rancune, 147–48

ratiocinative, the, 155, 203–4, 209

reality, 167, 242n. 3, 246n. 5; clinical reports and, 98; death of God and, 87; the epistemological and, 93; the metaphysical and, 82–85; Nietzsche on, 44–45; the ontological and, 69–70, 72; perspectivism and, 75, 78–80

reality principle, 7, 8, 54, 79, 224

redemption, 47, 98, 102, 150–51

reduction (analytical), 36–38, 45

Rée, Paul, 181, 188, 189, 192, 193, 194, 196

regulation of populations, 18–19

Reich, Wilhelm, 7, 10–11, 16, 17

repetition, to repeat, 54, 60, 113

repression, 8, 10–12, 14, 16, 26, 30

transgression, 85, 147, 148
transitional space, 118–19, 127, 168; eternal
  return and, 148; the infant and, 115;
  Nietzsche and, 112, 195; Winnicott and,
  33, 115, 119
truth, the true, 69–76, 73–80, 81, 217, 223,
  241n. 3, 244n. 14; metaphor and,
  166–67; the metaphysical and, 82–85;
  monisms and, 38; the moral and, 209;
  nature and, 165; Nietzsche and, 176; transitional space and, 118; will to power and,
  44; women and, 178; Zarathustra and,
  154

unconscious, the, 63, 90, 147
Untimely Meditations (Nietzsche), 6, 113,
  129, 168, 196
ur-fascistic, the, 227–29, 236
utilitarian, the, 2, 8, 32, 58, 218

vagina, the, 162, 163, 165, 176
value judgement, 1, 201, 209
values, 79, 87, 235; the capitalist and, 233;
  eternal return and, 142, 145; good and
  evil and, 43; in human life, 23; interpretation and, 83; Marcuse and, 7; metaphysical, 73; moral, 245n. 19; the moral and,
  209; the overman and, 180; the political
  and, 225; the will and, 219
violation, 48, 85–86, 177, 181, 213

Wagner, Richard, 128–29, 136, 145, 171,
  173, 188, 196
warrior, the, 166, 247n. 16; as blond beast,
  219; noble, 211, 212–14, 215; paranoid-
  schizoid position and, 62; wisdom and,
  180
weakness, the weak, 48, 57, 212, 216
will, 47–48, 151, 170, 185, 217, 219, 224
will to know, 9, 13, 166, 222
will to power, 39–51, 167, 205, 218, 242n.
  3, 246n. 5; aggression and, 59; the analyst
  and, 63–65, 68; analytic reduction and,
  37–38; Anna case, 106; asceticism and,
  216–17; the bourgeoisie and, 17; capitalist production and, 232; in clinical psychoanalysis, 93; conscience and, 125; creativity and, 134; critical theory and, 2–4;

cruelty and, 213–14; the dialectical and,
  202–4, 206–8; eternal return and, 139,
  148, 245n. 18; Europe and, 223; Foucault
  and, 9, 15, 222; Freud and, 55; the infant
  and, 115; interpretation and, 81, 83;
  Maya case, 102, 103, 104; the metaphysical and, 72–73; minimum defense and, 2,
  104, 106; the moral and, 209, 211–12;
  Nietzsche on, 225; overcoming pain and,
  59–60, 65, 93, 194, 207; overcoming
  resistance and, 56–58; the overman and,
  182; perspectivism and, 33, 68, 75, 80,
  85–87; the political and, 223–25, 232,
  234; psychoanalytic redefinition of, 3–4,
  9, 37, 58–59, 68, 93, 102–5, 158, 222;
  sexual liberation and, 20; suffering and,
  231; suspension of, 63–65, 68, 93, 108,
  109; tolerating anxiety and, 2, 104, 106
Will to Power, The (Nietzsche), 33, 38, 39,
  48, 52
Winnicott, Donald, 25, 26, 94; transitional
  space and, 33, 115, 119
wisdom, 62, 166, 171, 180–81, 215, 245n.
  21; wild, 183
womb, the, 162–63
women, 69, 231; as analysts, 222; the assimilative and, 41–42; in *Beyond Good and
  Evil*, 69, 95, 178, 181; in *The Gay Science*,
  62; Nietzsche and, 127, 132, 171–82,
  188–89, 192, 197; the patriarchal and,
  241n. 12; sexual desire and, 189;
  Zarathustra and, 185
"Women's Time" (Kristeva), 113
words, 167–68
work, 22, 90, 224–25
working class, the, 226–27
World as Will and Representation, The
  (Schopenhauer), 47

yin-yang, 205, 206–7, 230

Zarathustra, 180–90; the ascetic and,
  219–20; creativity and, 60; discharge and,
  45; eternal return and, 139, 140, 145,
  148–56, 159; the melancholic and, 123;
  overcoming and, 43, 56–57; Salomé and,
  194–95; transitional space and, 168; will
  to power and, 44